O9-AIF-203

Doing
Business
Tax-Free

NOV   2001

Doing Business Tax-Free

Perfectly Legal Techniques to Reduce or Eliminate Your Federal Business Taxes

SECOND EDITION

Robert A. Cooke

John Wiley & Sons, Inc.

New York · Chichester · Weinheim · Brisbane · Toronto · Singapore

343.73
C

This book is printed on acid-free paper. ∞

Copyright © 1995, 2001 by Robert A. Cooke. All rights reserved.

Published by John Wiley & Sons, Inc.
Published simultaneously in Canada.

No part of this publication may be reproduced, stored in a retrieval system or transmitted in any form or by any means, electronic, mechanical, photocopying, recording, scanning or otherwise, except as permitted under Section 107 or 108 of the 1976 United States Copyright Act, without either the prior written permission of the Publisher, or authorization through payment of the appropriate per-copy fee to the Copyright Clearance Center, 222 Rosewood Drive, Danvers, MA 01923, (978) 750-8400, fax (978) 750-4744. Requests to the Publisher for permission should be addressed to the Permissions Department, John Wiley & Sons, Inc., 605 Third Avenue, New York, NY 10158-0012, (212) 850-6011, fax (212) 850-6008, E-Mail: PERMREQ@WILEY.COM.

This publication is designed to provide accurate and authoritative information in regard to the subject matter covered. It is sold with the understanding that the publisher is not engaged in rendering professional services. If professional advice or other expert assistance is required, the services of a competent professional person should be sought.

Library of Congress Cataloging-in-Publication Data:

Cooke, Robert A., 1931–
    Doing business tax-free : perfectly legal techniques to reduce or eliminate your federal business taxes / Robert A. Cooke.—2nd ed.
       p. cm.
    Includes index.
    ISBN 0-471-41821-8 (pbk. : alk. paper)
    1. Corporations—Taxation—United States.   2. Tax planning—United States.
    I. Title.
HD2753.U6 C56 2001
343.7306'7—dc21   2001017632

Printed in the United States of America.

10 9 8 7 6 5 4 3 2 1

CONTENTS

INTRODUCTION

Saving Tax Money

Yes, it is possible for your business to prosper for 36 (or more) months without paying any federal income tax and probably no state income tax. (Of course, there are some less severe taxes, such as sales tax and license fees that are unavoidable, but this book is about the onerous income taxes and a little bit about estate taxes.)

Is it really possible to not pay income taxes for at least 36 months? Here's a brief look at one of the examples in Chapter 8: If you publish a newsletter, you can spend your entire advertising budget for next year in December of this year. All that advertising and promotion expense is deductible this year, but the additional income that results from those advertising dollars does not show up on your tax return for one, two, or three years later. How much later depends on the length of the subscription.

What if you are not in business? Can you reduce or wipe out your income tax? How about turning your hobby into a business, so you can deduct the expenses? The IRS says that's okay *if* you earn a profit in three out of five years. If you meet that test, the IRS will agree with you that your hobby is a legitimate business. However, if you have to earn those profits, you may end up with *more* tax to pay. What if you don't pass that three-out-of-five-years profit test? Are you shot down? Not necessarily. The IRS says that if the facts and circumstances indicate that you entered the activity with the objective of making a profit (even if you lose instead), it may still be a business. How do you set up the facts and circumstances so that the IRS will let you deduct your hobby/business expenses? We talk about that in Chapter 5.

Arrangement of This Book

What you will find here, of course, are legal ways to avoid paying income taxes,[1] and you will find them in an easy-to-use format. Unlike most tax-planning books, this is not a laundry list of tax rules compiled by an erudite tax attorney or CPA. Rather, it is a discussion, written in "English," of how you can use the tax rules to your advantage. The second edition includes new rules about S corporations, tax classifications of Limited Liability companies, and amortizing the cost of goodwill and other intangibles.

In writing this book, I have omitted many IRS compliance etails, which change almost daily. What this book does contain are tax-saving *concepts and ideas,* and it explains how you might apply them to your situation. Description of the details, however, must be left to the latest IRS regulations. As you read the explanations and many examples, you will gain an understanding of business tax-planning maneuvers and will be able to formulate a game plan. Then you can take your plan to a tax professional for an opinion as to the game plan's legality under current law, for fine-tuning the procedures, and for filling in the tax forms after the no-tax game has been played.

Why didn't I include all the details of the tax rules, so you can do it all yourself? The quickest way to pay more tax than you need to is to buy an eight-dollar "How to Prepare Your Income Tax" book and do it all yourself. Buying the book won't hurt you, but doing all your own tax work can, for several reasons:

1. By the time you prepare last year's income tax return, it's too late to do any tax planning. The die is cast, so, with few exceptions, you must pay whatever the bottom line of the tax form says you must pay.

[1]Tax "avoidance" covers the *legal* methods of reducing or eliminating your taxes. Tax "evasion" (not covered in this book) is the term used for the illegal maneuvers that can put you behind bars.

2. By the time the book is written, printed, and distributed to the stores, our whimsical Congress and IRS will have changed some of the laws and regulations.

3. Presumably, your knowledge of tax law would be the result of a few hours of study. A tax professional who works in the area full-time, subscribes to various tax newsletters and loose-leaf research services, and ties into an electronic data base that reports federal court decisions will be far more adept at maneuvering to avoid taxes.

4. Some of the tax forms have become so complicated that they can be filled in correctly only by a tax professional using a sophisticated tax software program. This is more apt to be the case if the business is a corporation, partnership, or limited liability company. The usual $30 or $40 program for individuals doesn't cover these, and the programs that do prepare taxes for these entities assume a comprehensive knowledge of tax and accounting rules on the part of the preparer.

Saving Money on Professional Fees

There is more money this book can save you. The most expensive way to use a tax professional is to have a vague idea of how you want to conduct your business, make an appointment with the professional, and spend several hours in his or her office discussing the alternatives you might pursue and being privately tutored in basic tax rules. Sure, you will hear some great ideas, and you will also receive a WHOPPING BILL.

The *money-saving* way is to learn enough about the tax rules and the way the IRS operates to be able to form ideas as to how to pay little or no taxes. Then buy just a little bit of a tax professional's time—just enough to research the latest rules and tell you if your idea will work. *This book helps you plan your own tax maneuvers and keep the professional's time (and cost) to a minimum.*

Also, to help you save on professional costs, the footnotes contain information of two types:

1. Interesting information—nice to know, but not essential.

2. References to the sections of the Internal Revenue Code, the Internal Revenue Service Regulations, and/or court cases upon which I based some of my suggestions. If you are a scholarly person, you can look up the references at a library that maintains tax material in its reference department. However, these footnotes are included for the professional to whom you take your ideas (generated by reading this book).

These technical footnotes are another MONEY SAVER. Here's why: In my practice, I often find a client seated across from me at my desk, describing a plan he or she has developed from reading a newspaper, magazine article, or some other source of do-it-yourself ideas. The client, of course, wants my opinion as to the feasibility and legality of the idea. This means I have to do two things:

1. Try to guess the code section, regulation, or court case on which the author of the article based the recommendation. This can be time consuming, particularly if I need to run down the author and call him or her to find out just what he or she has in mind.
2. Research recent developments in the tax area to determine if the rules have changed and if I agree with the article.

Number 1 usually takes far longer than Number 2. So that you don't have to pay your professional for time spent doing what I described, I have included technical references in the footnotes. You will save money, as you need to pay your professional only for conducting the procedures described in Number 2.

Almost every rule we have ever learned has its exceptions, and the tax rules are not exempt. Those exceptions are the reason that the erudite books written for the tax professionals are filled with "lawyer" phrases such as "in most cases," "with certain exceptions," "generally," and other cover-yourself terms. For the most part these terms are omitted in this book in order to make it easier to read. But please bear in mind that this entire book should be prefaced by "with certain exceptions" and those other terms. When you take your plan to your lawyer, CPA, or other professional, he or she should fill you in on the details of the pitfalls that exist because of those "certain exceptions."

A Philosophy

I have been involved with income taxes since 1956, and I have seen the rules grow from a relatively simple system to a morass of rules involving regular tax, alternative minimum tax, and many other taxes, often with requirements that two or more sets of records be maintained for the same transactions. Most tax professionals I know will admit, privately, that the income tax area has become too big and complicated for one individual to understand completely. A sensible way to spend our human resources composed of those employed by the IRS and those who battle the IRS? Hardly.

The alternative? A national sales tax *instead* of the income tax. Such a system would encourage the investment in our country for which our elected officials seem to pine. Yes, such a tax would make this book obsolete, but I would gladly forgo the royalties if I could see the income tax pass over the horizon into oblivion. I hope you will join me in supporting the embryonic movements that could make that happen. In the meantime, this book should help you see at least some of your income tax burden pass into that oblivion.

Doing Business Tax-Free

1

Pay No Income Taxes

WORKING FOR A SALARY OR LIVING OFF DIVIDENDS WON'T DO IT

If your only working endeavor is for a salary and your only other income is from interest and dividends from major corporations, you cannot, legally or illegally, escape income taxes (unless your income is miserably low). Your employer will provide you with a W-2 form, and the corporations or governments that pay you interest or dividends will send you a 1099 form. This is a convenient service, for it relieves you of a detailed bookkeeping chore. Unfortunately, it is also a convenient service for the IRS, for your employer and the other payers of income will send copies of those forms to the IRS. That means the IRS knows how much money you made and will expect to see those same numbers listed as income on your tax return.

Why do your employer, the bank, and other sources of income provide this information to the IRS? Because they are required to do so and would be assessed substantial penalties if they failed to reveal your financial secrets to the IRS!

What if you ignore the W-2 and the 1099 and report much less income? The IRS Big Brother computer now matches most of those W-2 and 1099 forms to individual tax returns, so you will be caught understating your income. That can bring bills for sizable penalties and, if you persist in such antics, can put you away for some hard time. In other words, don't try it!

METHODS THAT *WILL* WORK

Okay, so you will stay within the law. How then can you reduce your taxes to zero? Consider these ideas:

1. Convert all of your investments to state and local tax-exempt bonds—and quit your job and any other activity that might generate taxable income. Unfortunately, the "quit your job" requirement makes this impracticable for most of us.

2. Work only part-time, or full-time in a low-paying job, so that your income will be offset by exemptions and deductions and you will have no taxable income. That might work if you can live in a dilapidated one-room efficiency and drive around in a '77 Chevy, but that's a rather unattractive way to live.

3. Be a passive investor in a business that, through accounting magic such as depreciation, will generate a "paper" loss that you can use on your own tax return. Until the mid-1980s many promoters sold real estate and other partnerships that would generate tax losses that far exceeded the amount you had to invest. The partnerships had the additional advantage of hired management. As an investor, you had to do nothing but enter the tax-saving paper losses on your tax return. Because you had to do nothing, these investments became known as "passive investments." Unfortunately, during the 1980s, Congress slammed the door on most of these tax shelters, leaving only some sophisticated areas in low-income housing and oil reclamation as viable *passive* tax-avoidance tools, and there aren't many of those about. At least, there aren't many that make economic sense. ("Economic sense" means that you are not throwing your money into a sink-hole just to create a tax deduction.)

4. Invest in a nonpassive activity. What does *nonpassive* mean? It means that you will have to participate actively in your tax shelter. In other words, you will have to operate

your own business (part-time or full-time). Then you will need to operate that business in such a way that expenses of operating the business will offset all other income or a substantial part of it. As this is the only method of tax elimination that is practicable and legal for most of us, it is the method to which most of the rest of this book is devoted.[1]

YOUR REAL GOAL

At the risk of your adding me to your "absurd individuals" list, I will ask, Why do you want to pay no income tax? Is it really because you are so upset over limousines for managers of our bureaucracy or free haircuts for Congress members? Perhaps if you are somewhat altruistic, you worry a little about the waste in government, but isn't it truer to phrase your concern as: Because I want the results of my efforts to result in as much cash as possible in my pocket?

There are three methods to accomplish that:

1. Increase the income you receive for the same amount of effort.
2. Reduce or eliminate your tax burden.
3. Combine 1 and 2.

INCREASE THE INCOME YOU RECEIVE FOR THE SAME AMOUNT OF EFFORT

Except for the token raises you may receive, there is not much you, as an employee, can do to accomplish this. (Raises inherent to promotions don't count. Promotions usually involve more effort, more responsibility, and more risk.) This method is also difficult for you as a self-employed person, for it involves more efficient utilization of facilities, employee training, delegation, and all the phases of what is called management. Much of that

---

[1]Don't be too disappointed if every idea we cover doesn't completely wipe out your income tax burden. Instead, use the ideas to substantially reduce your tax bill, and enjoy some of that money you have been sending off to Uncle Sam and, perhaps, to your state governor.

is not tax-related and therefore beyond the scope of this book. Where management decisions have an impact on taxes, they are covered.

REDUCE OR ELIMINATE YOUR TAX BURDEN

There are various ways to accomplish this. Here is how one married couple can reduce their income tax and put more money into the family pockets:

Isaac has a full-time job in the insurance business, earning $100,000 per year. His wife, Mabel, had put her efforts into raising two children. Now that the children are teenagers, she has extra time on her hands. Years ago, she took a woodworking course in high school and has often found that making a few wooden knickknacks for the house relaxes her. Now she has decided to fill her time with more extensive woodworking pursuits. She buys more-sophisticated power tools and goes into business as Mabel's Tables, operating in their garage.

Because of the purchase of many power tools[2] and certain other deductible expenses, she incurs a loss of $15,000. The comparison of the family income-tax picture, with and without Mabel's Tables, is shown in Table 1.1.

The starting of Mabel's Tables has saved the family $4,200. (Of course, the IRS still has to be convinced that Mabel's Tables is really a business and not a hobby. For a discussion of this, see Chapter 5.)

Often, you can do even better in the tax deduction department by changing the status of your full-time pursuits from that of an employee to that of a self-employed business owner. People who work in their own businesses can often pay less tax because . . .

- They may be able to deduct the expense of offices they maintain in their homes.

---

[2]See the discussion, later in this chapter, about Section 179 and how the purchase of some equipment can be 100 percent deductible in the year you purchase it.

**Table 1.1   Isaac's and Mabel's Federal Income Tax
with and without Table Business**

	Family Employment Is Isaac's Job	Family Employment Consists of Isaac's Job and Mabel's Business
Isaac's salary	$100,000	$ 100,000
Loss from Mabel's Tables	—	(15,000)
Gross income	100,000	85,000
Income tax*	$ 15,531	$ 11,331

*Computation assumes four exemptions, itemized deductions of $13,000, and 2000 tax rates.

- Some of their automobile expense may be claimed as a business expense.
- They may be able to divert some of the income from a business to children or other members of the family who are in a lower tax bracket.
- They may be able to convert some vacation travel expense into a legal tax deduction as business travel.
- They can accumulate wealth in the form of business goodwill, on which they will pay only capital gains tax when they sell the business sometime in the future.
- They may be able to create paper losses in the start-up period that can generate refunds of taxes paid in previous years.

These are all covered in later chapters, with specifics on what the tax law and IRS rules will let you do and how you build up evidence that you are following the rules. Even if you cannot completely eliminate your tax burden, these suggestions should help you keep more money in your bank account.

2

Organize Your Business for the Smallest Tax Bite

In what sort of legal form should you organize your business? Should you operate as a sole proprietor, a corporation, or as some other entity? A little thought and planning in this area can save taxes. No, your business form alone won't make all of your taxes go away. It has to be combined with suggestions that come later in this book, but making the right decisions as to the type of organization for your business can be a big start toward saving serious dollars.

The choices include doing business as a sole proprietor, in a partnership with some other person, as either of two types of corporations, or as a limited liability company. Within some of these classifications are some finer distinctions, each of which is treated a little differently by IRS rules.

Want a simple rule of thumb that would make the choice for you? Sorry, there isn't any. Even if there were one, it wouldn't last long. As Congress changes the rules and the tax rates, your choice of organization can become the structure to avoid. Add to this the fact that the level of income, both of the business and of its owner(s), plays a major part in determining the best form in which to do business.

Probably the simplest way to explain all this is to describe each form of business organization and the tax characteristics of each and then to compare the alternatives.

THE SIMPLEST FORM—THE SOLE PROPRIETORSHIP

Almost everyone has been a sole proprietor at some time in his or her life. When you were younger, did you ever mow lawns, baby-sit, or clean swimming pools? If you mowed the lawn, you might have collected $10 from the homeowner. If you mowed enough lawns or did other tasks, you might have earned enough to make yourself eligible to pay income tax. (You did pay it, didn't you?) When you earned that first dollar, paid to you for providing a service, as opposed to hourly pay or salary, you were a sole proprietor.

You can assume this mantle for your business with no effort other than creating a product or service and selling it to others for a price. True, your city or county officials may require you to purchase an occupational license, but even if you do business without buying such a license, you are still a proprietor, and the IRS will expect you to send it a share of your profit. (The IRS does not care whether you bought a local business license, although the purchase of such a license can help prove that you really are in business.)

How the IRS Taxes Sole Proprietorships

If your part-time business earns a profit, there's bad news. The profit from that business is added onto the income you already make, which means it is taxed at the tax bracket you are already in, or it may even move you into a higher tax bracket.

If your business operates at a loss, there's good news. The loss will be subtracted from your present income, reducing your tax and perhaps moving you into a lower tax bracket.

Let's look at three scenarios of what could have happened to Horace Hare:

Horace is single and has a full-time job paying him a salary of $80,000 per year. He starts a sideline business of upholstery repair. Table 2.1 is the computation of the income tax results of Horace earning only his salary, his salary and a sideline-business profit of $20,000, and his salary and a sideline-business loss of $20,000.

When Horace's upholstery business earns a $20,000 profit, the bad news is an increase of $6,216 in his income tax. Not only does this

Table 2.1   Horace Upholstery—Sideline as a Sole Proprietorship

		Salary Only	Salary plus Profit	Salary minus Loss
1	Horace's salary	$ 80,000	$ 80,000	$ 80,000
2	Business profit or (loss)	0	20,000	(20,000)
3	Total income (total of lines 1 and 2)	80,000	100,000	60,000
4	Personal exemption	(2,800)	(2,800)	(2,800)
5	Itemized deductions	(13,000)	(13,000)	(13,000)
6	Taxable income (line 3 minus lines 4 and 5)	64,200	84,200	44,200
7	Income tax* on income shown in line 6	$ 14,575	$ 20,791	$ 8,971

*Federal income tax rates for 2000. State income tax may also be incurred.

additional income create a bigger bite, but that $20,000 is also taxed at 31 percent, whereas his $80,000 salary is taxed at a rate of 28 percent or less. (For an explanation of how percentage brackets work, see Appendix B.)

If Horace loses $20,000 in his sideline business, that loss is also bad news. However, he can have some solace from the fact that the loss reduces his income tax by $5,604.

"But," you say, "my job doesn't pay $80,000!" Of course, most jobs don't come with that sort of income. However, I chose the figures for the previous example because they display the impact of income taxes without complications that arise from Social Security taxes. That's because the major part of the Social Security tax is collected on only the first $76,200 of income (in 2000).

So what if your numbers are below that $76,200 cutoff? Assume the same facts as in the previous example, but change Horace's day-job salary to $50,000. The numbers now look like Table 2.2.

Table 2.2   Horace Upholstery—Sideline as a Sole Proprietorship

		Salary Only	Salary plus Profit	Salary minus Loss
1	Horace's salary	$ 50,000	$ 50,000	$ 50,000
2	Business profit or (loss)	0	20,000	(20,000)
3	Total income (total of lines 1 and 2)	50,000	70,000	30,000
4	Personal exemption	(2,800)	(2,800)	(2,800)
5	Itemized deductions	(13,000)	(13,000)	(13,000)
6	Taxable income (line 3 minus lines 4 and 5)	34,200	54,200	14,200
7	Income tax on income shown in line 6	6,171	11,771	2,134
8	Social Security tax on salary*	3,825	3,825	3,825
9	Social Security tax on net income from the upholstery business*	0	3,060	0
10	Total income tax and Social Security tax	$ 9,996	$ 18,656	$ 5,959

*Social Security taxes are 7.65 percent on Horace's salary and 15.3 percent on his net income from the upholstery business.

The tax due to the sideline business is greater at this level because of the Social Security tax levied on self-employment income at the rate of 15.3 percent. Notice that although the $20,000 loss in the last column serves to reduce the income tax on Horace's salary, it is of no help in reducing Social Security tax on his salary. In other words, a loss on a sideline business cannot offset salary income for Social Security tax purposes.

There is a moral here. If Horace's daytime job were as an independent contractor (operating his own business), he could offset the $50,000 income with the $20,000 loss. That is, the incomes and losses of sole proprietorships can be netted together for social security taxes. But business losses and salaries cannot be combined to reduce Social Security taxes.

When to Operate as a Sole Proprietor

As should be obvious from Horace's situation, if you expect a loss in your business and you have significant other income, operating as a sole proprietor makes sense. (Also consider operating as an S corporation, discussed later.)

If you expect a loss and have little or no other income, the decision is more complex. The consideration then has to do with carrying losses to other years and whether you can do that better as a sole proprietorship or as a corporation. (For a discussion of net operating losses, see Chapter 4.)

If your business earns a profit and you do have significant other income, then you may be better off operating as a corporation.

THE REGULAR, PLAIN-VANILLA CORPORATION
(C-TYPE, AS THE IRS CALLS IT)

What Is This Corporate Animal?

The term *corporation* usually evokes thoughts of General Electric, Shell Oil, Microsoft, or other large firms operating globally. Yet the great majority of corporations are smaller entities, each owned by very few people. In fact, many are owned by just one individual. As you, too, can own a corporation, let's review how the corporation evolved, what it is, and how it is taxed.

As Europe moved into the Renaissance period six centuries ago, monarchs and their governments wanted to expand. In the late Renaissance, this expansion included the exploration and colonization of the New World. Building ships and crewing them required considerable investment, usually more than any one regent had. Therefore, these monarchs sought ways to attract investors from the rising merchant class. Suppose Tony, the goldsmith, invested in a pool, or partnership, of merchants to build a ship. What if the ship developed leaks and sank? Eric, who owned the furs on board the ship, might sue Tony and the other partners for the value of the soggy furs now in Davy Jones's locker. What if the other partners had little money and property, while Tony had much gold in his safe? Tony might be the only one able to pay a judgment Eric might obtain. Tony could end up losing far more than his share of the ship enterprise! Of course, Tony anticipated such a result, so he declined to invest in the royal enterprise.

The solution? Issue a royal decree that investors in the ship enterprise could not lose more than they invested in it—each investor's liability was limited to that person's investment. This type of enterprise became known as a corporation, and because a corporation issues a stock certificate to each investor to document how much of the corporation the investor owns, the investors became known as *stockholders* or *shareholders*. As a creditor could not "reach through" the corporation to the assets of the investors, the corporation took on the aspect of a separate person. In fact, it is sort of a superperson, because it never has to die of old age. It can exist forever if it doesn't get killed by insolvency and bankruptcy or if it is not eaten by another corporation.

How the Corporation Is Charged Income Tax

Until 1913, doing business as a corporation made sense, for it provided the advantage of limited liability and few, if any, disadvantages. But the infamous Sixteenth Amendment to the U.S. Constitution, ratified in 1913, brought a serious disadvantage to corporations—the income tax! Corporations are charged income tax much as are individuals: The more profit a corporation makes, the higher the percentage of its income it pays.[1] Look at Table 2.3. This is what will happen if Horace Upholstery operates as a corporation and generates a taxable income of $20,000.

---

[1]Although this used to be an accurate description of our progressive tax-rate structure, there are now some aberrations. For discussion, see Appendix A.

Table 2.3   Horace Upholstery—Operating as a Corporation

1	Taxable income of Horace Upholstery Corporation	$20,000
2	**Subtract corporation income tax (@ 15%)**	**3,000**
3	Remainder (line 1 minus line 2) that the corporation can pay to Horace as *dividends*	17,000
4	**On his individual income tax return, Horace must pay this tax on the dividend on line 3***	**5,270**
5	**Total corporation and individual income tax (line 2 plus line 4)**	**$ 8,270**

*Assumes a salary from his day job of $80,000.

This tax bill represents about 46 percent of the earnings of the business. As a sole proprietor, Horace has to pay only $6,400 tax on that additional $20,000. The higher tax bill with the corporate setup demonstrates the infamous *double taxation of corporations.* That $20,000 income is taxed on the corporation income tax return and again, as a dividend, on the owner's individual income tax return. (What better way to destroy individual initiative!)

How to Avoid This Corporate Tax

If Horace Upholstery Corporation has additional expenses of $20,000, that will reduce the corporation's income to zero, and there normally is no income tax on zero income. But how can he do that without having his corporation buy a bunch of deductible gadgets and services he doesn't need? He can have the corporation pay him a salary, as shown in Table 2.4.

By taking the corporation profits out as salary, Horace has reduced his total income taxes by $2,070. So the rule must be that it is always better, taxwise, to take out corporate profits as salary. But like most all rules, this one has exceptions. For instance, this Horace example assumes a daytime job that is above the level ($76,200 in 2000) that is subject to most of the Social Security tax. If Horace's salary from that job is $50,000, Horace will have to pay full Social Security tax on the salary

Table 2.4 Horace Upholstery Corporation Pays Horace a Salary

1	Taxable income of Horace Upholstery Corporation	$20,000
2	Subtract salary paid to Horace (a deductible expense to the corporation)	20,000
3	New taxable income of corporation (line 1 minus line 2)	0
4	Income tax on new taxable income (line 3)	0
5	Additional income tax Horace must pay on his $20,000 salary (line 2) from Horace Upholstery Corporation	6,200
6	Total income tax (corporate and individual) Horace pays on his business profits* (line 4 plus line 5)	$ 6,200

*This represents about 29 percent tax. As this salary is added to the salary from Horace's full-time job, it raises him into a higher tax bracket.

Summary:

Total income taxes if corporation profits are paid out as dividends (from Table 2.1)	$8,270
Subtract total income taxes if corporation profits are paid out as salary to stockholder	6,200
Saving in taxes by taking profits as salary	$2,070

from the upholstery corporation. In that case, the results are reversed from the example. It will cost Horace and his corporation $900 more in income and Social Security taxes than it would if the corporation paid income tax on the $20,000 profit and paid Horace a dividend of the remaining $17,000.[2]

Before you become discouraged, be aware that there is a way to have the best of both worlds—no double taxation and less Social Security tax. We will discuss the how of that under S corporations.

[2]If you make this calculation yourself, remember that both the employer and employee portion of Social Security on the salary from the upholstery corporation are, in effect, coming out of Horace's pocket.

Low Tax If You Leave the Money in the Corporation?

Suppose Horace can provide for his needs and wants adequately from his regular job's $80,000 salary:

Horace is operating his upholstery business partly as tax shelter and partly to build a business that will help him earn money after retirement. He therefore does not take any dividends or salary but leaves all of the profits in the business. He can let these profits sit in a savings account and earn interest, or he can buy some sophisticated sewing machines, a computer, and other equipment. (Buying equipment will provide some further tax reduction. For discussion, see Chapter 3.)

If he operates as a sole proprietor, he will pay $5,883 of income tax on that profit, as we saw earlier in this chapter. He will pay this regardless of whether he draws the money out of the business or leaves it there.

However, if he operates as a corporation (C type), he will be taxed in the lowest corporation tax bracket (15 percent of the first $50,000), so he will pay only $3,000 on his $20,000 profit. The comparison looks like Table 2.5

Remember that this works only if Horace leaves the profit, or at least most of the profit, in the business. Someday, he may want to take some of the profits out of the business. At that time, taking them as salary will avoid the double taxation of corporate profits.

The Penalty for Keeping Too Much Money in a Corporation

There is no problem with accumulating corporate profits in a corporation, if that accumulation is under $250,000. The IRS can tax profits that are kept in the business beyond the $250,000 at a rate of 39.6 percent. This is *in addition* to income tax! How do you avoid this tax? By convincing the IRS that you are keeping the money in the corporation to meet the reasonable needs of the business, to expand, or to meet any contingent liabilities that may be out there.

For instance, Horace Upholstery might have used some substandard springs in fixing chairs. If those springs suddenly erupt, poke through the upholstery, and injure a sitter, Horace's

Table 2.5   Horace Upholstery—Sole Proprietorship versus Corporation

Tax on the $20,000 upholstery profit, when Horace acts as a sole proprietor and the profit is added onto his salary, putting him in a high tax bracket (from Table 2.4)	$6,200
Subtract corporate tax when business is incorporated and profit is left in the business	3,000
Tax saving when profit is left in the C corporation business	$3,200

corporation could be sued. If his product liability insurance has a $50,000 deductible, the need to cover the deductible should justify his keeping an extra $50,000 in the corporate bank account.

More Tax Rules When the Big Bucks Roll In

The accumulated earnings tax demonstrates a major quirk of our income tax system: As a business grows, some of the tax rules change, and the rates go up. If we project to the future when Horace is manufacturing thousands of stuffed chairs and shipping them all over the world, the numbers might look something like Table 2.6.

Table 2.6   Horace Upholstery Corporation—Years in the Future

1	Taxable income of Horace's corporation	$500,000
2	**Subtract corporate income tax**	**170,000**
3	What's left paid out as dividends*	330,000
4	**Tax on dividends on line 3 (paid by owner of corporation as part of individual income tax)**	**105,000**
5	**Total corporate and individual income taxes (line 2 plus line 4) on business income**	**$275,000**

*Of course, few corporations will pay out all of the profits as dividends. Corporations generally keep some cash for expansion, contingencies, and such matters. In this example, to keep the comparison as simple as possible, Horace pays out all of the profits.

If Horace foolishly decides to handle his affairs this way, he ends up paying the feds more than half of his profits—and more tax to the state government.

Horace can reduce the double taxation by paying the profits to himself as salary, but now, with $500,000 in income, we have another factor. The IRS says that salaries paid to owners of corporations can be no more than reasonable. If Horace takes a $500,000 salary to reduce the corporate taxable income to zero, the IRS might say it is an unreasonable amount. What amount is reasonable? Lots of business owners have fought the IRS in court on this question. Some have won. Some have lost. The rules seem to be that the salaries should be about the same as those that other companies in similar businesses and of similar size pay. So although the president of General Electric may receive a salary of several million dollars, Horace Upholstery does not compare in size. The IRS could well determine that Horace's salary should be no more than $300,000 per year. What happens when the IRS, two years after the corporate tax return is filed, so decides? Can Horace pay the other $200,000 back to the corporation? Generally not, although there are exceptions. (For discussion of these exceptions and other ways to make an overlarge salary palatable to the IRS, see Chapter 6.) That $200,000 is disallowed as a deductible expense to the corporation and is then classified as a dividend, which is not deductible by the corporation. So the corporation has to pay tax on the $200,000 profit, and Horace also has to pay tax on the $200,000 dividend. Table 2.7 shows what this total tax bill looks like.

Taking too much money out of the corporation has cost Horace and his corporation $61,250 extra in his tax bill. (He pays double tax on the dividend.) Note that because Horace takes out all the profits as salary, he will probably have to loan his corporation the funds with which to pay that additional tax.[3] This can lead us into the questions about loans between a major

---

[3] With foresight, Horace may have been able to avoid this unfortunate situation. His corporation could have had an agreement with all employees that if the IRS disallowed any part of a salary as excessive, that employee would return the excessive amount to the corporation. (There is little danger that the IRS will ever find the salaries of nonstockholder employees to be excessive, so these agreements affect only stockholder employees.)

Table 2.7   Horace Upholstery Corporation
If the IRS Disallows Part of His Salary

		Corporate and Individual Tax Returns as Filed	Corporate and Individual Taxes After IRS Adjustment
1	Taxable income of Horace Upholstery Corporation before subtracting Horace's salary	$500,000	$500,000
2	Subtract Horace's salary	500,000	300,000
3	Remaining corporate taxable income	0	200,000
4	Corporate income tax on remaining taxable income	0	61,250
	Horace's personal income		
5	Salary	500,000	300,000
6	Dividend	0	200,000
7	Horace's total personal income	500,000	500,000
8	Individual income tax on dividends and salary	169,600	169,600
9	Total corporate and individual income taxes that Horace and his corporation pay (sum of lines 4 and 8)*	$169,600	$230,850

*Social Security taxes are omitted in this example as they would be approximately the same both before and after the IRS adjustment.

stockholder and his or her corporation. (For discussion, see Chapter 6.)

More Stockholders?

One of the nontax advantages of doing business as a corporation is the ease with which some or all of the company can be sold to other individuals, who then become stockholders. What effect does having more than one owner, or stockholder, have on the tax picture of the corporation? Essentially, none. It makes no difference whether there is one stockholder, as in Horace Upholstery Corporation, or thousands, as in IBM. The same tax rates and the same limitations on accumulated earnings apply to the corporation.[4]

Personal-Service Corporations

Personal-service corporations are corporations that provide services in the fields of health, law, engineering, architecture, accounting, actuarial science, performing arts, or consulting. These corporations do not enjoy the graduated corporation tax scale that provides, for example, 15 percent tax on the first $50,000 and 25 percent on the next $25,000. Instead, they are taxed at 35 percent on every dollar of profit. Also, they are subject to the accumulated earnings tax when that number reaches $150,000, instead of the $250,000 applicable to other corporations.

Why use a corporate structure with this tax burden? Some personal-service corporations were set up before the rules changed to single out these folks for the honor of paying higher income taxes, and there are other obscure tax rules that might make such a corporation workable. The best procedure with such a corporation is either to take all the profits out as salary, or to elect to file as an S corporation.

PARTNERSHIPS

In the past few years, partnerships have become somewhat passe as a business form, having been replaced by the *limited*

[4]The accumulated earnings tax is still a major consideration for corporations with few stockholders. However, for large corporations with thousands of stockholders, it usually isn't. The reason: For the IRS to be able to make that additional 39.6 percent accumulated earnings tax stick, there must be one or a few major stockholders who can control the corporation and the dividend policies such that they, the stockholders, will have a tax benefit. In the case of companies like IBM and General Motors, there are no stockholders with enough stock to wield that sort of power, so the IRS does not assess the accumulated earnings penalty.

liability company (LLC) form. However, as LLCs are a hybrid of a corporation and a partnership, it helps to understand this new breed by discussing partnerships and corporations first.

By definition, partnerships consist of two or more people or entities that band together to operate a business. Therefore, an individual such as Horace cannot operate as a partnership unless he expands by teaming up with someone else who becomes his partner. Although partnerships are usually composed of two or more people, corporations and other entities (such as trusts) can become partners.

Types of Partnerships

General partnership   This is the entity most of us are familiar with or have been involved in at some time. If Horace sold half of his business to Harry and together they cut fabric and hammered tacks, they would be general partners in a general partnership. It is not necessary that they be equal partners. Horace can sell just 10 or 20 percent of his business to Harry, or Horace and Harry can start the business together. But if Horace contributes more time or money to the business, he logically has the bigger partnership share. The downside to this partnership arrangement is the unlimited liability of each partner. Consider the following example:

The Amalgamated Technical Tool Company manufactures an automatic upholstery machine that will remove old upholstery from a chair, cut new upholstery, fit it to the chair frame, stitch as necessary, tack it to the frame, and compute the bill for the customer—all without human intervention. The machine costs $300,000, but Harry is convinced it will benefit the business, so he signs an order for a machine to be delivered to the partnership. If the partnership does not have the $300,000 with which to pay for the machine after it is delivered and the bill arrives, the Amalgamated Technical Tool Company can sue not only the partnership but also Harry and Horace. Horace might have to sell his yacht to pay the debt that Harry creates, even though Harry incurred that debt without Horace's knowledge.

(If Horace and Harry set up a corporation, Horace can keep his yacht. The Amalgamated Technical Tool Company can sue and cause the upholstery corporation to sell its assets to pay the bill, but it cannot force Horace to sell his personal assets.)[5]

Taxation of partnerships   Unlike the case with C corporations, there is no double taxation of partnerships. Rather than paying taxes, a partnership reports only (to its partners and, of course, to the IRS) how much it has earned. Each partner then adds his or her share of the partnership profit to his or her personal income. Also, earnings reported by any partner, if that partner is active in the business, are subject to Social Security tax.

This is not always an advantage:

What if Horace and Harry want to leave all of the profits in the business to purchase new equipment? If the business is incorporated and the profits are less than $50,000, they pay only 15 percent tax and have 85 percent of their profits left with which to invest in equipment. As partners, they add the profits to their other income and, in Horace's case, pay approximately 30 percent in income tax, plus Social Security, to the IRS. This leaves less than 70 percent of the profits to use for expansion.

Limited partnership   This form of partnership was popular in years past, as it allows all but one of the partners to have limited liability. The partner who assumes that burden is known as a *general partner.* (If someone tells you that he or she is a general partner, there is no way of telling, without additional information, whether they are a general partner in a general partnership or in a limited partnership.) Like general partnerships, they are no longer in favor, as the LLC form of doing business has virtually replaced it as a popular choice. The following description is included for information, in case you are offered the "opportunity" to make an investment in a limited partnership.

---

[5]There are exceptions, as when fraud is involved.

The word *limited* refers to the limited liability of certain partners in a partnership, who are then known as *limited partners.* These folk then enjoy the same protection of their personal assets as do corporate stockholders. To have this status, they must be so designated in the partnership agreement and, in some states, must not have any active management role in the partnership. These limited partnerships were the legal-form of vehicles of choice for most real estate ventures until 1986, when Congress and the IRS changed certain rules. It used to be that if such a partnership had losses, the limited partners could use those losses to offset other income, such as salaries. The new rules state that limited (inactive) partners cannot use those losses to offset salaries, business profits, and certain other income. The result is that the losses go unused (until years later when the partnership interest is sold), so structuring limited partnerships with the expectation of losses now seldom makes sense.

LIMITED LIABILITY COMPANY (LLC)

The LLC is a recent development, brought about because many foreign countries permit this type of organization, so as global trade and cross-border commercial alliances increased, so did the demand by U.S. enterprises for a matching business form in this country.

In a federal system such as ours, creating a new business form is not simple, for it is created by each state individually. That is, it took almost 20 years for all of the states to pass laws that enabled the creation of LLCs. (I hear that we should be amazed that it happened in 20 years, but I'm not sure whether we should wonder why it took so long or be awed that it happened so quickly.)

What Is an LLC?

An LLC can be described as a business form that has the advantages of both a corporation and a partnership without some of the disadvantages. Each owner (called a *member*) has limited liability, just as do the stockholders of a corporation. That is, a member of an LLC cannot lose more than he or she invested in the enterprise, regardless of what financial difficulties it encounters. (As in the case of corporations, there are exceptions where fraud or malfeasance is involved or, in the case of professionals, where there is an act of malpractice by the professional.)

At the same time, an LLC can be taxed as a partnership, thereby sidestepping the double taxation that a corporation can incur. As in a partnership, the profit of the business is allocated to the individual owners, and each of them pays individual income tax on his or her share of the income. (For simplicity, I've referred to members or partners as "he" or "she," but be aware that corporations, partnerships, other LLCs, and other organizations [e.g., a nonprofit operation] can be members of an LLC or partners in a partnership.)

Recent Changes in the LLC Rules

If you last read about the development of LLCs a few years ago (as in the first edition of this book), you will find some important changes in what follows:

Number of members   As previously mentioned, all 50 states now enable the formation of an LLC within their boundaries. However, there are variations in the rules among the states. For instance, some states allow one individual or other entity to form an LLC. Other states require that there be at least two members of an LLC. The requirement that there be two members is more consistent with the concept that an LLC is a partnership that has limited liability for the partners, but it may be unfair to deny a sole proprietor the limited liability he or she would have by joining with one other person in the enterprise.

Taxation of LLCs   There's a surprise here: The IRS actually simplified a rule! Until 1998, the IRS had some rigid rules as to what had to be included in the articles of organization of an LLC.[6] If those items did not meet IRS specifications, the LLC

---

[6]The old requirements revolved around four factors: continuity of life, centralized management, limited liability, and free transferability of ownership.

might find that it gets to pay income tax as if it were a corporation—double taxation, in other words. Each state passed its version of what its tax experts thought would best enable its LLCs to qualify to be taxed as partnerships. Obviously, with 50 different statutes to be interpreted, the IRS was swamped with ruling requests, and the prospect of the courts becoming clogged with taxpayer appeals of the IRS's decisions called for a simple solution: The IRS gave in. It promulgated a new policy by which each LLC could elect how it was to be taxed, and the old rules were discarded. At the same time, the IRS issued a form on which the LLC could make this decision by simply checking a box, so this new policy has become known as the *check-the-box regulations*. (Actually, most LLCs don't even need to submit this form. The rule is that if an LLC fails to submit the form, it will automatically be taxed as a partnership, and that process is known as the *default election*.)

S CORPORATIONS—THE BEST OF ALL WORLDS, IF THE WORLD IS SMALL

Years ago, Congress legislated this fickle creature into our tax code to relieve small businesses of the double taxation of corporate profits. When originally enacted, these corporations were called *subchapter S corporations*, named for the pertinent section of the U.S. Code. Later legislation changed the name to simply *S corporations*. (Here is one of those rare instances when something in the tax law was actually simplified.)

With very few exceptions, new corporations are set up, or chartered, by the state, not by the federal government. The C corporation and S corporation designations are a tax status conferred by the IRS on these state-chartered corporations.

When Horace decides to incorporate Horace Upholstery, he applies to the state for a corporate charter. After he pays the state fee and submits the required paperwork, the state creates a new entity, Horace Upholstery, Inc. (Horace can choose the name, as long as there is not another corporation already in existence with that name.)

He then has to decide whether he wants the corporation to be taxed as a C corporation or an S corporation. He records his decision by filing, or not filing, a request with the federal government (the IRS) to be taxed as an S corporation.[7]

In other words, the department of the state government that oversees the granting of corporate charters does not care what tax status the owner(s) of the corporation choose(s). They only care that the incorporation fees are paid and that the related paperwork is in order.

The state tax department, on the other hand, may want to know whether or not the corporation will be taxed as an S corporation. (Some states follow the federal rules on taxing S corporations, and some states tax all corporations as C corporations, regardless of the federal tax status. The tax department of your state can tell you which rules your state follows.)

How S Corporations Are Taxed

An often-used, simple explanation of S corporations is that they are corporations that are taxed like sole proprietors (if there is only one stockholder) or partnerships (if there is more than one stockholder). For corporations that have been in S status since day one of their corporate life, that is true. For corporations that spent some time as C corporations before electing S status, that is not always true. Specifically, if the corporation owned property at the time of the S election, the property later appreciated in value, and the S corporation subsequently sold it, then the corporation would pay corporate tax on the gain involved in the sale and the stockholders would pay more tax on that gain. That is, the double tax would apply. Also, there are rules as to how much passive income an S corporation that was formerly a C corporation can earn without becoming liable for corporate income tax on that passive income.[8] Generally, though, the tax-

---

[7]That request (*election* in IRS-speak) is filed on Form 2553 and is due by the fifteenth day of the third month of the corporation's tax year (March 15 for a corporation on a tax year ending on December 31).

[8]*Passive income* consists of royalties, rents, dividends, interest, annuities, and gains from sales or exchanges of stocks, bonds, and other securities.

able profit of an S corporation is split up among the stockholders according to their share of stock ownership, and each stockholder reports his or her share of that income on the individual income tax return.

Although most small business corporations have only a few stockholders, you should be aware that S corporation status cannot be held by a corporation with more than 75 stockholders. There are other technical requirements that make it imperative you confer with a tax professional before asking the IRS to grant S status.

Social Security Tax and the S Corporation

Assume that Horace has no other income except his $20,000 profit from Horace Upholstery, Inc., and that he takes the profits out as salary. His Social Security taxes total $3,060. He pays this in two ways: As an employee of his corporation, he pays 7.65 percent of $20,000, or $1,530. His corporation, as his employer, also pays $1,530. As Horace owns the corporation, both sides of the Social Security tax actually come out of his pocket. Can Horace reduce his Social Security tax? You bet. He can pay himself only a $5,000 salary and take the rest of the profit as a dividend. Because dividends are not subject to Social Security tax, Horace and his corporation would have to pay only $382.50 each, or a total of $765.[9]

There are a couple of caveats of which you should be aware. The IRS, of course, is aware of this maneuver, so their auditors will insist that the owner of the corporation take a reasonable salary before paying himself or herself a dividend. When Horace takes only a $5,000 salary, he needs to be able to prove that he is working only part-time at his corporate business, for the $5,000 is less than minimum wage for a full-time pursuit of 2,000 hours per year. It is also helpful if he can prove that the other $15,000 is a reasonable return on his investment in the business.

[9]Dividends, when they come out of S corporation earnings, are technically called *distributions*.

When you use maneuvers like this to reduce Social Security tax, remember that such reductions in your payments to Social Security will probably reduce your old-age pension. The solution is to put the savings on Social Security taxes into some sort of private retirement fund.

Also, let me remind you that this procedure of taking profits as dividends only works for S corporations. If you take dividends from a C corporation, you will end up paying double taxes. This brings up one further complication: If you have a C corporation and convert it to an S corporation without taking all of the profits out of the corporation before it is converted, be careful. If you take out, as dividends, more profit than the corporation earns when it has S status, you will be taking out those old C corporation profits, and they will still be subject to double taxation.

Will taking dividends from an S corporation always generate this kind of savings in Social Security tax? Not necessarily.

Assume again that Horace has a full-time job that pays him $75,600 per year, plus Horace Upholstery, which generates a $20,000 profit. (At this writing, only the first $76,200 of earnings are subject to the basic OASDI[10] 6.2 percent tax.) Through his full-time employment, Horace has already paid the 6.2 percent tax on $75,600, so he and his corporation pay that rate on only $600 more. The other 1.45 percent of Social Security tax is levied on all earnings, without limitation, so he and his corporation pay that on all of his salary. Now, if he takes out all profit from Horace Upholstery as salary, his total Social Security taxes will be $655. Taking a $5,000 salary and $15,000 in dividends will generate Social Security taxes of $220, a savings of only $435.

This maneuver is probably still worth doing, but the benefit is not so great if most of the Social Security tax burden has already been met through other employment.

---

[10]Old-age survivors, and disability insurance.

SUMMARY: A COMPARISON OF BUSINESS FORMATS

Sole Proprietorship or Partnership

Income will be added to other earnings, possibly resulting in a higher tax bracket. Added earnings are subject to medicare tax and perhaps OASDI tax. Liability is unlimited.

C Corporation

If earnings are left in the business, the tax rate may be lower than the individual tax rate paid by a sole proprietor. If earnings are withdrawn as dividends, they are taxed twice. Liability is limited.

S Corporation

Earnings are taxed only once but at the owner's individual tax rate. The owner may escape some Social Security tax on earnings by withdrawing profits as dividends. Liability is limited.

LLC

Earnings are passed through to the owner and taxed at the individual's rates. Double taxation is avoided but without the restrictions of S corporations. However, all earnings, whether paid to the owners or not, are subject to Social Security taxes. Liability is limited.

CONCLUSION

After reading this chapter, you are likely to ask "So what is the best form of organization?" Unfortunately, there is no easy answer, but you can make certain computations that help. Start with a forecast of what your business will earn or lose during its first two or three years of operation. For each year, work out the total income taxes, both business and personal (including any other job and investment income), for each type of organization. Don't forget to include computations of Social Security taxes and your spouse's income and deductions.

3

Jump into Business and Keep the IRS from Becoming a Greedy Partner

There are endless decisions to make if you are about to enter the world of the self-employed. However, as far as tax considerations go, we can divide the decisions into three major questions:

1. In what industry (such as retail, wholesale, personal service, construction) should you operate?
2. What legal form (sole proprietorship, corporation) should your business take?
3. Should you start from scratch or buy a business?

This chapter discusses question 3.

TAX DEDUCTIONS INVOLVED IN STARTING AND RUNNING A BUSINESS

First, let's look at some misconceptions, sometimes called "theories," about starting a business.

The World of Theories

The dream world   You start a business. You spend lots of your money. You borrow more money and spend that also. You travel through six states, checking with the owners of similar businesses to determine whether you really can make money in your business. (You have to travel to other states to talk to people who will not be your competitors. The local folk, who may be your competitors, may not tell you much, or they may give you wrong information.) You buy equipment. You engage a lawyer, a CPA, and a management consultant.

You have spent $100,000 getting your business started, so you have an initial $100,000 loss that will offset your other income (as salary from a full-time job). If you had taxes withheld from your salary, you could be in for a big tax refund.

But even though you have what you think is an enormous initial loss, you could still owe some tax from that first year of business. The economic and accounting theory that can shoot you down follows.

The nightmare world   That $100,000 you spent to get your business started will benefit you for years, as many years as your business lasts, and that may be a long time. The $100,000 may even benefit your children when they inherit your business. If your business is incorporated, it may last forever (at least in theory). Therefore, the cost of the equipment and all the other expenses you incurred in starting your business should be applied to the period during which you will benefit from those initial expenses. In other words, that $100,000 is an investment on which you will earn profits. It will never be an expense that can be deducted from income.

An analogy would be your investing the $100,000 in stock in General Motors. You would not be able to deduct that as an expense because it is an investment. Similarly, that $100,000 you invest in your own business should not be deductible.

The real world   Does the above scare you? Don't despair. Congress has seen fit to provide some relief to those who are willing to take the risk of starting a business and perhaps providing employment to others. Let's cover the types of initial expenses separately.

Equipment Purchases

Depreciation made easy   This is the first exception to the "investment will last forever" rule. Equipment, as we all know from experience, does not last forever. However, it does last more than one year, so the theory is that the cost of equipment should be spread out over several years. When accountants prepare financial statements, they compute depreciation over the expected useful life of the equipment. Look what happens to Art:

When Art starts Art's Auto Repair, he purchases a hydraulic lift, an electronic engine analyzer, and much other equipment that a modern auto shop needs. The cost of his equipment totals $50,000. (Art writes a check, but as far as depreciation computations are concerned, it does not matter whether he uses his own funds or borrows them.)

When Art's accountant prepares the financial statements for the auto repair shop, he (with Art's help) estimates that the equipment will last 10 years. (With today's technological advances, it will be obsolete much sooner, but 10 years makes the math simple.) The accountant divides the $50,000 by the 10 years of expected life and comes up with an annual equipment-ownership cost of $5,000. That goes on the profit-and-loss statement as a depreciation expense of $5,000.

The IRS used to compute depreciation the same way, but this led to endless arguments. Years ago, for tax return purposes, Art would have estimated that the equipment would last only 2 years so that he could have claimed a depreciation expense ("write-off") of $25,000 ($50,000 ÷ 2 = $25,000) in each of the first 2 years that he owned the equipment. The IRS auditor would have insisted that the equipment should last 20 years, so Art's annual depreciation would have been only $2,500 ($50,000 ÷ 20 = $2,500) each year. Art's $25,000 deduction would have saved him much more tax than the IRS auditor's computation of a $2,500 deduction. (Admittedly, the total deduction was (and is) $50,000 over many years, but see Chapter 8 for the reasons deductions in early years are better than deductions in later years.)

The IRS has now set up definite guidelines as to the lives of various pieces of equipment and for the computation of depreciation. The IRS rules about computing depreciation are complex and take up many pages. The computations vary with the year in which the equipment was purchased, the type of equipment (or the type of real estate improvements), and even within which quarter of the year the equipment was purchased. This is well beyond the scope of this book. The depreciation computations are best done by a tax professional, who will do it with special computer software. However, for your planning purposes, you should be aware of certain options.[1]

Although Art can't take the $25,000-per-year deduction, he can take advantage of what is called Section 179, Election to Expense Depreciable Business Assets. This is a gift to small business from your local member of Congress and his or her cohorts in Washington. It allows an individual or a corporation to take an immediate deduction for the year in which the equipment was purchased of up to $20,000[2] of the cost of the equipment. That's $20,000 that can be deducted in this year, instead of having to spread the deduction over several years as a depreciation deduction.

If you are really creative, you have now thought about setting up several corporations and having each one buy $20,000 worth of equipment. Good thinking, but it won't work. The staffs of the congressional committees also hire creative people, and they expect you to dream up that scenario, so they limit this gift to only one deduction per controlled group of corporations. Whether you have your S corporation or your partnership purchase the equipment, the deduction is limited to $20,000. This purchase also eats up your personal right to a $20,000 equipment purchase expense deduction (you can't get another $20,000 deduction by operating another business as a sole proprietor). Also, there is a reduction in the $20,000 if you purchase over $200,000 worth of equipment in one year.

[1]If you insist on knowing more about depreciation, start by ordering the free Publication 946 from the IRS. Warning: It's not recreational reading.
[2]This limit on a Section-179 deduction will increase to $24,000 in 2001 and 2002, with another increase to $25,000 scheduled for 2003 and subsequent years.

Table 3.1   Art's Auto Repair
Depreciation during the Year He Purchased $50,000 of Equipment

1	Cost of equipment	$50,000
2	Section-179 expense of equipment	20,000
3	Remaining cost of equipment (line 1 minus line 2) (this is the "declining balance")	30,000
4	Remaining cost divided by life (seven years)	4,286
5	Multiply line 4 by 2 (this is the "double" part)	8,571
6	Divide line 5 by 2 (the IRS lets you have only 6 months of depreciation in the first year)	4,286
7	Total deduction (Section-179 expense on line 2 plus depreciation expense on line 6)	$24,286

In addition to this gift, Congress and the IRS also let you compute depreciation by the *double-declining-balance method.* Assuming that the equipment that Art purchases is assigned an expected life of seven years by the IRS tables, his depreciation of the $50,000 worth of equipment could look like Table 3.1. As you'll see, Art actually gets a depreciation deduction of $24,286. However, the second year will not come out as well, which Table 3.2 demonstrates. If Art buys more equipment in year two, he can take Section 179 expense deduction and depreciation on that additional equipment in the second year.

There are other options to depreciation. Art can use a longer expected life of equipment and take depreciation as the accountant might do for the financial statements. Art can divide the cost of the equipment by the expected useful life and take the same depreciation deduction every year. (This is called *straight-line depreciation* because a graph of the expense would be a straight line.) Why would Art do that? He probably won't. But there are situations where it might be the appropriate action. For instance, if your earnings this year will be $100,000, you have already paid the maximum OASDI part of Social Security. Then if you expect to make only $50,000 in the next few years, you might want to save as much of your depreciation deduction

Table 3.2   Art's Auto Repair
Depreciation during the Year *after* He Purchased $50,000 of Equipment

1	Cost of equipment	$50,000
2	Subtract Section-179 expense and depreciation taken in previous year (from Table 3.1)	24,286
3	Remaining cost of equipment (line 1 minus line 2) (this is the "declining balance")	25,714
4	Remaining cost divided by life (seven years)	3,673
5	Multiply line 4 by 2 (this is all the depreciation Art can deduct in year two)	$ 7,347

as possible for those later years, as a business deduction at that level of income not only reduces income tax, but also reduces Social Security tax.

Investment tax credit—there it was, now it isn't, but??   This was a gift to business that Congress enacted and repealed several times over the last two or three decades. At this writing, it is in the repealed status, but who knows what Congress will do next year or thereafter? If you find yourself in a business that could use some new equipment, you might want to prod your representative occasionally about reenacting this benefit.

What this amounted to was a sharing of your equipment cost by the government. If you bought a piece of equipment for $100, Uncle Sam paid $10 of the cost, and you paid only $90. The government did not send you a check, but it did give you a tax credit, which amounts to the same thing. (For a discussion of the difference between a deduction and a tax credit, see Appendix B.)

I mention this on-and-off tax benefit because if it is enacted again, you should pay close attention. There will probably be a date on which it is effective and a date on which it terminates. Plan your equipment purchases to take advantage of the period during which it is effective.[3]

[3]There is still investment tax credit available for rehabilitation of historic

Intangibles—Amortization Made Easy

What is an intangible?   The dictionary defines an *intangible* as something that cannot be touched. The most obvious examples of business-related intangibles are patents and copyrights. You can't touch a patent. If you patent your Quick-Fizzle Can Opener, you can touch the can opener, and you can touch the document from the patent office, but you can't touch, feel, or spray-paint a patent. It's the exclusive *right* to manufacture and sell your can opener for a period of years. (I could steal the piece of paper generated by the patent office from you, but that would not mean I had your patent rights.) Similarly, a copyright is the *right* to publish and sell a writing or work of art. It's not the actual book or painting. There are other intangibles, as we shall see shortly. They're significant as you can deduct the cost of some intangibles, but often the cost is deducted over several years.

Amortization is similar to depreciation, but rather than being a method of deducting the cost of equipment over time, it is a method of deducting some intangible costs over time. A class of intangible costs is accumulated, totaled, and listed on a company's books as an asset, almost like a piece of equipment. Accountants and other tax professionals refer to this process of accumulating certain expenses as *capitalization*. Then, each year, part of that accumulated total of expenses is deducted from income. That deduction is called *amortization*.

A major difference between depreciation and amortization is that there is no such thing as a Section-179 expense deduction for amortization. Neither is there any double-declining-balance amortization. Amortization is determined by dividing the cost of the intangibles by a number of years. How many years? In most cases, the tax law provides that number. Let's look at some specific examples that arise in starting up a business from scratch.

---

buildings, certain buildings built before 1936, certain solar and geothermal property, and for reforestation. The rules are complex, but if you are in the unusual position of being able to take advantage of one of these credits, consult with your tax professional.

Organizational costs   Organizational costs arise from incorpo-rating a business and include attorneys' and accountants' fees for such procedures as filing the necessary papers with the state and drafting bylaws. These can be amortized over 60 months (or longer, if you so choose). Similarly, legal and other profes-sional fees incurred in setting up a partnership can be amortized over 60 months. The amortization expense for the first year of the business must be claimed on the first tax return of the busi-ness. Otherwise, the organization costs can never be amortized or deducted in any way, until years hence when the business may be dissolved.

Start-up expenses   This category includes:

1. Costs of investigating a business before a decision is made to enter, or to start up, the business.[4]
2. Business start-up expenses. These are expenses that occur after the decision is made to start a business and before the business begins operations.[5]

Although it would be nice if you could deduct these inves-tigatory and start-up expenditures immediately on your tax re-turn, the tax law says no. In theory, these costs, like an investment in the stock of a publicly held corporation, should never be deducted, as they are part of your investment. How-ever, at times Congress ignores theory and becomes generous, so the tax law allows the total of these costs to be amortized over 60 months.

---

[4]Generally, if the business is not started after the investigation stage, the costs of investigation are not deductible. However, some courts have allowed investigation expenses to be deducted even though the business was not started at that time. Actually funding the business and starting it would seem to assure you of being able to deduct (amortize) investigation expenses. At any rate, keep track of your investigation expenses, even if you do not start the business. Seek *knowledgeable* professional help on a decision as to whether to deduct the expenses.

[5]There are obtuse descriptions in the Internal Revenue Code Section 195 and related IRS regulations as to what costs can be included in these categories. If you anticipate incurring substantial start-up or pre-opening costs, you would be well advised to review these rules with a tax professional.

Note that these amortization rules are for new business start-ups. Costs of expansion of an existing business are deductible in the year the business incurs the costs.

Expenses of investigating a business that is never started
Wouldn't it be nice if we could deduct such expenses? Any time we traveled to Colorado or to the Virgin Islands, we could investigate the start of a business there and deduct the cost of a vacation trip. The IRS staff are aware that we would all do this, so they disallow deductions for investigating a business that never starts. Although the IRS regulations seem to allow deduction of legal expenses incurred in investigating a business that does not start or is not purchased, expenses of searching for, advertising for, and traveling to a proposed location are not deductible.

Where you can economically do it, the key seems to be to fund the business and actually start it. Then, if you close it, all the costs of investigation could be deducted. Or, if you are already in the business and searching for a site for expansion, the investigation costs should be deductible.

Because it's possible to lose a lot of after-tax dollars in investigating a business purchase or start-up, the pertinent Revenue Ruling (77-254) is reprinted in Appendix C-1. It is not easy reading, but it may help you decide whether you really want to take a look at that hot-dog stand in Vail.

There are several court cases involving people who have tried to deduct these unsuccessful investigation expenses, but almost all decisions have sided with the IRS.[6]

Intangibles—Immediate Expense Deduction Made Easy

Research expenses   In spite of itself, Congress sometimes passes laws that are logical. If the United States is to be competitive in our world economy, we should have brilliant people researching new processes and developing new products. Although most large companies have the financial resources to

[6]One case that allowed deduction of investigation expense where a business was not started is *M.S. Finch,* DC-Minn. 4-65 civil 149 6/30/66, 66-2 USTC ¶9542.

pursue research that will make them more competitive, not all the best minds are in the conglomerate world. To encourage those who would rather develop new products in the small entrepreneurial arena, Congress enacted Section 174, which, according to reports from pertinent congressional committees, is intended to level the playing field of small and large companies, insofar as research and development are concerned.

Research expenses can be deducted by a business as they occur, even if they arise during the start-up period.[7] There is no need to accumulate or capitalize and then amortize these expenses over time, although you can elect to handle them that way if that works out better for your tax picture.

Tax credit for research expenses   As an alternative, you can elect to claim a tax credit for part (as much as 20 percent) of your research expenses. In other words, Uncle Sam will reimburse you for as much as 20 percent of what you spend on research. If you are eligible for and do claim the credit, you can deduct as an expense only what is left of the expense after applying the credit. In other words, if you spend $100 on research and claim a credit of $20, you can deduct only $80 as a research expense.

Determining how much, if any, of the credit is not simple. The form on which you do that, with the instructions, are reprinted in Appendix C-2. If you peruse both, you'll understand why I say that it wouldn't be worth the trouble if all you had was $100 of research expenses. However, if you have spent many thousands on research, it may be worth the trouble and the expense of the professional you probably will need to fill in this form.

If you might be in a situation to receive the credit, you should also be aware that the IRS has issued Proposed Regulation 105170–9 relative to the research credit. Although it was issued in December 1998, it is not yet a final regulation, which means that it is not authoritative but merely represents how the IRS thinks. It's lengthy and complex, so it is not included in this book.

---

[7] *E.A. Snow,* 416 US 500, SupCt 73-641 5/13/74, 74-1 USTC ¶9432.

This credit is due to expire on June 30, 2004. However, it has also been scheduled to expire in 1995 and 1999, but Congress extended the life of the credit each time. Will it be extended in 2004? Sorry, my crystal ball is broken.

What are research expenses? The IRS regulations define them as

> expenditures incurred in connection with the taxpayer's trade or business which represent research and development costs in the experimental laboratory sense. The term includes generally all such costs incident to the development of an experimental or pilot model, a plant process, a product, a formula, an invention, or similar property, and the improvement of already existing property of the type mentioned.[8]

The definition does not include

> expenditures such as those for the ordinary testing or inspection of materials or products for quality control, efficiency surveys, management studies, consumer surveys, advertising, or promotions.[9]

There are some court cases that further define what are, and what are not, research expenses. If you are starting a business where you think you will have research expenses, particularly during the start-up period, describe your expenses to your tax professional and have him or her do the tax research as to the probability that the IRS will allow you to deduct immediately the research expenses. (For a discussion of the effect of immediate deductions versus amortization or later deduction, see Chapter 8.)

Software development costs   The IRS considers the costs of developing computer software to be so similar to research and development costs that the software development can be handled the same way. These costs can be deducted as paid (cash basis) or incurred (accrual basis). The good news is that this applies to both software that is developed for one's own use as well as for sale to others. If you are thinking of writing software as a business, this could result in some immediate

[8]IRS Regulation §1.174-2.
[9]Ibid.

deductions for you. The caveat is that you have to be able to prove that you are developing commercially viable software. (Sales in later years should prove that.) Also, you cannot deduct the value of your own time. (For details of what the IRS thinks about this point, see Revenue Procedure 69-21 in Appendix C-3.)

Advertising expenses   When you advertise your product or service, you may be reaching prospective customers who will not actually do business with you until next month, next year, or five years from now. That is why advertising experts advise that advertising must be repeated time and again. You would think, then, that the IRS would insist that because advertising benefits future years, it should not be deducted from income until those future years. In other words, those advertising costs should be amortized over several years. You would have been right many years ago, but by World War II, the courts had knocked that out of IRS thinking. Today advertising can be deducted immediately.

Circulation expenses   Ever wonder why you receive so many invitations to subscribe to newsletters, magazines, and other periodicals? In addition to the fact that so-called junk mail supports the postal system, the publishing of periodicals can generate high profits and as a side benefit, Congress has created special sections of the Internal Revenue Code for this industry. It allows periodical publishers to deduct current expenses for increasing circulation, the concept being that this is just a special form of advertising. At the same time, however, periodical publishers do not have to report the income that may come from that advertising until, sometimes, years later. (Full explanation of how this concept works involves accounting methods and net operating losses, which are covered in later chapters. For an illustrative example, see Chapter 8.)

Coping with the Rules as You Start Your Business

Now that you are aware of depreciation, amortization, investigatory costs, organizational costs, start-up expenses, and research expenses, what is the best plan? The answer will vary with each situation. For instance, what other income do you have? If you are keeping your full-time job and starting a side-line business, you will want to structure your activities so that as much expense as possible can be deducted, probably creating a loss that can offset some or all of your other income. If, on the other end of the situation spectrum, you have no other income and have had little income in the last three years, it may not make much difference whether you can deduct an expense this year or have to spread the expense out over the next five years.[10]

For most situations, though, the immediate deductions are preferable. How do you make them immediate when start-up costs have to be amortized over five years? Remember, costs of expanding an already operating business do not have to be amortized. They can be deducted now. Therefore, if you can, start your business in a small way, spending as little start-up money as possible. Once it's rolling along, start expanding. Now what would have been start-up expenses are immediate deductions.

Unfortunately, this tactic will not make equipment purchases immediately deductible. What you pay for equipment still has to be deducted over several years as depreciation expenses, with one exception: You can deduct the Section-179 expense every year. If you bought $20,000 or less of equipment every year, you could then immediately deduct all of your equipment purchases.[11]

TAX DEDUCTIONS INVOLVED IN BUYING A BUSINESS

If you buy a going business, you may not have to worry about start-up expenses and organizational costs, but there are other things to worry about. One area of concern is what you are buying. Are you buying the assets of a business or a whole business, lock, stock, and barrel? If you are buying a sole proprietorship, you usually are buying the assets of the business.

---

[10] A current loss could be carried back to the three previous years, generating a tax refund provided there was taxable income in the last three years.
[11] There is an exception to this exception: Automobiles and light trucks are subject to further limitations.

Buying a Sole Proprietorship

Let's look at what happens when Jennifer decides to go into the hardware store business:

Jennifer buys Herman's Hardware Store from Herman, who wants to slow down now that he has passed 60. Herman has always operated as a sole proprietor. The market value of his business assets are listed in Table 3.3.

Note that this list is the market value of the assets, which is not necessarily the value that appears on Herman's books. His father, who started the store, bought three dozen goose yokes in 1927 for $5 apiece. They are listed in Herman's book inventory at $180, but as no one uses goose yokes today, the market value is probably zero. However, they may be rare collectors' items that are worth $100 each. In that case, they would be included in the market-value inventory figure at $3,600. Similarly, the value of equipment on Herman's books is the original cost of the equipment minus the depreciation expense that has already been deducted on his tax return. The actual value of the equipment on the used equipment market may be much different.

As $700,000 is the value of Herman's business assets, we might assume that Jennifer would pay Herman $700,000 for them, but that is not often a reasonable assumption. Why would Jennifer buy Herman's store fixtures, equipment, and inventory, some of which Herman's father purchased in 1925? Why wouldn't she buy new equipment and fresh inventory and start her own hardware store?

Herman, like his father before him, has been very attentive to his customers, making sure that they were satisfied with their purchases and that what he did not have in stock for a customer, he usually procured by the next day. The result is that he has a loyal clientele, including some large contractors. To obtain the goodwill of those

Table 3.3   Herman's Hardware Store Assets (Market Value)

Accounts receivable	$ 30,000
Inventory	583,000
Furniture, fixtures, equipment	87,000
Total assets	$700,000

already existing customers, Jennifer buys Herman's assets (and the right to his business name) from him. In fact, the value of that customer goodwill is so great that she pays $1,000,000 for the $700,000 worth of assets. (For our computations, it does not matter whether she writes him a check for the $1,000,000 or pays him a little cash and signs a note for the remainder of the $1,000,000.) Now, Herman's assets that Jennifer purchased look like Table 3.4.

As Jennifer looks in her checkbook to find the $1,000,000 to pay Herman, she plans how much of that purchase the IRS will let her deduct from her income. What the IRS will let her do is this:

Jennifer can deduct depreciation on the furniture, fixtures, and equipment. As she can take that extra Section-179 $20,000 deduction in the first year she owns the equipment, her total depreciation will be approximately $34,000.

Fortunately, she buys this business after July 1993. The rule used to be that what one spent for goodwill could never be deducted. Now the rule is that goodwill that arises in the purchase of a business can be deducted as amortization over 15 years.[12] That is not as good as an immediate deduction, but it's better than it was.

Table 3.4   Herman's Hardware Store
Assets Purchased by Jennifer (Market Value)

Accounts receivable	$ 30,000
Inventory	583,000
Furniture, fixtures, equipment	87,000
Goodwill	300,000
Total assets	$1,000,000

However, there is an even better way for Jennifer to structure her purchase:

Herman wants to slow down, not become completely inactive, so Jennifer can structure her offer as $800,000 for the assets and $200,000 to be paid as a consulting fee to Herman at a rate of $50,000 per year for four years. (Like any salary or consulting fee,

[12]IRC §197.

*the $50,000 is fully deductible in the year Jennifer pays it to Herman.)
The IRS will not let part of a purchase be a consultant fee or salary to
the seller unless the seller actually performs services of a value equal
to the consulting fee. In this case, if Herman puts in a few hours each
week at the store, cementing Jennifer's relationship with his old customers and helping her in other management tasks, he should be
worth the consulting fee. What sort of money does this maneuver
make for Jennifer? Table 3.5 compares these two ways for her to buy
the business.*

*This maneuver of paying a consulting fee instead of buying good-
will has resulted in additional cash for Jennifer of approximately
$17,600 this first year, and it will generate the additional cash over
the next three years.*

Buying an Incorporated Business

Suppose Herman had some years ago incorporated his business:

*When Herman incorporated his business as Herman's Hardware
Store, Inc., he had the corporation issue 100 shares of common stock
to him, and he still owns all of the stock. Jennifer can purchase the
business by paying Herman $1,000,000 for all of his stock. She will
then own the corporation, which will continue to operate just as when
Herman owned it. However, there is no difference between Jennifer
buying stock in Herman's Hardware Store, Inc., and her buying stock
in Apple Computer. None of that $1,000,000 is deductible until she
sells the stock to someone else in the future.*

What can Jennifer do? She can buy the assets of the business
from the corporation, just as in the previous example, and deduct the amortization of goodwill. She can also hire Herman as
a consultant for the $50,000 per year. Herman would be left with
a shell corporation with nothing in it but the cash and promissory notes that Jennifer pays for the business.

Table 3.5 Herman's Hardware Store Purchase by Jennifer (Market Value)

	Purchase with No Consulting Fee	Purchase Includes Consulting Fee
Structure of Payments		
Jennifer pays Herman, in cash and promissory notes	$1,000,000	$ 800,000
Herman to receive a consulting fee of $50,000 per year for four years	_____	200,000
Total payment by Jennifer to Herman	$1,000,000	$1,000,000
What the Cash and Promissory Notes Bought		
Accounts receivable	$ 30,000	$ 30,000
Inventory	583,000	583,000
Furniture, fixtures, and equipment	87,000	87,000
Goodwill	300,000	100,000
Total	$1,000,000	$ 800,000
*Deductions, First Year**		
Depreciation (approximate)	$ 34,000	$ 34,000
Amortization of goodwill	20,000	6,667
Consulting fee	_____	50,000
Total deductions relative to purchase of business	$ 54,000	$ 90,667
Cash from deductions (@ 48%)†	$ 25,920	$ 43,520

*These computations assume that the business was purchased on January 1. Numbers would be different for other dates of purchase and other than calendar tax years.

†The computation of the cash generated by the deductions is based on a federal income tax rate of 28 percent, self-employment tax rate of 15.3 percent, and an assumed state income tax rate of 4.7 percent.

If Herman has a C corporation, he may have some trouble taking that money out of his shell corporation without paying tax on the dividends he pays himself, but there are ways around that. (For discussion, see Chapter 6.)

Buying a Corporation for Its Accumulated Tax Loss

This could be a one-word paragraph: "Don't." Years ago, you could buy a corporation that had a lot of losses accumulated over the years and use those losses to offset other income you had. Congress has done a rather thorough job of eliminating that practice. In simple terms, the law does not allow a tax loss to go with the corporation when there is a major change in ownership. If you are buying a corporation that has carryover of losses and various credits, be sure you have a competent tax professional review your plans before you act.

Buying a Franchise

If you read the advertisements in various business magazines and newspapers, you're aware of the multitude of franchises available in areas such as fast food, restaurants, motels, retail stores, house cleaning, and almost any other type of business. Whether the purchase of them makes good business sense, we will leave to other books. The tax aspects, since August 1993, are relatively simple.

The initial lump-sum fee that you pay, that gives you the right to use the franchiser's name and the right to expect some management help from the franchiser, is now considered to be in the nature of goodwill. You cannot immediately deduct it, but you can amortize it over 15 years.[13]

The recurring, monthly fee that is usually a percentage of sales is considered to be a contingent fee and deductible when you pay it. You may jump at the conclusion that you are therefore better off paying a small lump-sum fee and a larger percentage of sales, as that will generate higher immediate tax deductions. Your theory would be correct, but consider the nontax consequences before you try to negotiate a change in the fee structure. If you trade a lower initial fee for larger monthly per-

---

[13]IRC §197.

centage fees, you may be locking yourself into an arrangement that eventually will be far more expensive than the tax you would pay.

If you read any older literature on the tax implications in franchising, you will find several complicated discussions as to the length of the franchise, renewal periods, and other items that had to be cranked into a complicated calculation. That has now been simplified by a 1993 change that specifies a 15-year amortization, regardless of the terms of the franchise agreement. In other words, there is no great area for tax planning in buying a franchise from a franchising company. However, you may be able to structure some of the payment to the franchiser as training. If it is pre-opening training, its cost is amortizable over only 5 years. If the training occurs after opening, you should be able to deduct it immediately.

If you buy a going business that includes a franchise (such as an existing McDonald's® Restaurant), your tax planning opportunities are more akin to buying any other existing business. The IRS will expect you to pay the current market price for the franchise. What price is that? Most likely, it is not the price the seller originally paid for the franchise. The market price may be the figure at which you could buy a franchise for a new location from the franchiser, or it may be some other figure. For instance, if new franchises are for 10 years with two 10-year renewal periods (a total of 30 years), that franchise is worth more than an existing franchise that will expire in 5 years. Of course, because the location already exists and has a steady stream of customers, the lower franchise value may be offset by a high goodwill figure. If there is substantial goodwill involved, you can use the same maneuver that Jennifer used in acquiring the hardware store: Try to negotiate a reduced price in exchange for a continuing consulting fee to the former owner of the franchise location. (Keep it legal by requiring that he or she show up and provide some services to you.)

4

Keep Two or More Sets of Books (Legally) and Other Accounting Tricks

DOUBLE BOOKKEEPING, DOUBLE FILE CABINETS, AND A DOUBLE LIFE

"Ho!" Frank told his customers at his bar, "I don't pay those greedy you-know-whats at the IRS all they want. I keep two sets of books, and I just tell them about the books that say my sales are abysmal and I lose money."

Frank was an affable fellow and talked this way to most of his friendly customers. The trouble was that one of his customers was one of those "greedy you-know-whats from the IRS." Now Frank tells his new friends, "Ho, I'll be out of this federal pen in a little under five years!"

Not reporting all of your income or taking deductions for expenses you did not have amounts to fraud. The IRS could just have assessed civil penalties against Frank and collected large sums of money from him. However, in his case, the IRS authorities decided to press criminal charges. When can the IRS press criminal charges? Any time fraud or other crimes are involved in a tax return. When are the IRS officials satisfied with civil penalties, and when do they press criminal charges? That's a decision that is made case by case, somewhere in the bureaucracy. Presumably, it depends on the severity of the fraud, but there is no dollar amount that triggers criminal prosecution.

Moral: Don't cheat by such acts as keeping false records.

Sometimes It Is Legal to Do the Bookkeeping Two Ways

Saying "don't cheat" is not to say that there are no instances in which you can legally keep what amounts to two sets of records:

Carl, who is in the clay flowerpot business, buys an automatic flower-pot machine for $150,000. (It automatically molds the flowerpots and fires them in a kiln.) He expects it to last for 15 years, so for his financial statements and his own records, which tell him where he is and what he is actually doing, he views the expense of having the machine (the depreciation) as the cost spread over its life ($150,000 ÷ 15 years), which equals $10,000 per year. For tax purposes, he deducts as much depreciation expense as fast as he can, using the Section-179 expense deduction and double declining balance over 7 years. Table 4.1 is a comparison of these two sets of depreciation records.

This gives Carl the best of both worlds. The high depreciation deductions in the early years reduce his taxes, but on his financial statements he shows only $10,000-per-year depreciation expense, so his profit looks higher on the report he gives his banker than it does on the tax return he sends to the IRS. (To find out how much money this might put in Carl's pocket, see Chapter 8.) That probably means he can borrow more money with which to enlarge his business. The good news is that keeping two sets of depreciation records is entirely legal.

There are other situations in which it is legal to keep two sets of records. Although research and development expenses can be deductible expenses as they happen, they can be set up on the company's books as an intangible and be amortized over several years. The same is true of circulation expenses. These situations and others, where two sets of records can be maintained, are discussed in later chapters.

Table 4.1   Carl's Flowerpot Machine (Cost $150,000)
Comparison of Two Sets of Depreciation Records

Year	Depreciation Expense on Financial Statements	Depreciation Expense on Tax Return
1	$ 10,000	$ 36,006
2	10,000	32,572
3	10,000	23,262
4	10,000	16,612
5	10,000	11,877
6	10,000	11,864
7	10,000	11,877
8	10,000	5,930
9	10,000	
10	10,000	
11	10,000	
12	10,000	
13	10,000	
14	10,000	
15	10,000	
TOTAL	$150,000	$150,000

WHAT YOU CHOOSE AS YOUR BOOKKEEPING METHOD CAN MAKE A DIFFERENCE

When is a sale a sale? When is it income?

When is an expense an expense? When is it a deduction?

There are choices, and the choices are yours, with some exceptions. There are some IRS rules to follow, and if you fail to make a particular choice (the IRS calls them *elections*), the IRS will make them for you.

The Cash Method

Most of us keep our personal affairs this way. You can't spend the money until you have it, so even though someone (like your employer) owes it to you, it isn't income until he or she pays it to you. Similarly, you do not consider an expense to be an expense (or a deduction) until you pay it some day. This concept has some advantages in its flexibility for tax purposes. For instance, you are probably familiar with the device of bunching medical bills for your individual tax return. In case your memory needs refreshing, here is an example of how it works:

> *In December of this year, Karen receives a bill for medical treatment she had in November. Her part of the bill is $2,000. She knows that sometime next year she will have to return for additional medical procedures and her part of that bill will be another $2,000. If she pays the bill she has just received before December 31 of this year, her medical deductions for this year and next year are as computed in Table 4.2. (Her employer pays all of her medical insurance premium.)*
>
> *However, if she pays that December bill for $2,000 next year, her computation will look like Table 4.3.*
>
> *By planning when to pay the medical bills, Karen has a medical deduction of $1,750 instead of zero. She has this flexibility because*

Table 4.2 Computation of Karen's Medical Expense Deduction

		This Year	Next Year
1	Adjusted gross income	$30,000	$30,000
2	Medical expense	2,000	2,000
3	7.5% of adjusted gross income on line 1 (only medical expenses in excess of 7.5% of adjusted gross income are deductible)	2,250	2,250
4	Deductible medical expense (line 2 minus line 3)	$ 0	$ 0

Table 4.3   Computation of Karen's Medical Expense Deduction

		This Year	Next Year
1	Adjusted gross income	$30,000	$30,000
2	Medical expense	0	4,000
3	7.5% of adjusted gross income on line 1 (only medical expenses in excess of 7.5% of adjusted gross income are deductible)	2,250	2,250
4	Deductible medical expense (line 2 minus line 3)	$ 0	$ 1,750

she is on a cash basis. She can put the deduction in whichever year is best for her, for the deduction is pegged to the year in which she pays the bill.[1]

The Accrual Method

If Karen, in the previous example, reported her income and deductions on the accrual method, she would not have been able to bunch her medical expenses into one year. The rules of the accrual method dictate that expenses are expenses in the year in which they are *incurred* rather than in the year in which they are paid. If Karen were using the accrual method and received the services in this year, she would have become legally obligated to pay for them this year, so they would have been an expense or deduction for this year only.

Can an individual or a business switch back and forth between cash and accrual methods of bookkeeping and reporting? No, not without the permission of the IRS. (Do you really want to ask the people at the IRS to pull your returns out of the file drawer and look closely at them? That is what you may be doing when you ask for any type of permission from them.) The exception to needing to ask permission from the IRS (relative to cash or accrual methods) concerns the first return that an entity

---

[1] There are some rules against prepaying an expected expense for next year.

files. At that time, the individual or business can select whichever method it wishes.

From what you read here, you may infer that tax returns must be prepared by the same method (cash or accrual) as that by which the books are prepared. Although Internal Revenue Code Section 446 seems to read that way, two private letter rulings the IRS issued in 1990 indicate that keeping your books by one method and preparing the tax return on the other is legal, provided you have prepared a schedule for your files that reconciles the two methods.[2] Your accountant can prepare this for you. (If he or she can't, get a new accountant.)

Because it is simpler and more flexible, most individuals use the cash method of reporting. However, even though an individual is on a cash method of recordkeeping, a sole proprietorship that the same individual owns can be on an accrual method. This is legal, even though the tax return for the sole proprietorship (Schedule C) is part of the owner's individual income tax return.

The Choice of Bookkeeping Method for a Business

Sales reporting—don't pay tax on money you have not received. If your customers or clients take weeks or months after you send a bill before they pay you, that would be a factor in favor of the cash method. You don't want to pay tax on money you have not received yet. There are a couple of caveats in this area. If you have completed the work for a customer and are due the money, you are not supposed to delay income by not billing until the next year. Billing in December and asking a customer not to pay you until January is not legal, either. Of course, you can hope he doesn't pay in December. If a customer pays in advance, that is usually income when you receive it, even if you have not yet performed the work for which he or she is paying.

If you or your accountant prepare financial statements based on the accrual method of accounting, you report income when the service has been rendered or goods delivered. However, the IRS has different rules. They state that if you receive advance

[2]IRS Letter Rulings 9103001 6/19/90 and 9113003 12/18/90.

payment, it is income when received.[3] In other words, as far as the income side of the picture is concerned, the accrual method has all the disadvantages.

Expenses—deduct them even if you have not written the check   If you use the cash method for reporting income, you have to use the cash method for expenses. (That may be a negative factor in your decision.) There was a time when the cash method was usually preferable to the accrual method, for cash-basis businesses could prepay many expenses for future years and take the deduction this year. Over the years, the law has been changed so that prepaying expenses does not generate a tax deduction until there has been economic performance. That is, if you pay your landlord three years of rent, you cannot deduct it until the time has passed when you occupied the space or until there has been economic performance. All this says that in the expense area, the cash method can work against you. Even if there has been economic performance, you cannot deduct the expense until you write the check. The only redeeming feature is that the cash method of bookkeeping is simple. It consists of a checkbook.

To summarize, if you always are paid promptly for your services, you may be better off with the accrual method, in which you can deduct the expense even if you have not paid for it. If your customers' payments are often tardy, you are probably better off with the cash method.

When Accrual Is Required (for Sales and Cost of Goods Sold)

For some businesses, there is no choice. Any C corporation with more than $5,000,000 in gross receipts must use the accrual method. Also any businesses (most retailers and wholesalers) that buy merchandise to resell to customers must keep their sales records and cost of goods sold on the accrual method but may elect either cash or accrual for expenses such as rent, insurance, and utilities.

---

[3]There are some exceptions, such as periodical circulation income and money held in escrow status.

Table 4.4   Ted's Tent Store—First Year in Business, Scenario One

Sales of 200 tents @ $200 each	$ 40,000
Minus cost of goods sold	
(200 tents, purchased @ $130 each)	26,000
Gross profit	$ 14,000

What impact does this required accrual method have on a merchandise business? Let Ted's Tent Store illustrate:

In Ted's first year in business, he deals in only one style of tent. He pays the manufacturer $130 each and sells them for $200 each. During the first year, he is timid, so he takes orders from 200 customers for the tents and purchases only 200 tents from the manufacturer. Ted collects cash from his customers when he delivers the tents and pays the manufacturer cash when he buys the tents wholesale. His gross profit computation looks like Table 4.4.

Now change the circumstances.

One hundred of Ted's customers buy tents from him during the Christmas season. They are people he has known and trusted for years, so he agrees to wait to be paid until after their payday on the first of January. That is, he collects only $20,000 for his sales. He computes the year's gross profit as in Table 4.5.

Ted makes this computation by the cash method, which for him is illegal. Ted's business is that of a retailer, and the requirement is that he compute his gross profit (or loss) using the accrual method. The requirement of accrual is that sales are recorded when the sale is

Table 4.5   Ted's Tent Store—First Year in Business, Scenario Two

Sales of 200 tents @ $200 each	$ 20,000
Minus cost of goods sold	
(200 tents, purchased @ $130 each)	26,000
Loss	$(6,000)

Table 4.6   Ted's Tent Store—Second Year in Business, Scenario One

Sales of 200 tents @ $200 each	$40,000
Minus cost of goods sold (300 tents, purchased @ $130 each)	39,000
Gross profit	$ 1,000

made, not when the customer pays, so his sales are $40,000 not $20,000.

Ted wants that loss to offset other income, but he is not dismayed. The second year he handles his purchases differently. Again he sells 200 tents, but he spends more by purchasing an extra 100 tents to have on hand. Then he wants to report, on his tax return, his gross profit as in Table 4.6.

Purchasing those extra tents seems to help. The gross profit is now only $1,000. Other expenses, such as rent and insurance, would erase that and create a loss for Ted. But alas, this is also illegal. The accrual rules state that he can deduct only the cost of the merchandise he sells. The extra 100 tents he purchases are inventory, which is an asset that will turn into a deductible expense only when it is sold. Table 4.7 illustrates the correct way of computing the gross profit when inventory is involved.

The cost of goods sold and the profit made can also be calculated by identifying the products sold, as in Table 4.8.

Moral: We cannot deduct the cost of merchandise we have not yet sold.

Table 4.7   Ted's Tent Store—Second Year in Business, Scenario Two

Sales of 200 tents @ $200 each		$40,000
Minus cost of goods sold (purchase of 300 tents @ $130)	$39,000	
Subtract cost of 100 tents left on hand at the end of the year	13,000	
Cost of goods sold		26,000
Gross profit		$14,000

Table 4.8   Ted's Tent Store—Second Year in Business, Scenario Three

Sales of 200 tents @ $200 each	$40,000
Minus cost of goods sold (200 tents actually sold)	26,000
Gross profit	$14,000

Is all hope of reducing profit in this area lost? Not necessarily. One choice that is left to business people is which inventory items they sell. The example of Ted's Tents continues:

During the third year the manufacturer increases the wholesale price of the tents from $130 each to $150 each. Ted had bought 300 tents at the old price of $130[4] and buys another 300 at the new price of $150 each. He sells 400 tents at $200 each. He can compute his profit in one of two methods of identifying which inventory he sold. He can consider that he sold the oldest tents first, which is called first-in, first-out, *usually abbreviated to FIFO. Or he can treat his inventory as if he sold all of the last tents he purchased before he sold any of the old ones. That method is called* last-in, first-out, *or LIFO. Tables 4.9 and 4.10 display the different results.*

Ted has reduced his taxable income by $4,000, and this method is legal.

Obviously, the LIFO works only if prices are rising, but as that seems to be the case during the last 50 years, most of us presume it will continue. Strangely, this area of identifying which inventory is sold and which is left on the shelf is one in which the IRS is not persnickety. Ted could actually sell the oldest tents first but treat it on his books as if he sold the newest ones first. Like several elections in the tax law, once you make a decision, you have to stick with it. If you decide to use FIFO

---

[4]These 300 tents consisted of the 100 left from the second year and another 200 that he bought at the beginning of the third year, before the wholesale price went up.

Table 4.9   Ted's Tent Store—Fourth Year in Business
Computation of Cost of Goods Sold by First-In, First-Out (FIFO)

Sales of 400 tents @ $200 each		$80,000
Minus cost of goods sold		
300 tents @ $130 each	$39,000	
100 tents @ $150 each	15,000	
Total cost of goods sold		54,000
Gross profit		$26,000

Table 4.10   Ted's Tent Store—Fourth Year in Business
Computation of Cost of Goods Sold by Last-In, First-Out (LIFO)

Sales of 400 tents @ $200 each		$80,000
Minus cost of goods sold		
300 tents @ $150 each	$45,000	
100 tents @ $130 each	13,000	
Total cost of goods sold		58,000
Gross profit		$22,000

identification of what was sold, you have to stay with that method virtually forever (in that particular business).

DON'T PAY TAX WHEN YOU MAKE A PROFIT SELLING YOUR OLD EQUIPMENT

Look back at the example of Carl's flowerpot machine at the beginning of this chapter:

In year eight, Carl deducts the last depreciation, so he has now deducted all of the cost of the flowerpot machine. The poor old machine has become somewhat wobbly and turns out lopsided flowerpots, so Carl would like to sell it. Sam, the used-equipment dealer, offers him $15,000 for it.

If Carl takes that deal, look what happens: The IRS uses a concept called *basis,* and it's easily defined as the original cost of a machine minus the total of the depreciation that has been deducted.[5] In other words, the basis decreases every year until all the depreciation has been deducted, when the basis becomes zero. When equipment is sold, any amount by which the sales price exceeds the basis is taxable gain. When Carl sells the flowerpot machine for $15,000, he subtracts his basis of zero from the selling price and pays tax on the difference of $15,000. He could pay no tax on that gain if he trades the old flowerpot machine for a new one:

If Sam sells Carl a new flowerpot machine for $200,000 and takes the old flowerpot machine as a trade, Carl's books for tax purposes will look like Table 4.11.

The basis ($185,000), not the sales price, is the number on which Carl computes his depreciations. He will have a little less depreciation than he would have had if he had paid $200,000 without a trade-in, but he will save several thousand dollars in the tax he would have paid if he had sold the old flowerpot machine separately.

Moral: Work out trades of assets whenever possible if the basis of the old machine is less than market value.

Trades can also avoid tax because no money changes hands:

If Carl's flowerpot machine is still in good shape but he no longer needs it, he might trade it for Bert's birdbath machine. Neither Carl nor Bert will pay any tax on the trade. Three-cornered trades will also work. If Carl transfers his flowerpot machine to Bert, Bert transfers his

Table 4.11   Purchase of New Flowerpot Machine with Trade-In

Price of new flowerpot machine	$200,000
Subtract trade-in allowance of old flowerpot machine	15,000
Basis of new flowerpot machine	$185,000

[5]You don't really believe anything in the tax law is this simple, do you? Basis can also be affected by improvements to the machine and other factors, but this simple definition serves the purpose here.

birdbath machine to Adam, and Adam transfers his bulldozer to Carl, there is still no tax to be paid by any of the three involved in the transaction, provided that only like-kind property (no money) changes hands.[6]

TAX LOSSES—LIKE MONEY IN THE BANK

Your banker and your accountant will not let you count this as cash in the bank, but it almost is, or rather, it will be, if you handle your tax affairs well. Business tax losses arise when you have more deductible expenses than you have revenue (sales and fees). Christine has this situation. Here is what it does for her:

Christine starts a boutique shop, specializing in fine china and crystal. In her first year, before she has built a clientele, her sales are small and expenses large. She has a loss of $15,000. Her husband, Charles, earns $80,000 per year in the insurance business. Table 4.12 looks at the effect of Christine's business loss on the income tax bite by comparing the couple's tax bill without and with the loss from Christine's business.

The $15,000 loss has saved the family $4,200 in income tax.

"So what?" you ask. "Christine has had to lose $15,000 in order to save the family $4,200 of income tax. Hardly sounds like a good deal." You might be right, but what if Christine and Charles have always hoped to be able to take some vacation time to tour Europe and that tour would cost about $15,000? If the china and crystal collecting is only a hobby, that $15,000 will have to come out of Charles's $80,000 salary *after* they paid the

---

[6]What is *like-kind property?* Personal property used in a trade or business is like-kind, so the equipment in our example qualifies. Real estate traded for real estate usually qualifies, but it does not if a residence is traded for rental property. The definition has been interpreted differently by various courts, so it would be wise to ask a tax professional for advice before consummating a deal you believe to be a nontaxable exchange.

**Table 4.12   Effect of Christine's Business Loss
on Family's Federal Income Tax**

	Family Income Consists of Charles's Salary Only (Christine Not in Business)	Family Income Consists of Charles's Salary and Loss from Christine's China Shop
Charles's salary	$80,000	$80,000
Subtract loss from Christine's China Shop	0	15,000
Family income	80,000	65,000
Federal income tax*	$10,513	$ 6,313

*The tax computation assumes two dependent children and standard deduction at 2000 rates. It also assumes the family has no income except Charles's $80,000 salary.

$10,000+ income tax. However, if Christine operates a fine china and crystal business that makes a buying trip to Europe a necessity, the $15,000 travel expense, in effect, comes out of the $80,000 income *before* the income tax is computed, so the result is a tax saving of $4,200. That tax saving did not really cost $15,000 to generate, as they would have spent the $15,000 anyway.

Of course, there is more to this maneuver than this simple example demonstrates. The IRS needs to be convinced that Christine's China Shop is really a legitimate business, and those feds also need to be convinced that Charles's travel expense was also a business necessity. Those hurdles are covered in Chapter 5.

Before we leave Christine and Charles, let's look at what happens if Christine's China Shop had a loss of $55,000, computed in Table 4.13.

Now there is no income tax to pay! Can you create this much loss and still have a cash flow that will allow you to eat and pay the rent? Yes, if you structure your financial life to create the right circumstances.

Table 4.13   Effect of Christine's Large Business Loss on Family's Federal Income Tax

	Family Income Consists of Charles's Salary Only (Christine Not in Business)	Family Income Consists of Charles's Salary and Loss from Christine's China Shop
Charles's salary	$80,000	$80,000
Subtract loss from Christine's China Shop	0	55,000
Family income	80,000	25,000
Federal income tax*	$10,513	$ 0

*Tax computation assumes two dependent children and standard deduction at 2000 rates.

Losses That Can Turn into Cash Refunds from the IRS

What if your business generates a loss and there is no other income from which to deduct that loss? (This might happen if you are single or your spouse is not employed.) Does that mean the tax benefit of that loss has vanished into the ether? Hardly. The tax law allows that loss to be carried back 2 years and forward 20 years. Again, Christine and Charles can demonstrate this concept:

Christine starts her business on January 1, and on that same date, Charles resigns from his job, so he can devote his full time to helping Christine in the china-shop business. As above, the business incurs a loss of $15,000, but now there is no salary from which the loss can be deducted. However, two years before, a summary of the couple's tax return looked like Table 4.14.

That $15,000 loss, that was of no tax benefit this year, can be carried back two years and applied to Charles's salary that year. Now the amended return that Charles and Christine file for that year looks like Table 4.15.

Table 4.14   Charles's and Christine's Federal Income Tax, Second Previous Year

Charles's salary	$60,000
Gross income	60,000
Income tax*	$ 6,319

*Computation uses rates, exemptions, and standard deduction for 1998.

Table 4.15   Charles's and Christine's Federal Income Tax after Carryback of Loss to Second Previous Year

Charles's salary	$60,000
Subtract loss from this year	15,000
Gross income	45,000
Income tax	$ 4,605

*Computation uses rates, exemptions, and standard deduction for 1998.

When the folks at the IRS receive that amended return, they will cheerfully (?) send a check for $1,714 ($6,319 − $4,605) to Christine and Charles.

What if the loss this year is $80,000? A portion of that loss can be used to offset completely the income of $60,000 in the second prior year, so the entire original tax of $6,319 will be refunded.

What happens to the $20,000 of loss that was more than was needed to wipe out the income two years ago? It is carried forward to the return filed last year, offsetting at least some of that year's income and generating a further refund.

Such losses, technically called *net operating losses,* can be carried back 2 years and forward 20 years, and you can elect not to carry the loss back but to only carry it forward. Why would you do that? You might have had two very low income years in the previous 2 years, so you might have been paying tax at only 15 percent. In the future, you might be paying at 28 percent, 31 percent, or higher. Saving that loss carryover to apply to income at a higher rate might make sense.

Don't Lose Your Loss

Although these net operating losses are like money in the bank, some people throw them away. If you have net operating losses in your corporation and dissolve the corporation, if you sell the corporation to someone else, or if you elect S corporation status, those losses may disappear without ever generating a tax loss for anyone.

5

Change Personal Expenses into Business Tax Deductions

Of course, the IRS standard line is that personal expenses are personal expenses and they never become business expenses. The IRS folks don't advertise the exceptions or the way to change personal to business expenses, but it can be done—if done carefully.

Some timid souls wonder if it is worth the risk of an IRS audit to take deductions that the IRS might question. Their thinking goes something like: "If I am in a 28 percent tax bracket and I come up with an additional deduction of $100, I will save $28. Is that worth the risk of having to face an IRS auditor?"

HOW MUCH ARE THE DEDUCTIONS WORTH?

For a $28 saving, it is obviously not worth bringing attention to your tax return. But think in terms of hundreds or even thousands of dollars' additional deductions. Also, the saving is not just 28 percent, it is more like the following example, in Table 5.1, from the life of Eric and Elaine.

Table 5.1   Eric and Elaine: The Effect of $10,000 Additional
Deduction Generated in Elaine's Business

		Present Tax Picture	Tax Picture with Additional $10,000 Deduction
1	Eric's salary	$ 60,000	$60,000
2	Profit from Elaine's sole proprietorship	40,000	30,000
3	Total income (line 1 plus line 2)	100,000	90,000
4	Federal income tax* on total income on line 3	14,733	12,129
5	Social Security tax, Eric's salary	4,590	4,590
6	Social Security tax, Elaine's self-employment	5,652	4,239
7	State income tax†	2,918	2,547
8	Total taxes (lines 4 through 7)	$ 27,893	$23,505

*Computed at 2000 rates, four exemptions, $13,000 in itemized deductions.
†State tax is an estimate, at 4 percent of taxable income. Your state, if it has state income tax, probably will have some other rate.

Eric is employed in a salaried position, and Elaine operates her own business. Their present tax situation is shown in the first column of Table 5.1. The second column reflects the change in the tax picture if Elaine converts $10,000 of personal expenses into business deductions.

This reduction in total taxes, due to a $10,000 additional deduction, is $4,388, or almost half of the deduction.

Worth trying to create such a deduction legally? For most people, the answer is probably yes.

WHICH SPOUSE SHOULD CREATE THE DEDUCTIONS?

Note that the results will not be so spectacular if Eric develops a sideline business with a $10,000 loss. That loss will not apply to reducing either his or Elaine's Social Security bill. Why? For Social Security tax purposes, losses from a business can be applied only to profits from a business. They cannot be applied to salary income. Note the difference from income tax rules, where business losses can be applied to salary income to reduce total income and the income tax thereon. Table 5.2 illustrates this. It is a copy of Table 5.1 with the addition of another column. This last column assumes that instead of Elaine generating additional deductions of $10,000, Eric starts a small business that has a loss of $10,000 during its first year.

If Eric, rather than Elaine, generates that $10,000 loss in a small business, the income tax bill is reduced by the same amount that occurs if Elaine generates a $10,000 loss. However, the total Social Security tax is not reduced, so the total bill in column 3 is $1,412 greater than in column 2.

Moral: Try to make any business deductions applicable to the spouse who owns the business, not to the salaried spouse.

WOULD YOU BE BETTER OFF AS A SELF-EMPLOYED CONTRACTOR?

This Eric-and-Elaine example also partly explains why working as a self-employed contractor on your full-time job may be preferable to working as an employee. Any losses in another business will help reduce the Social Security tax. Also, deducting business expenses is easier for a self-employed person than for a salaried person:

Janice does sign painting and sign maintenance for the city school system. Late each afternoon she is expected to prepare a report, complete with worker-hours and other costs, so it can be on the maintenance superintendent's desk at 8:00 A.M. the next morning. She is provided with a desk and a computer on which to prepare her report and do other administrative chores.

Table 5.2   Eric and Elaine: A Comparison of
$10,000 Deduction Generated in Elaine's Business versus in New
Business Started by Eric

		Present Tax Picture	Tax Picture with Additional $10,000 Deduction by Elaine	Tax Picture If Eric Starts Business and Has $10,000 Loss
1	Eric's salary	$ 60,000	$60,000	$ 60,000
2	Profit from Elaine's sole proprietorship	40,000	30,000	40,000
3	Loss from Eric's business			(10,000)
4	Total income (lines 1 through 2)	100,000	90,000	90,000
5	Federal income tax* on total income on line 3	14,733	12,129	12,129
6	Social security tax, Eric's salary	4,590	4,590	4,590
7	Social security tax, Elaine's self-employment	5,652	4,239	5,652
8	State income tax†	2,918	2,547	2,547
9	Total taxes (lines 4 through 7)	$ 27,893	$23,505	$ 24,918

*Computed at 2000 rates, four exemptions, $13,000 in itemized deductions.
†State tax is an estimate, at 4 percent of taxable income. Your state, if it has state income tax, will have some other rate.

However, the physical condition of the schools' signs is abysmal. The workload is heavy, so she usually works in the field until at least 5:00 P.M. She then has to drive downtown, prepare the report, and drive to her house 15 miles away. It is often 8:00 P.M. before she arrives home, much to the displeasure of her husband and children.

To make life a little easier for both herself and her husband, she buys her own computer and a fax machine. Now she heads home at *normal quitting time, prepares her report after dinner, and faxes it to the downtown office. As the machines are strictly for her job, can she deduct their $2,000 cost on the couple's tax return, as Section-179 expense of equipment purchases? (For explanation, see Chapter 3.) No! Because the employer provides her with the necessary tools (desk and computer) and the place to use them, her purchase of a computer and fax machine is strictly for her own convenience, and therefore the cost cannot be deducted on the tax return.*

What if the school board tells her that she must have a computer and fax but that she must buy them herself as there were none available for her to use? Then the $2,000 may be deductible. But as she is an employee, the deduction must be made as a "miscellaneous deduction subject to a 2 percent floor." What does that mean? Table 5.3, computing the tax for Janice and her husband George, explains.

Table 5.3   Janice and George—Pertinent Sections of Tax Return

	Computation of Adjusted Gross Income	
1	George's salary	$35,000
2	Janice's salary	38,000
3	Interest income	2,000
4	Total (adjusted gross) income (total of lines 1, 2, and 3)	75,000
	Computation of Itemized Deductions	
5	Employee business expense (computer and fax)	$ 2,000
6	The IRS requires them to subtract 2% of adjusted gross income from most employee business expense (line 4)	1,500
7	Deductible employee business expense (line 5 minus line 6)	500
8	Other itemized deductions (mortgage interest, taxes, etc.)	12,000
9	Total itemized deductions (line 7 plus line 8)	$12,500

Because Janice is an employee, $1,500 of her business-related expenses is not a deduction but disappears into the IRS ether. As this couple is probably in the 28 percent tax bracket, they are paying $420 tax ($1,500 x 28 percent) on money they cannot personally use.

What if George and Janice rent their home and therefore do not have enough itemized deductions? They will have to take the standard deduction and can deduct none of the $2,000 cost of the computer and the fax machine!

Perhaps Janice can change her arrangement with the school administration. If she quits her job and contracts for sign painting and maintenance, then she will be self-employed and she can deduct the whole $2,000 cost of the computer and fax.

If you can change your status from that of employee to that of a self-employed contractor and you have some expenses that can be deducted as business expenses, you probably should make that change. However, before you settle on a contract price with your former employer, be sure you are compensated for the extra expense of paying all of your Social Security and other benefits.

Suppose you currently earn $50,000 per year as an employee and have employer-paid benefits of medical and life insurance that will cost you $12,000 to replace. Your compensation, then, as a contractor should be at least that computed in Table 5.4.

As not all of the former employee benefits may be deductible from your compensation as a self-employed contractor, you should ask for a few thousand more.

Table 5.4   Computation of Minimum Contract Price to Equal Previous Salary

1	Former salary	$50,000
2	Employer's share of Social Security tax previously paid by employer (7.65%)	3,825
3	Other benefits	12,000
4	Minimum contract amount necessary to be equivalent to salary (total of lines 1, 2, and 3)	$65,825

This maneuver pays off only if you have some business expense that you can deduct as self-employed.

In the example in Table 5.3, Janice has the expense of the computer and the fax machine. Assuming she is no longer provided a desk and computer by the school administration, her office is now her home, so she can deduct her expenses of driving to the various schools.

As you are no doubt aware, the IRS will not let just anyone change from employee to self-employed status. There are certain tests one must meet to be considered self-employed, and the IRS will apply them to your enterprise, whether it is a part-time enterprise or your full-time employment. Usually, the IRS would prefer that you be an employee. Not only will you have fewer opportunities to take deductions and lower your tax bill, but your employer will withhold income taxes and relieve the IRS of having to collect money directly from you.

The Tests: Employee or Self-Employed Contractor?

The principal test is that of control and direction. If John, her boss, tells Janice when to report to work, what signs to paint or repair, and when to leave, she is an employee. If, on Monday morning, John gives her a list of signs to be painted and repaired with the only time requirement being that the work be completed within seven days, she may be able to be a self-employed contractor. Some of the other factors that would strengthen the argument in favor of her being self-employed are:

- John does not pay Janice by the hour, but she is paid per a contract between Janice and the school board for the end result of her efforts.

- John has no right to instruct Janice on when, where, or how the work is to be done. He can only tell her what must be accomplished and when it is due. It is up to her to decide on the when, where, and how.

- John provides no training for Janice.
- Janice is not an executive of and does not make any decision for the school administration.
- Janice can hire and fire assistants as she chooses, without seeking any approval from John. The employees would be paid by Janice, not the school board.
- Janice also does sign work for other entities (government and business).
- Janice need not provide daily reports as to hours worked.
- John does not pay any of Janice's expenses. Her contract price should cover those, so she pays them herself.
- John does not provide any tools for Janice. She buys and maintains her own tools.

(John can be anyone in authority in the school administration.)

These tests are but a partial list of the factors the IRS will consider in determining employee versus self-employed status. The complete IRS guideline is in Revenue Ruling 87-41. Part of that ruling is reprinted in Appendix C-4. It is fairly readable, so study it if you think you might be able to operate as a self-employed contractor and enjoy the possibility of more tax deductions.

Penalty for the Wrong Status and How to Avoid It

What if Janice, with the approval of the school board, does change to a self-employed status, and IRS auditors subsequently decide that she does not meet their guidelines? The school board is penalized in that it is responsible for the income taxes and Social Security that should have been withheld from payments to Janice. Janice is penalized because she would lose the deductions for expenses such as the computer and the fax machine.

You can avoid the risk of this penalty. The employer (the school board in our example) can file a Form SS-8 with the IRS. This form requests a ruling on the status of a worker. (A copy of the form is in Appendix D.)

CONVERTING A HOBBY INTO A LEGITIMATE BUSINESS

Business magazines and books are full of suggestions for success from prosperous entrepreneurs. The most frequent advice is to make sure you find much of your business to be fun, for a new business requires time, time, and more time from its owner. The same is true for a part-time business, for it will take hours out of the day, after the regular job, that would otherwise be spent in recreation or relaxing. What better way to be sure your business will provide some pleasure than basing it on your hobby?

If you collect stamps, start a stamp-trading business; if your sport is sailing, start a business of providing sailing lessons. Surely you can dream up a business that is based on your avocation.

But here comes the IRS! The folk who audit your tax return seem to think that if a business is pleasurable, it must be only a hobby, and therefore none of the expenses should be deductible. Fortunately for the rest of us who are not the IRS, the federal courts have often disagreed with the IRS on this point. In a tax court case, the judge said:

> Business will not be turned into a hobby merely because the owner finds it pleasurable; suffering has never been made a prerequisite to deductibility. Success in business is largely obtained by pleasurable interests therein.[1]

However, the kindhearted IRS will let you deduct expenses of a hobby up to almost the limit of the income from the hobby:

Sally is an avid sailor who often enters her boat in formal sailboat races. To help defray expenses, she gives sailing lessons in the spring and summer, for which she collects a fee. The financial summary of her operation, at the end of the year, looks like Table 5.5.

Sally has a full-time job selling advertising, from which she earns $50,000 per year. If the IRS allows her to treat the sailing lessons as

---

[1] *Jackson* 59 TC 317 (1972).

Table 5.5   Sally's Sailing School

Sale of lessons		$ 2,000
Subtract expenses:		
Painting boat	$ 500	
Rigging repair	900	
New spinnaker sail	1,400	
Insurance	1,200	
Slip rent	3,000	
Total expenses		7,000
Loss (excess of expenses over income)		$(5,000)

a legitimate business, she can deduct that $5,000 loss from her $50,000 salary, so she would have less income tax to pay. However, inasmuch as Sally presumably enjoys the time spent as a sailing instructor, the IRS initially will take the position that the sailing lessons are a hobby. Therefore, Big Brother will say Sally can apply the sailing expenses to the sailing income and not to any other income. That is, she can deduct only $2,000 of sailing school expenses. As it is a hobby, she cannot use the other $5,000 of expenses to offset other income and reduce the tax on that other income. To add insult to injury, the tax law also prescribes that the $2,000 of expenses must be claimed as miscellaneous itemized deductions, subject to the 2 percent of gross income floor.[2] And it can be even worse. What if Sally does not have enough other deductions to itemize and she has to take the standard deduction? She will then have no benefit from the hobby expenses, but she will be privileged to pay income tax on the $2,000 income from sailing lessons. Fair? Congress thinks so!

Whether or not the sailing business is a hobby or a bona fide business does make quite a difference, as computed in Tables 5.6

---

[2]If there were taxes or interest on part of a residence included in the sailing school expenses, they would be deductible in full as taxes or interest. Only the remainder of the $2,000 expenses would be subject to the 2 percent floor. (Source: The General Explanation of the Tax Reform Act of 1986, Staff of the Joint Committee on Taxation, 83.)

Table 5.6   Sally's Income Tax Picture
If Her Sailing School Is Only a Hobby

Salary from advertising business		$50,000
Sales of sailing lessons	$2,000	
Subtract sailing school expenses (listed in Table 5.5) allowed as deductions (only to the extent of income and further reduced by the 2% of adjusted gross income floor)	1,000	
Income from sailing school		1,000
Total income (adjusted gross income)		$51,000
Federal income tax*		$ 7,291

*One exemption, itemized deductions of $10,000, 2000 rates.

Table 5.7   Sally's Income Tax Picture
If Her Sailing School Is a Business

Salary from advertising business		$ 50,000
Sales of sailing lessons	$2,000	
Subtract sailing school expenses allowed as deductions (all of expenses listed in Table 5.5)	7,000	
Loss from sailing school		(5,000)
Total income (adjusted gross income)		$45,000
Federal income tax*		$ 5,611

*One exemption, itemized deductions of $10,000, 2000 rates.

Table 5.8   Sally's Income Tax Picture
Comparison of Hobby to Business

Sally's income tax if sailing school is a hobby (from Table 5.6)	$7,291
Subtract Sally's income tax if sailing school is a business (from Table 5.7)	5,611
Income tax *saved* if sailing school is a business	$1,680

through 5.8. (This example assumes Sally itemizes her personal deductions.)

Like most of us, Sally can use an extra $1,680 in her bank account. To have that extra money, all she needs to do is convince the IRS that Sally's Sailing School is a legitimate business and that she is operating it with the expectation of making a profit. How does she do that? There are two methods:

1. Meet a safe-harbor test.
2. Create facts and circumstances such that her intentions of making a profit are obvious.

Let's discuss each method in turn.

Safe- (Almost) Harbor Test (Three-of-Five-Years Profit)

This is often called by the informal name of "hobby loss rule." Actually, the so-called rule is a computation that serves as a guide in determining whether an enterprise is a hobby or a business.

Rule: If an enterprise shows a profit in three out of five consecutive years, it may be presumed to be a business rather than a hobby.[3]

Does this mean that if your enterprise, or Sally's Sailing School, makes a profit in three of five years, the IRS is forbidden to question your motives in operating the enterprise? No. What passing this test does do for you or Sally is that it shifts the burden of proof from you to the IRS. If Sally's Sailing School generates a loss every year from the day she starts the business until five years hence, the IRS will most certainly attack her loss deductions, claiming she is not operating a business but a hobby for which she cannot claim loss deductions. As she has

---

[3]There is one exception to this three-of-five-years rule. Horse farms that breed, show, train, and race horses need show a profit in only two out of seven consecutive years. Why this special rule for horses? It may be the nature of the business, or perhaps several members of Congress own horse farms.

not met the three-of-five-years profit test, it will be up to her and her professional advisor to prove to the IRS, or perhaps the Tax Court, that she really is in business.

If, on the other hand, she does meet the test of three-out-of-five-years profit and the IRS auditor takes the position that the sailing school is operated only for her pleasure (a hobby), that auditor has to convince his or her IRS supervisors, the IRS appeals staff, and perhaps a federal judge that the school really is a hobby. What are the chances an IRS auditor will put forth that much effort over a few thousand dollars of deductions? Not much, unless there appears to be gross manipulation of numbers, as the examples in Tables 5.9 and 5.10 demonstrate. Table 5.9 reflects the actual history of Sally's Sailing School over five years. Table 5.10 reflects the same total results over the five years, but after being massaged with some accounting magic.

The operating results as listed in Table 5.9 would not, of course, pass the test of making a profit in any three out of five consecutive years. The same overall results in Table 5.10 would, on the surface, appear to pass the test. How can Sally, or her accountant, accomplish the results in Table 5.10?

The additional $3,000 loss in year one can be generated by changing the method of claiming depreciation in that first year. In year two, Sally can simply not pay $4,000 worth of bills until January of year three, thereby showing a profit in year two and a loss in year three. She can do the same thing in year five,

Table 5.9 Sally's Sailing School Actual Yearly Results (losses in parentheses)		Table 5.10 Sally's Sailing School Manipulated Results (losses in parentheses)	
Year 1	$(5,000)	Year 1	$(8,000)
Year 2	(3,000)	Year 2	1,000
Year 3	(6,000)	Year 3	(10,000)
Year 4	1,000	Year 4	1,000
Year 5	(2,000)	Year 5	1,000
Total	$(15,000)	Total	$(15,000)

delaying the payment of several bills to year six, which is beyond the test period.

Will this work? Will the IRS blindly accept such manipulation of numbers? This area is an excellent example of the obfuscation of our tax laws. The Internal Revenue Code and the IRS regulations refer only to "profit," without any definition as to how "profit" is to be determined. Presumably, then, if the method by which the profit is determined is legal under other parts of the federal tax laws and regulations, it is legal for determination of profit for this test. Sally's business would qualify for cash-basis accounting, and Table 5.10 is a reflection of cash basis (recording expenses when they are paid). (For explanation, see Chapter 4.) Therefore, it would seem that the second method of computing yearly profits would fly.

However, the Internal Revenue Code does require that any method of accounting that a business uses must "reasonably reflect profits," and it grants the IRS authority to impose a different method on a business if the present method of accounting is not reasonable in the opinion of the IRS. Will the IRS agree that the method in Table 5.10 reasonably reflects profits? Who knows?[4]

My personal opinion, and that's all that it is, is this: The IRS auditor would probably accept using any method of depreciation that is acceptable on an income tax return, so the increased loss in year one would stand. However, he or she would probably claim that the bunching of expenses into two years is artificial and was done only to meet the test of three-out-of-five-years profit. Would I try this scenario? Maybe, but I would also take all the actions discussed further in this chapter. I say "maybe" for this reason: If I obviously manipulate the books to meet the test, I am, in a way, admitting that I think the sailing school is a hobby and that I therefore must use this maneuver. If I report the profits as in Table 5.9, I am taking the position that the sailing school is a legitimate business and can back that up with procedures covered later in this chapter.

---

[4]Unresolved questions such as this are why the federal Tax Court had a backlog of 15,500 cases as of January 2001.

I do not recommend any outright dishonesty to make a hobby meet this test. For instance, if Sally has a loss of only a few hundred dollars in one year, she could put a few hundred dollars of her own money into the business and record it as a sale of lessons, thereby changing one loss year into a profit year. This is clearly fraudulent and could bring forth criminal penalties. Similarly, an overly creative accountant could probably come up with some fraudulent bookkeeping maneuvers for accrual-basis books that would accomplish passing the test but land you in trouble. (For explanation of accrual basis, see Chapter 4.) Make sure you have a reputable accountant.

Other Ways to Make Your Business Not a Hobby

First, let's clear up a general misunderstanding. In the barber shop, beauty parlor, or by the pool, you will hear the statement that "unless a business makes a profit in three out of five years, it is not a business but a hobby, and the losses cannot be used to offset other income in the current year or carried over to offset profit in other years."

Wrong!

This three-of-five-years rule is only sort of a safe harbor that shifts the burden of proof from the taxpayer to the IRS. The basic rule laid out in the Internal Revenue Code[5] is not some sort of numbers test but a test of the facts and circumstances. The IRS regulations[6] set forth nine tests to help the IRS determine whether or not an enterprise is a business or a hobby. As attested by the number of court cases that taxpayers have waged (both winning and losing) on this point, these tests are not definitive but are only guidelines. In fact, the regulations refer to them as factors, rather than tests. The nine factors are:

1. Manner in which the taxpayer carries on the activity.

2. Expertise of the taxpayer or his or her advisors.

3. Time and effort expended by the taxpayer in carrying on the activity.

---

[5]IRC §183.
[6]IRS Regulation §1.183-2(b). (Reprinted in Appendix C-5.)

4. Expectations that assets may appreciate in value.

5. Success of the taxpayer in carrying on other similar or dissimilar activities.

6. History of income or losses with respect to the activity.

7. Amount of occasional profits, if any, that are earned.

8. Financial status of the taxpayer.

9. Elements of personal pleasure or recreation.

Let's discuss each factor in more detail.

The Nine Factors

1. Manner in which the taxpayer carries on the activity.   You need to be businesslike in the operation of your business. Some of the ways of appearing businesslike are these:

(a)   Open a separate checking account for your business and use it only for business receipts and disbursements. Do not play "put-and-take" for personal needs from this account. Take only periodic draws (or salary) and, if the business needs more cash, loan it in a lump sum to the business and record the cash receipt as a loan. (For a discussion of capital contributions versus loans from business owners, see Chapter 6.) If your business is incorporated (either C or S corporation), be sure to sign (as president) formal promissory notes from the corporation to you, and be sure the corporation pays the interest to you.

(b)   Set up a formal bookkeeping and accounting record. The best bet is to have an accountant set up a system and have someone knowledgeable in bookkeeping keep journals and ledgers for you. (These do not have to be the old-fashioned pen-and-ink "books." Computer programs create the same type of records more efficiently, but buy *business* software. Do not use personal-finance software.) Most IRS auditors, appeals officers, and Tax Court judges have had some training in accounting and bookkeeping. They will not be impressed by your own peculiar homegrown bookkeeping system. Use professional help.

(c) Maintain all business records in orderly files.

(d) Have and use professionally printed letterheads, business cards, invoices, and other forms.

(e) Make a sincere effort to promote your business. Of course, you should have brochures and do some advertising, as well as make presentations to prospective customers. Be sure to record, as in your daily planner, every promotional activity you undertake. This would include one-on-one sales pitches, presentations to groups, phone calls, and everything else that would indicate you are sincere in your efforts to attract more customers.

2. Expertise of the taxpayer or his or her advisors. It would seem obvious that anyone entering a business should have some knowledge and skill relevant to the business. Let's look at Sally and Herman:

Sally has had years of sailing experience and is well qualified to teach sailing skills to others. On the other hand, Herman, who has never been on any boat (except for the Staten Island Ferry), decides that he would like to try sailing and buys a sailboat. To try to deduct the expenses of his new hobby, he sets himself up as a sailing school and gets a few of his friends to pay him token amounts for an afternoon of sailing. (Actually, the sailing lessons are nothing more than social events, and the token payments are enough only to buy the refreshments.) Sally should pass this test. Herman obviously flunks.

Herman might be able to claim to pass this test if he hires Sally to run the sailing school, but if she devotes only a little time to Herman's enterprise and his payments to her are small, he might still fail. Perhaps the best case for passing this test on the basis of expertise of advisors is to purchase a franchise. You may never have been in the hamburger business, but if you purchase a McDonald's™ franchise, you are purchasing the corporation's expertise and advice that should make you successful.

Also, of course, it is hard to believe that the IRS would consider a fast-food business to be a hobby.

3. Time and effort expended by the taxpayer in carrying on the activity.   The IRS is more likely to accept an enterprise as a business if the owner puts substantial effort and time into its pursuit, and the argument is even stronger if he or she gives up other vocational pursuits to concentrate on the enterprise in question. Let's look again at Sally:

Sally has a full-time job, so the pursuit of her business is limited to evenings and weekends. She could have a problem because of this, but she might successfully argue that her business can operate profitably only in evenings and on weekends, as those are the hours when customers have time available to take sailing lessons.

In the same vein, if Sally buys two or three more sailboats and hires instructors, her argument that the sailing lessons are a business is much stronger. After all, she can enjoy sailing only one boat at a time. Owning a fleet of boats would indicate a profitable-business intent. Then again, this logic might not hold if her additional boats are substantially different sizes. For example, if she owns a small, open boat for day sailing, a 30-footer for coastal cruising, and a 50-footer for trips to Bermuda, her enterprise might still be a hobby. In other words, there are no concrete rules.

---

4. Expectation that assets may appreciate in value.   Even if the day-to-day operations of the business do not generate a profit, the enterprise may still be considered a business if it is reasonable to expect that the assets can be sold at a profit at some later date. Sally could have a problem with using this rule to build her case, for nearly all boats decline in value with age.

Businesses that could use this argument would include real estate operators, who may lose money on rentals of certain parcels of real estate but can expect to reap a big profit when the parcel is sold some years hence.[7]

---

[7]Ownership of real estate can be a business if it is actively managed (participated in) by the owner. For many of us, though, ownership of real estate,

You might say "Ah ha!" and think that this rule makes it easy to consider your art, or antique automobile collection, a business. However, I doubt that the expectation of later profitable sales will make the 1932 Packard in your garage into a business. However, if you acquire several other classic cars, rented a building in a tourist area and opened a classic-car museum, you probably are in business. Then you could argue that even though the receipts from admission into your museum do not cover all of your expenses, the expectation that the Packards, Hupmobiles, and Stutzes will sell someday at huge profits makes your car-collecting enterprise into a business.

5. Success of the taxpayer in carrying on other similar or dissimilar activities.   This seems to say that if you have been successful in making a profit in other businesses, you are more likely to convince the IRS that your present enterprise is a business.

6. History of income or losses with respect to the activity.   This factor would seem to be redundant with the three-of-five-years profit rule. However, it does mean that the IRS auditor should not rule out the possibility that an enterprise is a business even if it doesn't meet the three-of-five-years rule. Suppose, for instance, that you have a business that shows a little less loss each year, and finally, in the fifth and sixth years, shows a profit. Shouldn't that make it a legitimate business?

Sally finds that her sailing school cannot meet the three-of-five-years profit rule but is still very much a legitimate business. The America's Cup races are sailed every four years. Because of the television and other coverage, public interest in sailing greatly increases in those "Cup years." Sally earns a $100,000 profit in those years in which the America's Cup is raced and loses $10,000 per year in each of the off years.

---

particularly if we have contracted with someone else to manage it, is a passive business, and losses from passive businesses cannot be deducted from a salary and/or a profit from a business you actively manage.

I would think her argument is strong, though a profit once every four years does not meet the three-of-five-years test.

You should be aware that the courts are often more lenient than the IRS in this area. In one case the Tax Court judge said:

> If the taxpayer has a good faith expectation of profit from a particular venture, irrespective of whether or not others might view that expectation as reasonable, his venture is a trade or business.[8]

7. Amount of occasional profits, if any, that are earned.   Profitable years should show significant profits. If Sally's Sailing School shows a profit of only $3,000 in America's Cup years after three years of losing $10,000 per year, her case would be weak, for the profit is small when compared to the losses.

8. Financial status of the taxpayer.   If the owner of the business has no other source of income, then he or she must have entered this enterprise with the expectation of making a profit, and the operation should qualify as a business.

On the other hand, if a business executive or a medical doctor operates a farm that continuously loses money, it is likely that the IRS will consider the farm a hobby, for there is an ample source of other income for the owner. If that owner has also built or remodeled a luxurious house on the farm, his or her case would be even weaker.

9. Elements of personal pleasure or recreation.   It is unlikely that anyone would set up a business for fat rendering or sewer cleaning because they enjoyed those activities as a hobby. Just the nature of the business would indicate that anyone entering the business does so for the money or the prospect of profit. Compare that to someone setting up a sailing school or buying a horse farm. The IRS will be strongly suspicious that the operation is really a hobby for which the owner wants to be able to deduct expenses from other income. Anyone doing that has to scrupulously follow my suggestions covered in the discussion of factors 1 through 8.

---

[8] *Francis X. Benz* 63 TC 375,383 (1974).

EXPANDING TO A BIGGER BUSINESS

Meeting at least some of these nine tests looks like a lot of hassle to go through. Is it worth it just to save a few hundred dollars? That's a personal decision that only you can make.

Can Sally wipe out even more taxes if she really jumps into this sailing business in a big way? Table 5.11 looks at Sally's Sailing School (Expanded):

Sally borrows $50,000 with which she buys two more boats, advertises her classes, and incurs other expenses that would come about with the expansion of the sailing school.

Applying this loss on Sally's individual tax return generates an income tax picture as in Table 5.12.

There may be one problem here. If Sally's Sailing School has a loss of $37,900, it will appear that Sally is not going to have much cash left out of her salary, and she does have to eat and have a place to live.

Before we look closer at that situation, let's talk about *cash flow.* The cash that results from the transactions in the sailing

Table 5.11   Sally's Sailing School (Expanded)

Sale of lessons		$ 17,000
Subtract expenses:		
Advertising	$ 5,500	
Depreciation	22,000	
Instructors, part-time	5,000	
Insurance	3,600	
Interest	5,000	
Maintenance, old boat	2,800	
Slip rent	8,000	
Travel expense	3,000	
Total expenses		54,900
Loss (excess of expenses over income)		$(37,900)

Table 5.12   Sally's Individual Income Tax

Salary from advertising business		$ 50,000
Subtract loss from sailing school		(37,900)
Adjusted gross income		12,100
Subtract		
Personal exemption	$ 2,450	
Itemized deductions	10,000	
Total subtractions		12,450
Taxable income (loss)		(350)
Income tax		$ 0

school is not going to equal the taxable income, as not all of the transactions in Table 5.11 are cash transactions, even though Sally keeps the sailing school's books on the cash basis. Depreciation is a bookkeeping entry; Sally never writes a check to anyone called "depreciation." (She does pay the boat dealer for the two boats, but because she borrows that money, that does not change her bank balance.) Also, even though she pays the bank loan department $7,000 during the year, only $5,000 of that is a deductible interest expense. The other $2,000 is a principal payment. Therefore, to see what her cash flow is for the year, we have to prepare a list as in Table 5.13.

Compare this with the cash flow Sally has without the sailing school business, displayed in Table 5.14.

The vacation in Table 5.14 is travel expense in Table 5.13. In other words, Sally has structured what might have been a nondeductible vacation into a deductible travel expense. This is explained later in this chapter.

In both Tables 5.13 and 5.14, the cash balance Sally has left at the end of the year is about the same. It might seem then, at first glance, that it makes no difference whether Sally starts the sailing school or not. However, without the business (Table 5.14) she ships almost $8,000 off to the IRS. With the business, she ships nothing to the IRS. Instead, she pays off part of a loan that pur-

Table 5.13   Sally's Cash Flow (with Expanded Sailing School)

Salary from advertising business		$50,000
Sale of lessons		17,000
Total cash inflow		$67,000
Subtract cash outflow		
Advertising	$ 5,500	
Loan payment	7,000	
Instructors, part-time	5,000	
Insurance	3,600	
Maintenance, old boat	2,800	
Slip rent	8,000	
Travel	3,000	
Personal living expenses	25,000	
Total cash outflow		59,900
Cash left at end of year		$ 7,100

Table 5.14   Sally's Cash Flow If Sailing Were Only Her Hobby (One Boat)

Salary from advertising business		$50,000
Insurance	$ 1,200	
Maintenance, old boat	2,800	
Slip rent	3,000	
Vacation	3,000	
Other personal living expenses	25,000	
Federal income tax	7,837	
Total cash outflow		42,837
Cash left at end of year		$ 7,163

chased additional boats, and she is building an intangible asset in a going business.

This may be going further into self-employment than you wish to, but the opportunity is there if you want to wipe out income tax for a few years and build equity (value of ownership) in a business.

DEDUCT OFFICE-IN-THE-HOME EXPENSES?

This is a deduction area that has received far more publicity and IRS attention than seems justified, for it generally does not result in a significant additional deduction. It may look large on your tax return, but examine it. Much of it probably is made up of mortgage interest and real estate tax that can be deducted anyway. Yet if your business should show a profit, you may want to take this deduction. The computation is rather mechanical, and following the instructions for filling in Form 8829, *Expenses for Business Use of Your Home,* will lead you through the arithmetic. A couple of factors, though, deserve some comment.

The Principal-Place-of-Business Requirement

In order for home office expense to be deductible, the home office must be (1) exclusively and regularly[9] used as your principal place of business; (2) used as a place where you meet with customers, clients, or patients on a regular basis; or (3) be a separate structure used in your business. The definition of "principal place of business" has been elusive and the source of many arguments between business people and the IRS. Congress finally made some changes in the law, effective in 1999. The test now is:

- You use it exclusively and regularly for administrative or management activities of your trade or business.
- You have no other fixed location where you conduct substantial administrative or management activities of your trade or business.

If you don't qualify by meeting those two rules, the IRS gives you two alternative rules:

[9]There are two exceptions to the "exclusively" requirement: certain inventory storage and day-care operations.

- If you have more than one location, what is the relative importance of the activities performed at each location?
- You can also consider the time spent at each location.

If these rules/guidelines leave you in a quandary as to whether you qualify for a home office deduction, call the IRS and order Publication 587, *Business Use of Your Home.* It provides these rules and some examples that may help you.

Caveat: Before you spend a lot of time on this decision, check the section about the home office effect on future gain on your home, which is in an italicized paragraph later in this section.

Sally, our sailing-school friend, cannot now take a home office deduction, even though she uses a room in her house to keep records and telephone prospective students. It seems obvious that the most important activity of the school is the instruction, which is done mostly on the water. Also, she spends most of her time allotted to the sailing school in this instruction.

What if she uses her home office to hold classes on navigation, knot tying, meteorology, and other subjects that enhance sailing skill? I doubt it would fly. The most important ingredient in learning to sail is the actual handling of a sailboat under way.

Net Income Limitation

For a business such as we have been discussing to this point, where losses from a small business will offset income from another business or salary, this factor almost makes computation of the home office expense a waste of time. The law states that the part of the home office expense that would create or add to a loss cannot be deducted. However, any such disallowed home office expense can be carried forward, or saved up, and used to offset income in a profitable year.

Sally, because she has a loss even without any home office expense, cannot use that expense to increase her loss. She can only save it for future use when she earns a profit. (She will still have to get around the principal-place-of-business requirement.)

Should you go through the computation and build up a reserve of home office expenses to deduct someday? If you want to build up such a carryforward item, you have to include the Form 8829, *Expenses for Business Use of Your Home,* in this year's tax return, listing the home office expenses and computing how much can be carried forward. Filing those Forms 8829, each one adding to the home office–expense carryforward, may bring a little extra attention to you from the IRS. I doubt that you find that desirable.

Another negative aspect of the home office deduction is the effect that depreciation (deducted as part of home office expense) can have on your tax return when you sell your residence.

Assume you pay $150,000 for your home and claim home office expense, which will include depreciation. In round figures, you claim 10 percent of the house as business use and deduct depreciation of $350 per year. Five years later you sell your home for $250,000, creating a $100,000 gain. If you had not claimed the depreciation on 10 percent of the house, there would be no tax on that gain, as it is under the $250,000/$500,000 exclusion allowed. But because you did claim depreciation, you have the privilege of paying tax on the portion of the gain that is attributable to your office portion. That's probably 20 percent tax on a $10,000 gain, or $2,000 that you ship off to Uncle Sam. What was the offset? The tax saving on a $350 deduction every year for five years. If you're in the 28 percent tax bracket, that amounts to a total tax saving of only $500. Yes, you do deduct a little insurance and house maintenance also, but will it all add up to the $2,000 tax on the gain?

In summary, I urge that you work out the numbers for a home office–expense deduction, compare them with what you could deduct anyway (interest and taxes), and make a decision as to whether it is worth the complications and possible extra concern directed at you by the IRS. Your time and attention might be better spent on making sure you conduct your business in such a manner that it will not be considered a hobby.

TRANSFORM VACATIONS INTO BUSINESS TRIPS

For many of us, our dream is to arrange our lives so that we can travel extensively and deduct all the cost as a business deduction. The current law and various court cases have decimated that dream, but there are some pieces of it that we can pick up and use.

There was a time when Sally might have been able to deduct the cost of a trip to watch the America's Cup races. She could have claimed that watching the professionals would enhance her knowledge of sailing, a skill she needed to continuously improve if her sailing school was to prosper. Actually, such a deduction would have been justified by its educational benefit. Unfortunately, this deduction is no more. A recently added section of the tax law[10] states that travel, as an education in itself, is no longer a deductible expense.

However, if Sally travels to San Francisco to attend a seminar training program on the operation of a sailing school, she can claim the travel expenses, plus the cost of the seminar, as a business expense. What can she deduct? The airfare (or the cost of train, bus, or her own automobile) to San Francisco and back, the hotel room, and 50 percent of the cost of meals. (Only 50 percent, rather than 80 percent, is now deductible, courtesy of the Deficit Reduction Act of 1993.) Note that the act of her spending the money to attend this seminar may strengthen her argument that she is serious about making a profit in her sailing school and thereby avoiding the hobby-loss classification.

Sally has a brother, Sam, who lives with his wife and a couple of kids in San Francisco. If Sally spends two days at the seminar and five days visiting her relatives, most of her business deduction is shot down. She can deduct only the hotel room and 50 percent of the meals for the two days of the seminar. The airfare is now just a

[10]IRC §274(m)(2).

personal expense, as most of the time on the trip is spent on personal pursuits. However, if she spends five days at the seminar and only two days visiting relatives, the main purpose of the trip is business and she can deduct all but her expenses for the two days she spends playing with her niece and nephew.

There is, however, one plan Sally can pursue that would enable her to have three days with her family and still deduct the transportation to San Francisco and back. If she attends the seminar on Thursday and Friday, stays with her family on Saturday and Sunday, and then negotiates for the purchase of another boat with a dealer in San Francisco on Monday, the two nonbusiness days of Saturday and Sunday will count as business days even though she spends them with her family. Then she will have five business days and can spend up to four more days with her brother. Her score will look like this:

Days actually devoted to business	*3*
Personal days that count as business days	*2*
Personal days that count as personal days	*4*

Count them up. Five business days and four personal days mean that the trip was predominately for business, so Sally can deduct the cost of the travel.

The theory here, which the IRS allows, is that a business-person cannot conduct business on weekends, so if he or she conducts business during the week and has plans to stay and conduct business the following week, his or her reason for staying over the weekend is for the purpose of being at that location on Monday, and thus the weekend days are business related. As yet, the IRS hasn't said that we can't enjoy ourselves on Saturday and Sunday.

There are a couple of caveats to cover before we leave Sally for a while. If the same seminar is offered in her hometown, or near it, the IRS may try to disallow the travel expense, maintaining that she chooses to go to San Francisco for purely personal reasons. If that is the case, how can Sally protect herself from such IRS attack? (1) She can make sure that she attends a seminar that is not offered at a closer location. (2) She can find that other scheduled activities (such as providing already booked sailing lessons) conflict with the dates of the local offering of the seminar. Also, it is very important that she keep copies of her schedules and lesson contracts so that she can prove this schedule conflict two years later when she might be unlucky enough to be selected for audit by the IRS.

Another admonition is to keep records of the travel—the more, the better. If you take a trip that is both business and pleasure, keep a log of activities so that you can prove the number of business days versus personal days.

One way to make a lot of travel a deductible business expense is to be in a business for which travel is the essential ingredient. A career as a travel photographer or writer could fit this description. If you have no experience and credentials as a photographer or writer, your chances of finding a publication or television producer who will foot the bill to send you, your camera, and your word processor around the world are nil. (I'm ignoring the exceptional situation where your uncle owns a prosperous travel magazine.) You will have to set up your own business as a freelance photographer and writer, and the "hobby-loss" rules we covered earlier in this chapter will pursue you:

Three years go by. You have spent $100,000 per year in traveling around the world, taking pictures, and writing about what you saw. Your sales of pictures and essays are zero. How strong will your argument be that you are really trying to make a profit in a bona fide business? Not very.

If you try this scenario, you should have some strong credentials that would indicate you can sell your photography and writing. That is, you need to have made significant sales of your output to the media, and that output needs to be travel related. Then, if you follow all the earlier suggestions for keeping your business out of the hobby classification, you may be able to deduct all that glamorous travel.

Are you scholarly? That can be another source of credentials for the deduction of travel expense. If you left school after the fifth grade and now want to spend a year in China looking at art, your travel expenses are surely personal. However, if you have a PhD in oriental art, you have a strong argument that your research may result in profitable sales of your scholarly writing. Indeed, if you have a teaching position in the same discipline, you can deduct such research expense even though you will receive nothing for your efforts other than your teaching salary.[11]

Deducting the Cost of Taking Other Family Members on Business Trips

This is another area in which Congress tightened the rules in 1993. No longer can you justify deducting your spouse's travel cost because the people with whom you were going to confer would also have their spouses present at related entertainment. Now there are three requirements you and your spouse must meet if his or her travel expense can be deducted as a business expense:

1. Your spouse must be an employee of the person paying or reimbursing the expenses. Presumably, if you are paying the expenses as an owner of a business, you will need to hire your spouse.

2. Your spouse's travel must have a bona fide business purpose. In other words, he or she must have a job in your business, and that job must make it necessary to be present on the business trip. While light duties such as taking notes of meetings and typing them might qualify, they often don't. Better that your spouse is an executive with decision-making powers over what is being discussed. That is, it should be essential that he or she be at meetings at the remote location.

3. Your spouse's expenses should otherwise be deductible. For example, generally, the cost of new clothes anyone purchases on a business trip is not deductible, so if your spouse purchases new clothes on the trip, they are not deductible, even if he or she meets tests 1 and 2. (This seems pretty obvious, but Congress saw fit to specify this point in the law.)

Moral: Involve your spouse in your business as much as possible if deductible travel is a possibility.

[11]IRS Rev. Rul. 63-275, 1963-2 CB 85.

As I do so often, I will add the advice to document his or her involvement. Write your spouse a letter, specifying duties, responsibilities, and hours you expect him or her to devote to the business. (That letter should cover both duties at home office as well as in travel work.) If you are operating as a corporation, specify your spouse's duties in the corporate minutes.

Before you put your spouse on the payroll, consider the consequences in terms of Social Security tax. Assume your self-employment income is $90,000, which puts you above the Social Security tax base ($76,200 in 2000). In order to be able to deduct your spouse's travel expense, you pay him or her $20,000 per year. This will cost your spouse and your business $3,060 in Social Security taxes (both employer and employee shares), without reducing your Social Security tax. If putting your spouse on the payroll allowed an extra travel deduction of $5,000 and you are in the 28 percent tax bracket, that deduction would save you $5,000 × 28 percent, or $1,400.

So to save $1,400 in income taxes, you and your spouse have paid $3,060 in Social Security taxes! Not a desirable trade-off!

Under those circumstances, go ahead and treat your spouse's travel as nondeductible expense. Remember that this is only the amount it costs both of you over what it would cost for you alone. If you are driving to a convention in Orlando and your spouse rides in the same car, the nondeductible expense is only his or her meals and the difference between the double and single rate for the motel room.

Foreign Travel

If you have a business reason for foreign travel, try to make the trip last only seven days. (Do not count the day of departure, but count the day of return.) You can play around with some personal sightseeing for up to 25 percent of your time and still consider the whole trip as business, and the whole cost of the trip is a deduction from your business income.

If you stay out of the United States for more than seven days, you have to allocate your expenses between time spent on business and time spent on pleasure.

MEALS AND ENTERTAINMENT DEDUCTIONS—
STILL WORTH 50 PERCENT

This is another area in which Congress and the IRS have come down hard. Business entertainment is no longer a way in which to wipe out much of your tax burden, but it can still help.

What you can no longer deduct includes a big party to which you invite people who might become your customers or clients. There has to be a stronger relationship with those whom you entertain. If you are thinking of buying, for a season of business entertaining, a skybox in your local football stadium, don't. Very little of skybox expense can be deducted.

What you can deduct 50 percent of is entertainment that is directly related to or associated with the active conduct of your business. IRS publication number 463, *Travel, Entertainment, and Gift Expenses,* explains the detailed rules as to what is meant by the terms "related to" and "associated with." Pertinent excerpts are reprinted in Appendix C-6.

BECOME A LITTLE MORE EDUCATED AND SAVE ON TAXES
WHILE YOU'RE DOING IT

You can deduct, as legitimate business expenses, the cost of education that maintains or improves the skills necessary for your present job or business. If the education qualifies you for a new trade or business or is necessary for the minimum skill levels for your present position, the education is a personal, nondeductible expense.

What's considered to be education? The rules are fairly liberal for a business owner. Education can consist of college courses (credit or noncredit), seminars, conventions, and courses offered by your trade association as long as the courses or seminars help you in your present occupation. As we saw previously, Sally is able to deduct the cost of attending a seminar in San Francisco because it helps her run her sailing school. However, if she travels to China for a course in oriental art, she is out of luck as far as finding a tax deduction in that trip, for it is of no help in either her sailing school or in her job in advertising.

The usual example of training that is nondeductible is that of an employee of an accounting firm who wishes to add the designation of certified public accountant (CPA) to his or her credentials. The cost of the college courses, including the accounting courses, the review courses that prepare one to take the CPA exam, and the cost of the exam are all nondeductible, for they all fall into the classification of attaining the minimum level of knowledge to become a CPA. Courses that accountants take, after they become CPAs, in advanced accounting and tax concepts are deductible, for these people are already in the CPA business.

Deciding where the dividing line is between basic education and deductible courses is a little more difficult where there is no certification to attain. For instance, if you think our example of Sally's Sailing School describes a fun business, you may want to open your own sailing school. However, if your only seagoing experience has been the Lewes-to-Cape-May Ferry and you have never been on a sailboat, you will have to take a course or so to learn the difference between bow and stern and between mainsail and jib. Such courses provide basic knowledge and would be nondeductible. If you then open your sailing school and subsequently take a course in sailboat-racing tactics, that should be deductible. Of course, if you don't open your business before you take the advanced course, you are apparently still gaining a minimum skill (or maybe just enhancing your hobby), so the advanced course would be nondeductible.

Moral: Open your business as soon as you have minimum skill level and knowledge, so the additional education (including travel to seminars and conventions) will be deductible. Better yet, convert your hobby into a business. If your business is based on your former hobby, you probably already have learned the basic knowledge in that field.

6

Taking Money Out
of Your Business

IT'S AS EASY AS WRITING A CHECK—BUT NOT QUITE

Writing a check to yourself is a satisfying act, for it means you have operated your business in such a manner that there are profits for you to take. But if you are going to pay as little tax as possible, it's an area that requires careful planning and execution.

When you take money out of your business, it may be taken as a draw, dividend, distribution, salary, loan, employee benefit, or legitimate business expense that has some personal benefit.

(My comments in this chapter assume you have read Chapter 2 or are already familiar with the various forms of business organization.)

DRAW

The term *draw* refers to the cash that a sole proprietor takes out of his or her business. Generally, it does not matter to the IRS whether he or she takes such a draw weekly, monthly, in an annual lump sum, or now and then as the money is available in the business checkbook. As it is the profit from the business that goes on the sole proprietor's individual income tax return rather than the cash drawn out, a draw has no tax effect.

However, there is an exception. If you have a business that grew out of a hobby or that can be seen as a hobby, you need to take every action you can to make your business appear businesslike (see Chapter 5). One such action is to take a draw of a definite amount on a definite schedule, as if it were a salary. (It is not a salary, so it is not subject to income and Social Security withholding. Those items are paid via quarterly estimated taxes that the sole proprietor should file as an individual.)

DIVIDENDS

A *dividend* is money that is paid by C corporations to owners of its stock. While many publicly held corporations pay significant dividends, payment of large dividends by a closely held corporation should be avoided if at all possible. Taxes on these dividends are paid twice: once by the corporation when it earns the profit from which the dividends will be paid and once by the stockholders when they receive the dividends (for examples, see Chapter 2).

Sometimes, though, the necessity to pay dividends is inescapable, as when the corporation has no other use for its earnings and needs to avoid the accumulated earnings tax (see Chapter 2).

In other circumstances, the payment of some dividends may be advisable. Although a small corporation should avoid paying much in dividends, taking a small amount of the profit out as a dividend is a good idea. If you take no dividends, the IRS agent is in a strong position to argue that since you had profits, you must have had dividends, so the loan you take from the corporation, or your year-end bonus, is really a dividend. If you do take some money in the form of a dividend, the agent can argue only about the amount, making his or her argument weaker.

Another negative aspect of dividends, besides double taxation, is the requirement that they be distributed equally per share of stock. If you own all of the stock in your corporation, that requirement is not a problem, but if you have minority stockholders, state corporation law requires that they also receive pro rata dividends.[1] For example:

When Corinne starts her corporation, she has more determination than money. Her Uncle Elmo therefore helps her but receives no cash payment. Instead, when the 100 shares of common stock are issued, Corinne receives 90 shares and Elmo receives 10 shares. If Corinne then receives a $900 dividend from the corporation, Elmo must receive a $100 dividend at the same time.

When you do pay dividends, be certain that your corporate minute book contains minutes of the board of directors meeting that declared the dividend. In an IRS audit, the agent will want to see the minute book. If the book is not in order and up-to-date, it can create problems. For instance, if the circumstances are such that you would have paid more taxes if you had operated as a sole proprietor instead of a C corporation and your minute book and state corporate franchise fees are not current, the auditor may take the position that the corporation never existed and recompute your tax as if you were a sole proprietor. That creates a problem, and a tax bill you don't need.

Until the early 1980s, subchapter S corporations could pay dividends, which were generally nontaxable. The same legislation that changed the name of these corporations to simply *S corporations,* also changed the term *dividends* to *distributions,* whenever such payments to stockholders are from S corporation earnings.

DISTRIBUTIONS (S CORPORATIONS)

Unlike dividends from C corporations, distributions from S corporations generally are not taxed twice. Similarly to a sole

---

[1]This assumes that your corporation has issued only one class of stock.

proprietorship, the corporation computes a net income and that income is added to the stockholders' individual income tax returns so that the stockholders, not the corporation, pay the income tax. Unlike the sole proprietor draw, dividends are formal. They should be authorized by a meeting of the board of directors, recorded in the minutes, and paid pro rata to the stockholders. This payment to the shareholders in proportion to the stock they own is very important. If a distribution is made to some stockholders and not to others, the IRS may consider that distribution to be the establishment of more than one class of common stock. Such establishment would disqualify the corporation from S status, perhaps causing such disastrous effects as double taxation of distributions. Of course, if there is only one stockholder, there can be no unequal distribution.

Another area that requires care deals with those corporations that did business as C corporations before electing S status. If the board of directors declares a distribution that is greater than the earnings the corporation has accumulated under S status, the directors are reaching back into the pool of C corporation earnings. That part of the distribution then becomes C corporation dividends, which are subject to double taxation. There are other complications that can arise when an S corporation has been a C corporation. If your corporation fits that description, you would be well advised to seek help from a competent tax professional.

Before we leave the subject of distributions from S corporations, let me remind you of the good news in this area: S corporation distributions are not subject to Social Security taxes, so there are situations in which it is wise to take a small salary and large dividends—within reason (see Chapter 2).

DISTRIBUTIONS (PARTNERSHIP AND LIMITED LIABILITY COMPANIES)

This section assumes that if you form an LLC and it has two or more members, it will elect to be taxed as a partnership. In one way, distributions from partnerships are similar to distributions from S corporations in that the partnership does not pay any income tax. The profit appears on the individual tax returns of the partners, and the partners pay the income tax. Unlike S corporations, however, the share of profits that is assigned to each partner does not have to be in proportion to his or her interest in the partnership. Similarly, the distributions do not have to be pro rata. They should be done according to the partnership agreement, but that agreement can call for the allocation of profits and distributions in any way that makes economic sense. (If it doesn't make sense, the IRS may determine that the partnership agreement is only a tax dodge and require a pro rata sharing of profits and distributions.)

An example of unequal distributions that probably makes economic sense would be the print shop operated by Patti and Prunella:

Patti is in the print shop every day, running the business from 7:00 A.M. to sometimes as late as midnight. Prunella puts up the $100,000 with which to buy the equipment and spends a few hours a week cultivating some of her contacts who can send business to the shop.

The partnership agreement calls for the division of profits and distributions in this order:

1. *A guaranteed distribution of cash and allocation of profits of $30,000 to Patti, to compensate her for her time.*

2. *A distribution of cash and allocation of profits of $5,000 to Prunella, to compensate her for the money invested.*

3. *Remainder of profits to be allocated equally, as are any additional distributions that the partners agree should be paid.*

4. *The allocation to Prunella of the profit or loss from any equipment that is sold.*

The impact of Social Security taxes is another difference between S corporations and partnerships. If the partnership's earnings are allocated to partners who are active in managing the partnership's business, all of those earnings are subject to self-employment Social Security tax (up to the annual limit), regardless of how much of the earnings are actually distributed to the partners.

SALARIES

Salaries paid to owners of a business by the business can be split into two classes: Those that are really salaries, subject to Social Security, other payroll taxes, and income tax withholding; and those that are often informally called salaries but are really distributions of profits.

Real Salaries, Subject to Payroll Taxes and Withholding

Stockholders in both C and S corporations can be paid salaries, provided they are active in the business in some capacity. Salaries should not be paid to sole proprietors or partners.

For profitable C corporations with stock owned only by the managers of the business, salaries are certainly a preferred way to take cash out of the business, for they avoid the double taxation of dividends. (Salaries are an expense that the corporation can deduct from income before computing taxable income. Dividends are not deductible by the corporation.) However, salaries do have to be reasonable. The IRS can disallow too big a salary (see section in Chapter 2, "More Tax Rules When the Big Bucks Roll In"). But there are some actions an owner of a corporation can take to try to overcome the problems in that area.

If you wait until the IRS audits your corporation and determines that your high salary was unjustified, you will have little choice other than to recompute the corporate tax without some of the deduction for your salary and to stroke a check to the IRS for the thousands of dollars of additional tax the corporation will owe. If you plan ahead, though, you can do this: When you hire executive employees, always require them to sign an agreement that if the IRS determines that their salaries are too high, they will refund that part that is disallowed to the corporation.

In addition, include a resolution to that effect in your corporate minutes. (If you were the only one to sign such an agreement, that might be a tip-off to the IRS that you think maybe your salary is too high.)

Another wise entry in your corporate minutes should first occur early in the corporation's life. Each year, the board of directors passes a resolution that you are worth some high figure (maybe $200,000 a year), but because of cash-flow problems, you are being paid only $30,000. That means the corporation has a moral obligation to pay you the other $170,000 some year when it can afford it. If you do that for 10 years and then the profits do pile up, you can start taking out the unpaid salary of $1,700,000 that has built up.

If you didn't put those resolutions in your minutes in the early years, do not despair. Put a resolution in the corporate minutes now to the effect that you are being paid an unusually high salary to compensate for many years of being underpaid.

I can't guarantee that either or both of these actions will work, but they are worth a try.

Salaries may or may not be a desirable way to withdraw cash from an S corporation, depending on the situations of the stockholders. If some of the stockholders are active in the business and some are not, then salaries become a necessity, for that is the only way to compensate the active stockholders for their time spent in the business. However, if all the stockholders are active in the business, in approximately the proportion of their stockholdings, salaries could be lower and dividends higher. Obviously, if there is only one stockholder, and he or she is the individual who runs the company, equitable compensation for time spent in the business is not a problem.

The tax situation of the stockholder-employee also needs to be considered. If the stockholder has other earned income taxable for Social Security and that income is over the Social Security limit ($76,200 in 2000), it makes little difference whether cash is withdrawn as salary or distributions, although distributions will avoid the 2.9 percent health insurance part of Social Security. If the stockholder has little or no other income, salary paid by the S corporation (up to the Social Security limit) is subject to the total Social Security tax of 15.3 percent.[2]

Salaries That Are Really Distributions

This misnomer often occurs in conversations about sole proprietorships and partnerships. These payments are not salaries but are distributions of profits, so they are not subject to Social Security and other payroll taxes when they are paid. However, the recipient of the distribution (the sole proprietor or partner) is liable for Social Security taxes and income taxes on the profits of the business. Note that this tax liability is on the total profits of the business, whether or not they are distributed to the owner(s) in cash or other assets.

DIRECTORS' FEES

Every corporation must have one or more directors, depending on state law. These are the people elected by the stockholders. The directors hold at least one annual meeting, at which they hire the officers of the corporation. This process is perfunctory in closely held corporations. Directors can be paid for their services, and such payment is not salary. However, it is self-employment income that must be reported by directors on their individual tax returns, and these directors' fees are subject to self-employment Social Security taxes. In other words, there is little tax saving to be gained from paying some of the profits as directors' fees.

LOANS TO STOCKHOLDERS

As you are no doubt aware, if you borrow money from your local friendly banker, that money is not income. It follows that

[2]These Social Security rates include both the employer and employee share of the tax. As far as salaries to stockholders are concerned, the stockholders are ultimately paying both sides of the tax, half out of their personal pockets and half out of the pocket of the corporation they own.

when you pay it back, the payment is not a deductible expense. Only the interest that you pay the bank is an expense, and that expense may be deductible in certain circumstances, such as interest on your mortgage or on money borrowed for business or investment purposes.

When you borrow money from your banker, he or she will scrutinize your financial life, apply formulas and grading systems, and perhaps loan you the money or perhaps not. At any rate, preparing the loan application and answering questions take time and are aggravating. It is far easier to borrow from someone or some institution who will ask no questions. If you own all the stock in your corporation and you tell your corporation to loan money to you, it certainly will do so, provided the funds are available.

In other words, if your C corporation has extra funds and you temporarily need extra funds, you can take one of three actions:

1. Increase your salary (resulting in more income tax and possibly Social Security tax).
2. Cause your corporation to declare a dividend (amounting to double taxation).
3. Borrow the money from your corporation (generating no additional taxes).

Presumably, you will elect number 3. Inasmuch as the IRS gets no more money from you when you go this loan route, its agents would much prefer to classify that payment as salary or dividend, and they will do just that when they audit you and your corporation, unless you follow some specific rules. These dictates are in various sections of the law, but they boil down to this:

1. Draw up a formal note to the corporation and sign it. Unless the note is for less than $10,000, it must specify the interest rate, the dates the interest payments are due, and the date on which principal payment(s) must be made.
2. Make the interest and principal payments to the corporation as specified in the note. If you can't make them, declare

a bonus for yourself with which you can make the payment. (Now you will have to pay tax.) Play it safe. Actually write the check from the corporation to yourself and another one from you to the corporation.

3. Have the note require that you pay at least the minimum interest rate that the IRS specifies. If you are using the proceeds of this loan for personal and nonmortgage purposes, the interest would be nondeductible to you but taxable income to your corporation.[3] Therefore, you will want to pay as little interest as possible. The rules as to minimum interest are complicated, so ask your tax professional to advise you as to the rate you should use.

PLAN FOR THE DAY YOU WILL BE TAKING CASH OUT— WHEN YOU *START* YOUR CORPORATION

You wouldn't start a corporation unless you expect eventually to withdraw some profit out of it. So when you set up a corporation, you need to plan ahead. The following example explains two of the alternatives in the funding of a C corporation:

Wanda started the Wanda Waterbed Corporation to manufacture waterbeds. She needed funds in the corporation for start-up costs, equipment, initial rent of a building, advertising, inventory, raw materials, and other costs totaling $1,000,000. Fortunately, she had that much in her savings account. She had the corporation issue her 10,000 shares of stock, at $100 par value, in exchange for $1,000,000 in cash. Now she owned the corporation and had the $1,000,000 in the corporation, so she was able to acquire a lease, equipment, and initial materials.

She started production and found that there was a large demand for her unique beds that not only had a relaxing wave motion but also generated the soothing sound of waves rolling up on the beach.

---

[3]If you have equity in your residence and the size of the loan justifies the expense, think about securing the corporate loan with a second mortgage (if that would meet the rules that make second-mortgage interest deductible).

Business boomed, and she took all the salary and bonuses her accountant thought that the IRS would allow but still needed to take more cash out of the corporation. There was little else to do but take a dividend of $100,000 and suffer the double tax.

What if, instead of causing the corporation to issue her a million dollars' worth of common stock, Wanda's corporation issues only 5,000 shares at $100 each, for which Wanda pays the corporation $500,000? The corporation still needs another half-million dollars to start business. Where will that come from? Wanda can loan her corporation that $500,000. Now, after she has taken all the salary and bonus she can, she will not have to take further cash as taxable dividends. Instead, she can cause the corporation to pay her back $100,000 of that $500,000 loan she made to it. (Loan proceeds and repayment of loans are not income.⁴) She will save as much as $39,600, the tax on the $100,000.

In addition, the corporation should pay her interest on the loan, so that will create some cash flow into Wanda's purse. Although that would be taxable interest to Wanda, it would be deductible by the corporation, which is more or less an offset when she owns all of the corporation.

So it seems that the more you loan your corporation and the less stock you buy, the better. But, you guessed it, the IRS has other thoughts, and its authority to recharacterize transactions means its thoughts will probably win. Suppose you funded your corporation to the tune of $100,000 this way: It issues you $5,000 of stock and borrows $95,000 from you. You would have what is called a *thin corporation,* meaning that the dollar value of the stock it issued is very thin compared to the amount of its debt to its stockholder(s). In this case, the ratio of debt to stock (often called *debt to equity*) would be a ratio of almost 20 to 1, and that is almost certain to be challenged by the IRS. (The dollar amounts of debt and equity have to be disclosed to the IRS on the annual corporation tax return.)

What should you do? The following are recommendations on the best way to handle loans from stockholders to corporations:

---

⁴If a corporation buys back some of its stock from a major stockholder, that flow of cash to the stockholder, unlike the money used to pay off a loan, is usually taxable.

1. Draw up a formal note and pay the interest when due. Be sure that the note has a maturity date.

2. Make sure that the note specifies at least the minimum rate required by the IRS. However, as this interest expense is deductible by the corporation, it may be easier to specify a higher interest rate and not worry about paying as little interest as possible. Ten percent is usually a safe number.

3. Don't try some absurd structure, such as $50,000 in stock and $950,000 in a loan. (This sort of ratio is known as a *thin corporation structure.*) The IRS will argue that the bank would not loan $950,000 to a corporation with only $50,000 in capital, so why would you make such a loan? Obviously, you created this capital structure only to avoid taxes, ergo the entire $1,000,000 is stock and cannot be repaid to you. Although some people have been successful in having the Tax Court approve a thin corporation structure with the loan nine times the amount of the stock, a safer course is to limit yourself to the loan being no more than twice the amount of the stock issued.

4. An even safer procedure is to make the loan only enough to fund needs of the corporation and an amount that obviously can be paid back soon. For example, the owner of an incorporated toy store can loan the corporation money for Christmas inventory in the fall, knowing that it will be paid back in January. The IRS will be hard put to classify that loan as an investment in stock.

The previous recommendations apply to C corporations and may appear to be unimportant if you elect S status for your corporation. However, S corporations can become disqualified from S status, and therefore, will be turned into C corporations. That possibility brings up another caveat if you elect S status or might do so in the future. Loan money directly to the corporation—do not guarantee a bank loan. Why? If you have losses in the S corporation, you can deduct those losses on your individual income tax return only to the extent you have put cash (or other assets) into the corporation by buying the common stock or loaning money directly to the corporation.

EMPLOYEE BENEFITS CAN HELP YOU EXTRACT PROFITS FROM YOUR BUSINESS

Generally, these plans allow an employer to deduct the cost of employee benefits in the year the employer pays for them. Yet the benefit is not taxable income to the employee now (for example, medical coverage) nor is it taxed in the future, when the employee retires and falls into a lower tax bracket (living on a pension plan). For many employee benefits, particularly pension plans, sole proprietors and partners are considered to be employees, so an employee benefit plan will benefit the owner of the business as well as the employees.[5] Years ago, pension plans were an excellent way for business owners to shelter a large part of their earnings, deferring taxes until they retired and fell into lower tax brackets. Congress has steadily chipped away at the benefits of high-income owners and executives, but you can still reap some personal benefit from them. Even if your business is a sideline to a full-time job that provides a pension, 401(k), and/or other plans, you may still be able to set up another pension plan for yourself based on your small business earnings.

Besides placing dollar limits on how much can be stashed into a pension plan, Congress has enacted antidiscrimination laws. That means that your employees have to enjoy the same benefits as you do, relative to salary levels. Of course, if you are a one-person operation, there are no other employees, so you cannot be guilty of discrimination in favor of the business owner (you). You are limited only by the rules about maximum dollars and maximum percentage of earnings that can be salted away.

If you have employees making average wages and your income from the business is substantial (over the Social Security tax limit), you may still be able to set up a plan that eventually puts most of the pension money in your pocket. Specifically, set up a plan that is integrated with Social Security. Such a plan allows you to consider the Social Security pension that your

---

[5]Even though owners of a business are considered employees for purposes of pension plans, they are subject to more stringent rules. The purpose of those rules is to prevent pension plans from generating proportionately higher benefits to the owners than to the other employees.

employees will get when you set up a plan for their retirement and so somewhat reduces their benefits in relation to yours.

Try to avoid a mistake many new entrepreneurs make. When they hire their first employees, there is no benefit plan in place, so they must pay a little more in cash wages to attract employees. Then, if the entrepreneur later establishes a plan, such as a pension plan, the employee will expect that to be provided in addition to the wages already being paid, plus inflation adjustments. For example:

When Wanda starts production in her factory, her corporation hires production workers at $12 per hour, which is a competitive rate in the area for such work, if all the pay is cash and there are no benefits. Later, she adds a pension plan and other benefits that cost $2 per hour per employee. She tells each employee that they must take a reduction in pay (to $10 per hour) so that she can afford to pay for the benefit package. Ho! Can you hear the employees accepting that? Besides, the IRS folks would probably disqualify the plan as an approved tax-deferred plan if they heard about that maneuver.

If, instead, Wanda starts the benefit package at the beginning of her enterprise, she probably can hire production employees at $10 per hour, because she could point to the benefit package they will also be receiving. At the same time, she will be able to provide herself with the same benefits, for she is also an employee of her business. In addition, in such areas as pension plans where benefits are calculated as a percentage of salary, her benefits will be greater, assuming she pays herself a salary commensurate with her responsibilities. (Just how much more will be subject to special rules for business owners.)

What is the most economical way to set up an employee benefit package? The rules are complex, so this is not a do-it-yourself area. In fact, many tax professionals will handle any tax problem except this, deferring instead to benefit consultants who specialize in this one area. Avoid anyone who wants to run up a fee of thousands of dollars to build a custom plan for you. There are off-the-shelf "prototype" plans around that have already been approved by the IRS. A good benefit consultant should be able to fit your business into one of those at a reasonable cost.

LET YOUR BUSINESS PAY YOUR MEDICAL BILLS

Some medical coverage for self-employed individuals occurs by law. The tax law allows self-employed individuals to deduct a percentage of medical insurance, as well as long-term care insurance, for themselves, spouses, and dependents. In 2000 and 2001, the percentage is 60 percent and rises to 100 percent in 2003.

If just you and your spouse are active in your sole proprietorship, this will work: Set up a medical reimbursement plan for employees of your business and make sure your plan covers spouses and dependents of employees. Hire your spouse as your only employee and immediately put him or her in the plan. Voilà! You are covered as his or her spouse. Note that this plan can cover not only insurance but also the out-of-pocket co-payments, dental bills, and so on.

TAKE YOUR HARD-EARNED MONEY OUT BY SELLING THE BUSINESS

As we are mere mortals, our productive years as managers of a business are finite. What happens when we can no longer function? We can install our children or other young relatives as managers and hope that they can continue on in a profitable mode. We can develop our best employees to take over. These possibilities involve estate as well as income taxes (see Chapter 7 for a discussion of estate taxes). However, if you sell the business while you are still young enough to enjoy your money, there is another way of taking money out of your business.

Selling the Corporation

After many years of hard work, Wanda increases sales to the point that Spongy Sofas International, Inc., a large furniture manufacturer, offers her $10 million for her corporation. If Wanda receives a *check for $11,000,000 from Spongy, her tax bite will be close to $2,000,000.[6] Her profit will be subject to capital gains tax, which in 2000 is a maximum of 20 percent. Having $9,000,000 (minus any state tax) in her pocket will not be bad, but it is not necessary to give that much to Uncle Sam.*

If, instead of cash, Spongy pays Wanda $11,000,000 worth[7] of its stock for her corporation and she follows IRS prescribed procedures, she will not pay any income tax on the sale proceeds. Assuming Spongy is a financially strong company and pays reasonable dividends, she can live off those dividends and still have assets worth the full $11,000,000. If this sale for stock (technically called a corporate reorganization*) complies with requirements of the Securities and Exchange Commission, she can sell just some of the Spongy stock for additional income or to diversify her investment portfolio. When she sells the stock, there will be tax due on the gain on the shares of the Spongy stock that she sells.*

Selling a Sole Proprietorship

Selling a sole proprietorship can create a bigger tax problem than selling a corporation. Why? The tax rules require that the money received be allocated to the various assets sold to the purchaser. Any profit on the asset of inventory items is taxed at regular income tax rates, not at capital gains rates. You may think that this isn't a problem, as you are earning only minor profits from your business and are in the 28 percent bracket anyway. However, the amount of the sale needs to be only a few thousand dollars to push you into the 31 percent, 36 percent, or even the 39.6 percent bracket for the year of sale.

Here's what can happen:

Wanda operates the Wanda Waterbed operation as a sole proprietorship instead of a corporation, and she sells the business to the Spongy Sofa Company as previously described. Seventy-five percent

[6]The gain on the sale is $11,000,000 minus Wanda's original cost of $1,000,000, or $10,000,000. The capital gains tax is 20 percent of that gain, or $2,000,000.
[7]Market value, not par value or book value.

of the $10,000,000 gain is allocated to the inventory of waterbeds in the warehouse. See Table 6.1.

If Wanda operates as a sole proprietorship and sells the business for $10,000,000, her tax will be $2,970,000 plus $700,000, or $3,670,000. That is $870,000 more in tax than it would cost her to sell the business as a corporation. Also, a sole proprietorship is not eligible for the corporate reorganization rules that would allow Wanda to receive the stock in Spongy without any tax bite.

The obvious action to take is to incorporate a business before you sell it. Can you do that a few weeks before you sell the business? If you do, the collapsible corporation rules[8] will require that your sale still be taxed as a sale of a sole proprietorship. You can usually avoid being shot down by the collapsible corporation rules in this area by incorporating at least three years before you sell the business. You should also have a good nontax reason for incorporating.

HOW TO SELL YOUR CORPORATION AND PAY TAX ON ONLY ONE-HALF THE PROFIT

Here's a recent gift from Congress and the IRS.[9] If you purchase stock in a small company that was issued after August 10, 1993, and you keep the stock for at least five years, one-half of the gain (profit) you receive upon selling it escapes tax, both regular tax

Table 6.1   Computation of Tax on Sale of the Wanda Waterbed Operation If It Is a Sole Proprietorship

	Inventory	Other Assets
Allocation of $10,000,000 gain	$7,500,000	$2,500,000
Tax rate	39.6%*	28%
Income tax	$2,970,000	$ 700,000

*This example assumes that Wanda has enough other income to put her in the highest tax bracket.

[8]IRC §341.
[9]IRC §1202.

and capital gains tax. The purchase of the stock can be made by cash or other property, so presumably you could exchange the assets of your sole proprietorship for stock in your new corporation and then be eligible to take advantage of this rule in five years.

There are some limitations. The gain on sale is limited to the higher of $10,000,000 or 10 times the basis (your cost, usually) in the stock. Corporations engaged in certain types of businesses are ineligible. Among them are:

- Accounting, actuarial science, architecture, athletics, brokerage services, consulting, engineering, financial services, health, law, the performing arts, or any business whose principal asset is the reputation or skill of one or more of its employees.
- Banking, financing, insurance, investing, leasing, or similar businesses.
- Farming, including raising or harvesting trees.
- Businesses extracting or producing natural resources eligible for percentage depletion.
- Businesses operating hotels, motels, restaurants, or similar businesses.

If you are not in one of the excluded businesses, make sure your attorney and accountant handle your corporate affairs in such a way that you will be eligible to exclude half your gain when you sell your corporation.

There is one downside to this forgiveness of gain. (Congress seldom gives you as much as it says it is giving you.) The remaining gain is taxed at 28 percent rather than the usual 20 percent. So, in effect, the section of the tax law amounts to a tax on the gain at 14 percent rather than 20 percent. That's nice, but not as nice as advertised!

INSTALLMENT SALE CAN SPREAD OUT THE TAX BURDEN

An installment sale of your business can mean you wait years to get all of your money. If you sold your business for $1,000,000 payable over 10 years, your cash flow would be only $100,000 per year, plus interest. Should you go that route? Think about these points:

1. **Is the buyer financially strong and likely to stay that way?** If not, try for a cash deal.

2. **Is the interest rate satisfactory?** The IRS requires that an installment sale involve interest as part of the payments, but as a seller you should want more. One good idea is to specify that the interest rate will change annually to so many percentage points above prime at a particular bank or above 90-day U.S. Treasury notes.

3. **What is the tax advantage?** If the deal is properly structured to comply with the installment-sale tax rules, you will pay tax only on the cash you receive each year. Assuming that your investment in the business is minimal, that you own the business for more than one year, and that the sale is otherwise eligible for long-term capital gains rates, there is some tax saving. If you have no other income during the year, file a joint return, and collect the one million in one year, only $38,000 of that $1,000,000 is taxed at 15 percent. (The rest is taxed at the maximum long-term capital gains rate of 28 percent.)

If, however, you receive and are taxed on only $100,000 each year and again have no other income and file a joint return, $43,000 of each $100,000 payment would be taxed at only 10 percent. There is an additional saving in the installments because there is less phaseout of personal exemptions and itemized deductions when the income is spread out over ten years (see Appendix A). The total tax saving over the 10 years of payments might be approximately $80,000.

If, in light of the previous example, it seems prudent to accept an installment payment offer for your business, your task then is to make sure the sale qualifies for installment-sale taxation. If it does not, you could be in trouble. For instance, if you accept a deal that will pay you $1,000,000 over 10 years but it does not qualify for installment-sale tax rules, you would have to pay the tax on the total $1,000,000 in the first year. That amount might be about $265,000. But you will be receiving only $100,000. Where are you going to get the other $165,000? (I told you that you might have a problem.)

If you are selling your sole proprietorship, all of your assets, except for inventory of goods for resale, should be eligible for long-term gains rates on an installment-sale schedule. Even the gain on the goodwill should be eligible for long-term gains rates and installment-sale treatment. If your business is incorporated and you sell the stock on the installment plan, you will have the problem of a large tax bill and no money.

(For other strategies you can use, which involve transferring some of the ownership of your business to other family members, see Chapter 7.)

7

Spread the Tax Burden Around the Family

You have done some creative tax planning, but it has gone a little off track. What you thought would be a business that would allow you to take some deductions against your regular income has turned out to earn its own profit. Now your income is even higher, and you are in the 36 percent tax bracket. The high income is nice, but it would be nicer if you did not have to send off 38.9 percent[1] of every additional dollar you make to the federal government and probably another 5 to 10 percent to the state government.

Meanwhile, your Aunt Sarah is retired, living on a small monthly Social Security check. Occasionally you buy some groceries for her, and you help her in other ways. If you could transfer some of your income to her, she could, by offsetting it with her personal exemption and standard deduction, pay no income tax, buy her own groceries, and have money left over.

Can you just tell your employer to pay part of your salary to Aunt Sarah? This assignment of income might have worked once, but it won't now. The assignment of income will not

---

[1] Thirty-six percent income tax + 2.9 percent health insurance tax = 38.9 percent tax.

transfer the tax obligation from the person who earned the income to the relative.[2]

SHIFTING THE TAX BURDEN TO AUNT SARAH

What can you do to shift the tax burden? There are ways.

Hire Aunt Sarah in Your Business

If Aunt Sarah can do some clerical work, answer the telephone, type letters, or perform any task that your business legitimately needs done, you can pay her for it. If she has no income other than Social Security, you can pay her up to $8,300[3] per year, and she will pay no income tax on it. She will, however, be subject to Social Security tax of 7.65 percent, and you will have to pay the other 7.65 percent, making a total family burden of 15.3 percent, but that is still significantly less than the 38.9 percent you are now paying. If you pay her more than the $8,300, you are accomplishing some tax saving, as her income tax (15 percent) and Social Security (15.3 percent) total 30.3 percent, which is still 8.6 percentage points under your bracket.[4] The advantage of paying Aunt Sarah more than escapes tax is smaller if you are in the 31 percent bracket, and it is virtually a wash if you are in the 28 percent bracket. Be sure you keep records of the work she does and can prove that the work is worth what you are paying her. (If you pay her, but she does no work, the IRS will call it a sham, and you, or your corporation, will get to pay the tax, at your high rate, on the income you paid Aunt Sarah.)

Incidentally, if you have an elderly relative who needs just one or two more years' wages covered by Social Security in

[2]IRS Regulation §1.102–1.
[3]Personal exemption of $2,800, standard deduction of $4,400, and the over-65 addition to standard deduction of $1,100.
[4]If you are in the 36 percent bracket, you probably have already paid the maximum OASDI tax of 12.4 percent, but you are still subject to the 2.9 percent health insurance tax.

order to get benefits from the Social Security Administration, this is an excellent way to make them qualified for the benefits.

Hire Your Children in Your Business

This works about the same way as hiring Aunt Sarah, with two exceptions:

1. You may have more of a problem justifying the salary paid to your child. Obviously, a two-year-old cannot perform any services, so you can't hire him or her. You could probably pay a seven-year-old a little money to empty waste baskets and end up being able to deduct the equivalent of an allowance. If you have a teenager who has taken a full load of computer courses, he or she may be extremely valuable to your business, particularly if you belong to the generation still frustrated by electronic files that mysteriously disappear and other quirks of electronic paper. People have justified a high enough salary to computer-literate kids to be able to deduct a salary high enough to put them through college, but you need to raise a near-genius to pull that off.

2. If the child is under 18 and he or she works for your sole proprietorship (or husband-and-wife partnership), neither your child nor you pay any Social Security tax on the wages.

Give Property to Aunt Sarah

Assume you own 1,000 shares of Amalgamated Consolidated Incorporated and that these shares pay a total of $7,000 a year in dividends. After you pay your income tax of 31 percent, you have only $4,830 left. If you give the stock to Aunt Sarah, she will receive the $7,000 in dividends, and she will get to keep the whole $7,000 (assuming she has no other taxable income, as just explained).

There are a couple of requirements and downsides to this maneuver. First, stock that generates $7,000 in dividends is most probably worth well over $100,000, and giving that to Aunt Sarah all at once can trigger some gift tax. (See the section on estate taxes later in this chapter.) Second, if you keep any strings attached to the stock (so you can pull it back from her later), the dividend will still be taxable to you, not to Aunt Sarah. Putting it in a trust for Aunt Sarah won't help, either, unless you make the gift and/or trust irrevocable. If Aunt Sarah has a son (your cousin) whom you detest, there is nothing you can do to stop her from leaving your stock to him. A worse scenario would be if you give her stock in your own corporation. Then your detested cousin might become your de facto partner!

Maybe your relationship is such that you can trust her to draw up a will that leaves the stock to you, but there is some risk. What if she fails to make a will and later marries for a second time? You have said good-bye to your stock.

Give Property to Your Children

Giving property to your children may make a little more sense, in that you are probably going to leave your assets to them anyway. However, when the children are of legal age (18 or 21, depending on your state laws), they can go on a wild spree, sell the Amalgamated Consolidated stock, and dissipate the proceeds. You could give the stock to your children in an irrevocable trust, not to be distributed until they are older (35 maybe), but that runs afoul of gift-tax planning. (See the section, later in this chapter, on one way to surmount this problem.)

Be Creative

Stella owned and ran a profitable storage warehouse operation, generating an income of $100,000 per year. Ben, her brother, was a widower and because of some major medical problems, was unable to work other than part-time. His $15,000-per-year income did not go far in supporting himself and his twin 16-year-old sons, Tad and Ted. Stella wanted to help and had several alternatives.

She could simply have given some cash to Ben each month to help with the expenses. She could have hired her nephews for part-time work, such as cleaning up the warehouse after school, or she could have been a little more creative. If Tad and Ted had worked for Stella, they would have been subject to a total of 15.3 percent Social Security tax each (one-half paid by Stella for each and one-half paid by each *twin). However, if they had worked for their father, there would have been no Social Security tax on their salaries until they were 18. Stella decided to sign a contract with Ben by which he was responsible to clean up the warehouse daily in the late afternoon. The contract price was $12,000 per year. Ben, in turn, hired his sons to do the actual sweeping and scrubbing at salaries of $5,000 per year for each son. Note that Ben made a little profit ($2,000) on the arrangement. These maneuvers made sense and had reasons for their existence other than tax avoidance, in order to withstand IRS scrutiny.*

How much did this arrangement save? Here's how the three alternatives compare (Table 7.1):

Table 7.1   Stella's Alternative Methods of Helping Ben Support His Sons (Her Nephews)

	Stella Gives Ben a Gift of $12,000 per Year	Stella Hires Her Twin Nephews at $6,000 per Year Each	Stella Contracts with Ben and Ben Hires His Twin Sons
Stella's tax picture			
Income tax	$20,980	$17,260	$17,260
Social Security tax	10,414	10,066	10,066
Total taxes	31,394	27,326	27,326
Ben's tax picture			
Income tax	308	308	608
Social Security on wages	1,148	1,148	1,148
Social Security on contract			306
Total taxes	1,456	1,456	2,062
Tad's and Ted's tax picture			
Income tax (total)		660	360
Social Security (total)		1,836	0
Total taxes		2,496	360
Total income and Social Security taxes on all four individuals	$32,850	$31,278	$29,748

In making these computations, I took a technical shortcut in the second column of figures by figuring the Social Security on Tad's and Ted's salaries at 15.3 percent. Actually, of course, 7.65 percent was paid by Stella for each, and 7.65 percent was paid by each of the boys. However, because it was all a cost that the family, as a whole, incurred when Stella payed salaries to Tad and Ted, I included all of this amount in the box with their salaries.

As the table indicates, Stella saved $3,102 ($32,850 − $29,748) by this creative planning. What else did she consider doing?

Because Stella had no children of her own, she considered giving Tad and Ted a piece of her business. The easiest way to do that was to incorporate and elect S corporation status, giving each of the twins a few shares of stock. In that manner, she channeled funds to them by declaring distributions, which are not subject to any Social Security tax. However, inasmuch as distributions are not earned income and Tad and Ted were Ben's dependents, they would not have been able to use the standard deduction of $4,400 but would have been limited to $700. This plan also has the disadvantage that Stella would never have gotten her stock back because she had to make an irrevocable gift if she wanted to shift the income tax burden to her nephews.

IRS' FINAL GIFT TO YOU—A TAX BREAK AT YOUR DEMISE (STEPPED-UP BASIS)

This is the ultimate, though not very satisfying, way to pay no tax. No, the IRS will not forgive taxes that you owe when you die. It will look to your executor to sell assets from your estate in order to pay any taxes you owe. However, Congress has mandated that the IRS do this for you, or rather, for your heirs. It's called *stepped-up basis at death,* and we can use Stella as the example to demonstrate.

When Stella started her warehouse business, she invested $250,000 in the business, most of which went for construction of the ware-

house. As she incorporated, this meant that her stock had a cost, or basis, of $250,000. When she died, she left her stock to Tad and Ted. They both now have other careers and do not have the time to manage the warehouse, so they sell the stock to another warehouse business for $750,000 in cash. As you are probably aware, for most sales of stock, you compute the taxable gain on the sale by subtracting the original cost[5] from the sales price. In other words, the taxable gain on this sale might be as in Table 7.2.

But it generally does not work that way at death. When Stella died, the basis of the stock (and almost all her assets) became the market value on the date she died, or possibly six months later. If Tad and Ted sell that stock shortly after Stella dies, the $750,000 they receive for the stock is probably the market value at the date of Stella's death, so they will pay no tax on the sale.[6]

This stepped-up basis concept applies not only to stock in a business but to most assets, including those in a sole proprietorship. In other words, it's good tax planning to hang on to your valuable possessions until you die. However, if your estate is worth (at market value) more than $1,000,000 (or a total of

Table 7.2   Sale of Stock in Warehouse Company By Tad and Ted

Proceeds of stock sale	$750,000
Subtract original cost of stock to Stella	250,000
Gain on which tax is paid (not really)	$500,000

[5]There are modifications, such as brokers' commissions and other costs of purchase and sale, but they are ignored here to keep things as simple as possible.

[6]This area is an excellent example of what ultimately must happen to an overly complex tax rule, of which our law is so full. In the mid-1970s, Congress changed this stepped-up basis rule to one that required that heirs had to compute any gain on sale of inherited assets using the basis of the decedent. That meant often futile searches of a decedent's records to find out what he or she had paid for various assets. Most people do not keep, or can't find, their own records of these transactions. To expect an heir or executor to find them was an illogical and ill-conceived idea. It took Congress only a couple of years to realize this and to change the law back to the stepped-up basis rule.

$2,000,000 for a married couple),[7] keeping all your assets may increase your federal estate tax. Read on to the next section.

ESTATE AND GIFT TAXES AND HOW TO AVOID THEM

While it's not something to look forward to, taxes on one's estate is the final way to spread the tax burden to the rest of the family. Estate tax is an area that is confusing, inasmuch as the IRS can attack you, and ultimately your heirs, in three directions:

1. Estate tax: A tax levied on the assets (minus liabilities) of the estate, technically called the *corpus* of the estate.
2. Gift taxes: A tax levied on gifts made while you are still alive.
3. Income tax on an estate: The income tax levied on the income that the assets in the estate earn while the estate is being administered and before all the assets are distributed to the heirs.

Estate and gift taxes are intertwined. Gift taxes paid during your life may reduce estate taxes paid after you die, but in total, there usually will not be any tax saving.

On what is estate tax levied? On just about everything: real estate, investments, annuities, some life insurance, household goods, and most importantly, the value of a business. Most of us have heard, correctly, that an estate with a value of under $1,000,000 will not be subject to estate tax. Then we do some mental arithmetic:

Residence is worth $250,000; automobiles are worth $40,000; cash and money in the bank is $5,000; and we originally started the business with $50,000. No way does that add up to $1,000,000,

---

[7]For purposes of this discussion, we'll assume all of us are going to live to at least the year 2006. For years, the estate and gift taxes kicked in at $600,000 ($1,200,000 for a married couple with a properly constructed will and trust). Recently, however, Congress agreed to increase this threshold gradually until it reaches $1,000,000/$2,000,000 in 2006. So, the examples in this section on estate and gift taxes are based on 2006 tax rates.

so there is no need to worry about estate tax. Wrong! The IRS will compute the value of the business by various methods, relying on "the facts and circumstances" of each case. The result is a value for the business that includes the goodwill and the earning capacity you have built up over the years.

For instance, the business in which you originally invested $50,000 now earns $300,000 per year, after it pays you and other executives reasonable salaries. The IRS could compute the value of your business by determining how much would have to be invested at some interest rate in order to earn $300,000. The IRS agent might assume that 10 percent is a reasonable interest rate. To earn $300,000 at 10 percent, one would have to invest $3 million. Now, your potential estate is worth well over $1,000,000, and you do need to consider this tax in your planning.

How do you organize your affairs so that you pay no estate tax? Sorry, but to lay the foundation for some explanations, we have to get technical. First, let's look at (and be scared by) the rates at which the IRS taxes estates (Table 7.3).

Notice that this table contemplates taxing every penny of every estate. However, every individual gets a one-time present from the IRS: A tax credit (that can be applied only against estate taxes and gift taxes) of $345,800. This is the amount of tax on an estate of $1,000,000. Hence the concept that there is no tax on estates smaller than that figure.

It's significant that this graduated tax schedule and offsetting credit has this effect: When the $1,000,000 credit is used up, the tax rate that will apply to the next dollar is 41 percent! There is no such thing as an estate's dollar being taxed at a reasonable rate. The tax rate is either zero or a confiscatory percentage. *Moral:* Use competent advisors who can create a will and trusts that may avoid some of this tax.

One way to avoid estate taxes, one might think, is to give away one's assets while one is alive so that they will not be in the estate. Unfortunately, the rule makers in Congress and the IRS closed this door long ago. They decreed that gifts would also be subject to a tax at the same tax rates as estate tax. Also, the gift and estate taxes would be levied on accumulated totals. For example:

Table 7.3   Estate Tax and Gift Tax Rates—2000

If the Amount Is Over	But the Amount Is Not Over	The Tax Is	Plus This Percent	Of the Excess Over
$ 0	$ 10,000	$ 0	18	$ 0
10,000	20,000	1,800	20	10,000
20,000	40,000	3,800	22	20,000
40,000	60,000	8,200	24	40,000
60,000	80,000	13,000	26	60,000
80,000	100,000	18,200	28	80,000
100,000	150,000	23,800	30	100,000
150,000	250,000	38,800	32	150,000
250,000	500,000	70,800	34	250,000
500,000	750,000	155,800	37	500,000
750,000	1,000,000	248,300	39	750,000
1,000,000	1,250,000	345,800	41	1,000,000
1,250,000	1,500,000	448,300	43	1,250,000
1,500,000	2,000,000	555,800	45	1,500,000
2,000,000	2,500,000	780,000	49	2,000,000
2,500,000	3,000,000	1,025,800	53	2,500,000
3,000,000	———	1,290,800	55	3,000,000

Four years ago, Dennis gave his daughter, Daphne, a taxable gift of $100,000. Dennis filed a gift tax return reporting the gift. From the table, he computed a tax of $23,800. However, he did not have to stroke a check to the IRS. On the return, he simply applied part of his lifetime credit of $345,800.

Three years later, Dennis gave Daphne another $100,000. Now the computations for his gift tax return look like Table 7.4.

Table 7.4 Dennis's Remaining Lifetime Credit

Lifetime credit		$345,800
Taxable gifts made this year	$100,000	
Taxable gifts made in prior years (since Dennis was born)	100,000	
Total gifts	200,000	
Gift tax (from Table 7.3) on $200,000	54,800	
Subtract lifetime credit applied	54,800	54,800
Tax due	$ 0	
Remaining lifetime credit		$291,000

Note that in computing a gift tax and the amount of the credit used, you start over from the first gift and recompute the tax. The result is that the second gift is taxed at a higher rate. (The last half of the second gift was taxed at 32 percent in the example, while the highest bracket applied to the first gift was 28 percent.)

When Dennis died the following year, his net estate was valued at $1,300,000. The computation of the federal estate tax is in Table 7.5.

Again, the prior gifts are added to the remaining estate. If Dennis had not made the gifts to Daphne, his estate would have had the

Table 7.5 Dennis's Estate Tax Computation This Year

Net value of estate	$1,300,000
Add taxable gifts made during lifetime	200,000
Total on which to compute tax	$1,500,000
Tax from Table 7.3	$ 555,800
Subtract lifetime credit applied	345,800
Tax due	$ 210,000

$200,000 still in it, so his estate still would have paid about the same tax.

I used the term *net estate* because there are certain deductions that can be subtracted from the total estate valuations. For instance, legal, accounting, and other administrative expenses related to the estate can be deducted from the gross estate.

Given that the gift tax and estate tax are structured like this, how can anyone take any action to avoid or reduce these taxes? Here are some methods:

- During each year of your life, you can exclude gifts of up to $10,000 to each person to whom you make gifts. Your spouse can join you in the gift, making a total of $20,000 you can give to each person.[8] (It does not matter whether the source of the gift is your money, your spouse's money, or joint money. Nor does it need to be money: It can be any property except a future interest.) So if you have five married children, you and your spouse can give away $20,000 to each child and another $20,000 to each child's spouse, making a total of 10 people receiving $20,000 each, for a total of $200,000. You can do this each year, so if you are wealthy, start gift giving early.

  If you give someone more than $10,000 (or jointly, $20,000), the $10,000 exclusion can still be applied. In other words, if you and your spouse give your single son, Charlie, $35,000 in one year, you can deduct the $20,000 exclusion and pay gift tax on (or apply the lifetime credit to) only $15,000.

- If you have assets that are appreciating fast, you can avoid gift or estate tax on what they will be worth years hence by giving them away before they appreciate. The gift tax is calculated on their value today, while if you hang on to them, the estate tax will be calculated on the value when you die (years hence, we hope). This is particularly apropos of your small business. As discussed earlier in this chapter,

---

[8]You have to file a gift tax return for any gift over $10,000, even though your spouse joins you in making the gift and there is no lifetime credit used.

the IRS will think your business is worth a lot more than you think it is. If you have children who appear to be interested in continuing the business, look into a program of giving them shares of the business each year, taking advantage of the $10,000 gift tax exclusion.

Set Up a Trust

An individual who has an estate of $2,000,000 may do this: Leave $1,000,000 outright to his or her spouse and create a trust to hold the other $1,000,000 of estate assets (cash, stocks, bonds, mutual funds, real estate, and anything of value). The $1,000,000 left outright can pass from the spouse to children or other heirs without tax, because of the estate and gift tax one-time-per-individual credit.

Gertrude had $2,000,000 worth of assets (cash, stocks, bonds, mutual funds, real estate, and anything of value). She died before her husband, Donald. As she had properly arranged her affairs, she left $1,000,000 to Donald with no strings attached. (There is no federal estate and gift tax on assets are transferred by gift or will to a spouse.) The other $1,000,000 was placed in a trust for the eventual benefit of their child, Cathy. However, as long as Donald lives, he can receive the interest or other investment income from the trust. The final effect is this: The $1,000,000 left outright to Donald is tax free, and Donald can pass it on to Cathy tax free, using his lifetime credit. The $1,000,000 in the trust eventually passes, in effect, from Gertrude to Cathy, and Gertrude's lifetime credit is used to offset the tax on that $1,000,000.

Make Gifts to Your Children

Obviously, transferring some investments, such as stock in Amalgamated Consolidated Incorporated and its income, to a child over 14 can cut the tax burden. (Unearned, or investment, income of children who have not turned 14 by the end of the calendar year is generally taxable to the parents as required by the "kiddie tax" rules.) Such gifts can be made in trust, but gifts in trust usually are not "present interests." (That is, the recipient of the gift, because it is in a trust, does not have the right to sell the investment, spend the proceeds, reinvest the proceeds, or do whatever he or she wishes with the investment.) A gift that is not a present interest is not eligible for the gift tax $10,000 or $20,000 exclusion, so such a gift can generate some estate and gift tax later, if not now.

Fortunately, Congress has authorized an exception to this rule. If the gift is made to a child in trust but the child can take the investment out of the trust at age 21, the gift is considered a present interest. The trouble most parents have with that is the relative immaturity of many 21-year-olds. It would be nice if the trust status could prevent an offspring from getting at the bulk of the money until he or she is, perhaps, 35.

Now comes the IRS to the rescue! (Actually, the IRS did not act out of its own generosity. It was prodded to do the following by several court decisions.) The IRS will consider the trust qualified for the gift tax exclusion if the child "has, upon reaching age 21, either (1) a continuing right to compel immediate distribution of the trust corpus by giving written notice to the trustee or (2) a right *during a limited period* [italics added] to compel immediate distribution of the trust corpus by giving written notice to the trustee, which if not exercised, will permit the trust to continue by its own terms."[9]

In other words, you could set up a trust for your child, divert income to his or her lower tax bracket, make the trust last to age 30 or 35 or whenever, and still take the gift tax exclusion. That is, you can do it if you give the child, at age 21, the right to terminate the trust as long as he or she does it within a certain period of time. Perhaps you can structure it this way: For 30 days after his or her twenty-first birthday, he or she can demand the proceeds of the trust. If the child does not take that action, the trust will continue on until whatever age you specify when you set up the trust.

Obviously, there is some risk of the child taking and dissipating the investments, but the risk is not as great as an arrangement that forces the child to manage the assets, starting on the twenty-first birthday.

[9]Revenue Ruling 74–73 1974–1 CB 285.

INCOME TAX ON ESTATES

Income tax rates on the income that an estate or trust earns are considerably higher than the taxes on individuals, up to the point that an individual has a taxable income of $250,000. If your heirs are at lower income levels, the planning for income tax on your estate is to make the terms of your will such that your executor can transfer earning assets to your heirs as soon as possible or at least make it possible for the income from the assets to be distributed to the heirs so that it will be taxable to the heirs rather than to the estate.

This section has only skimmed the estate and gift tax area, but it should be enough to make you aware of those taxes and the planning opportunities that exist. It is certainly an area that needs input from your accountant and an attorney versed in estate planning in the state of your residency. (Many federal estate tax rules vary from state to state, depending on state law.) For instance, I did touch on the fact that, because each spouse has a lifetime estate and gift tax credit of $1,000,000, it is possible to structure an estate plan that will avoid tax on gifts and estates totaling $2,000,000. A knowledgeable attorney can structure trusts that take advantage of that total credit and can, therefore, eliminate estate tax. If the IRS thinks your small business is worth a million dollars, you need that planning.

SPREAD YOUR INCOME AMONG SEVERAL
C CORPORATIONS

If you look at the corporate income tax rates in Appendix A, you will see that the first $50,000 of income tax that a C corporation earns is taxed at 15 percent. So if you expect $250,000 of taxable income in your business, set up five corporations and split up your operation so that each corporation earns $50,000 and pays only 15 percent tax. You have saved a bundle instead of paying 34 percent or more on your earnings.

Will that plan work? If it were 1955, yes, but not in the twenty-first century. Long ago Congress inserted sections in the tax law that permit "controlled" corporations only one $50,000 bracket to be taxed at 15 percent and only one $25,000 bracket to be taxed at 25 percent.[10] In other words, if you try the tax avoidance of spreading your business among five corporations, each one will be taxed at 15 percent only on the first $10,000 ($50,000 ÷ 5 corporations) of taxable income and at 25 percent on only $5,000 of taxable income ($25,000 ÷ 5 corporations).[11] The rest of the income will be taxed at 34 percent. (The tax rate effectively will be more than 34 percent; see the corporate rate section of Appendix A.)

Does this explanation mean you should forget about multiple corporations as a means of tax avoidance? Not necessarily. If you have other unrelated (not your family members) owners of the corporations *and you have other than tax reasons for having the several corporations,* you may be able to use the lower tax brackets for each corporation. The tax law provides various tests that determine if two or more corporations are under common control. If you can manage to fail the tests, you could use the low-rate brackets for each corporation. (This is one time in your life when failing a test works to your advantage.) The pertinent regulations are not simple and can be misinterpreted easily, so use professional help to determine if your situation can fit the requirements for using several low-percentage brackets. Part of the regulations are reprinted in Appendix C-7. I did not include them with the expectation that you will completely understand them, but reading them will give you some thoughts you can take to your tax professional.

---

[10]IRC §1561.

[11]The corporations could agree among themselves to split up the $50,000 and $25,000 brackets in any way they please. The income brackets do not have to be split evenly among the corporations.

8

Pay Taxes Late, Years Late, Without Penalty or Interest

Most of us are aware that if we can save a dollar and put it in the bank, we can earn interest. As the bank and mutual fund advertisements say, "Let your money work for you." Similarly, we can let Uncle Sam's money work for us. If we owe him a dollar but can figure out how to put off paying him (without interest or penalty charges) for a year and then send him the dollar, we get to keep the five or so cents interest that the dollar earned while we kept it. Of course, worrying about the interest on a dollar is hardly worth the time involved, but if it's thousands of dollars, such worrying can pay off in a big way. Two examples, both extensions of examples from earlier chapters, illustrate how dramatic the results of delaying the due date of taxes can be.

CIRCULATION EXPENSES KEEP THE TAX MAN AT BAY

In Chapter 3, we touched on the tax law benefits for publishers of periodicals. The regulation allows for "the deduction . . . of all expenditures to establish, maintain, or increase the circulation of a newspaper, magazine, or other periodical. . . ."[1] This

[1]Regulation §1.173–1.

deduction is allowed regardless of the time when the revenue generated by the expenditures may show up.

This regulation is somewhat counter to the principle in accrual-method accounting that expenses should be "matched" to the revenue they produce. Yet the rules specifically state that both cash- and accrual-method businesses can take advantage of this immediate deduction. (For a discussion of cash and accrual methods of accounting, see Chapter 4.)

Although this rule allows deduction of expenses before they have generated income, another rule[2] allows a publisher of a periodical to defer paying tax on receipts for subscriptions until receipts have been paid. If a publisher receives $30 in payment of a three-year subscription, the publisher need report income of only $10 per year for each of the three years. (The publisher must be using the accrual method to make use of this rule.) This example illustrates what all this means:

Ned determines that there is a market as yet unserved by a newsletter, to wit, the vast population of scholarly people who are put off by newsletters devoted to commonplace activities. So Ned starts Ned's Nerd Newsletter, an annual publication to be published and mailed in February of each year.[3] To publish the newsletter, he sets up a C corporation, called the Ned's Nerd Newsletter Corporation.

In December of his first year, he rents a mailing list of nerdy people and mails out 20,000 direct-mail solicitations for three-year subscriptions at $50 each. By December 31, 400 people send in a positive response, each including a check for $50. Ned's cash situation then looks like Table 8.1.

Because Ned mails out the direct-mail solicitations in December and the newsletter is not printed until February, his corporation does not have any cost of producing and mailing the actual newsletter until February. If Ned's corporation files its income tax return using the cash method, it pays tax of $1,500 on the $10,000 of cash income computed in Table 8.1. However, this is not an industry in which any

---

[2]IRC §455.
[3]This is not a realistic schedule for a newsletter, but it makes a complicated example a little simpler.

**Table 8.1   Ned's Nerd Newsletter Corporation
Cash Receipts and Disbursements—
First Year of Business**

Receipts: 400 subscriptions (three years) @ $50 each	$20,000
Subtract cost of printing and mailing direct-mail solicitations	10,000
Remaining cash	$10,000

rational person would use the cash method. Ned's Nerd News-letter Corporation computes its income tax for this first year on the accrual basis, with the special rules for periodical circulation, as in Table 8.2.

If Ned operates this business as a sole proprietor, he can apply this loss to his other income and reduce his individual tax. However, as he is operating this business as a C corporation, the loss becomes a net-operating-loss carryover to be used to offset corporate income in future years.[4]

In February of the second year of this business, Ned produces and mails 400 copies of the newsletter. In December of that year, he again mails direct-mail solicitations—25,000 of them this time. His cash inflow and outflow for the second year look like Table 8.3.

Again, the corporation is ahead as far as cash is concerned, but there is still no income tax, as computed in Table 8.4 by the accrual method. (If the corporation reported to the IRS by the cash method, it would owe $8,500 × 15%, or $1,275 income tax.)

**Table 8.2   Ned's Nerd Newsletter Corporation
Computation of Income Tax (Accrual Method)—
First Year of Business**

Income (no newsletter produced this year)	$ 0
Subtract expenses: Cost of printing and mailing direct-mail solicitations	10,000
Net operating loss	$(10,000)

[4]The loss cannot be carried back, as the corporation was not in existence in prior years.

**Table 8.3   Ned's Nerd Newsletter Corporation
Cash Receipts and Disbursements—
Second Year of Business**

Cash received in December for 500 additional subscriptions		$25,000
Subtract cash disbursements:		
Cost of printing and mailing newsletter in February	$ 4,000	
Cost of printing and mailing 25,000 direct-mail solicitations in December	12,500	
Total cash disbursements		16,500
Additional cash generated		$ 8,500

**Table 8.4   Ned's Nerd Newsletter Corporation
Computation of Income Tax (Accrual Method)
Second Year of Business**

Income: One-third of payments ($25,000) received for three-year subscriptions in first year		$ 6,700
Subtract expenses:		
Cost of printing and mailing newsletter in February of second year	$ 4,100	
Cost of printing and mailing direct-mail solicitations in December of second year	13,000	
Total expenses for tax purposes in second year		17,100
Net operating loss, second year		(10,400)
Add net operating loss carried over from first year (from Table 8.2)		(10,000)
Total net operating loss to carry over to third year		$(20,400)

**Table 8.5   Ned's Nerd Newsletter Corporation—
Net Operating Loss to Carry Over to Next Year**

First year	$(10,000)
Second year	(20,400)
Third year	(24,700)
Fourth year	(22,200)
Fifth year	(16,900)

So it goes. The Ned's Nerd Newsletter Corporation generates cash each year but pays no taxes because it does not pay tax on that revenue until one, two, or three years later. If Ned continues to increase his solicitation mailing by 5,000 pieces each year and continues to have a 2 percent sign-up rate and the same cost for producing the newsletter, his corporation will continue to generate net-operating-loss carryovers as in Table 8.5.

The accumulated net operating losses start to diminish in the fourth year. Eventually they will run out, and the corporation will have to pay income tax. However, before that happens, Ned should start another newsletter that will throw off more paper losses.

So, what are you waiting for? Start your newsletter business!

WHY CLAIM DEPRECIATION EXPENSE AS FAST AS YOU CAN?

In Chapter 4, while discussing the subject of some records for financial statements differing from those for tax returns, we used an example of a flowerpot machine that Carl, a contractor, had purchased. We computed the depreciation of that machine at the fastest rate the IRS would allow so that most of the depreciation deductions occurred early in the 15-year life of the flowerpot machine. The question that sometimes arises is, "Why bother with that extra computation of fancy depreciation? In the end, both methods will result in the same total of deductions." (The total depreciation deduction for all years will equal the cost of the equipment.)

There is good reason to take the deductions early, and it has to do with the extra money from the early deductions and what can be earned with that money. Let's digest this in two bites:

First, Table 8.6 lists, in column 2, depreciation expense computed in the basic, straight-line method that Carl prefers to use in his financial statements, for it makes the picture he gives his bank look better. (A smaller depreciation expense results in a larger profit figure.) Column 3 lists the fastest depreciation the IRS allows, consisting of Section-179 expense and double declining balance over seven years. (For explanations of depreciation, see Chapter 3.)

The fourth column lists the difference between the basic straight-line depreciation and rapid depreciation. The negative numbers in parentheses in column 4 indicate that the straight-line depreciation is greater than the fast depreciation in later years, as the fast depreciation has already been fully deducted.

In the fifth column, I computed the cash flow into and out of Carl's bank account. (The cash flows out of the account are the negative amounts.) The tax rate was computed by adding a federal income tax rate of 28 percent, a Social Security tax of 15.3 percent, and a hypothetical state tax of over 4 percent, giving us a total rate of 48 percent. For each dollar of additional deduction with which Carl comes up, he saves 48 cents of the tax that would have come out of that dollar.

The next bite (Table 8.7) takes the extra cash these early deductions put in Carl's pocket and computes what he will have, at the end of 15 years, if he puts that extra cash in an investment account that earns 8 percent per year, which is reinvested in the account. As you can see, by the time the rapid depreciation has played out in year 8, Carl's investment account has grown to over $55,000. Thereafter, he has to take money out of his account to pay taxes because he has used up all the tax depreciation to which he is entitled. (The tax payments are the negative amounts in column 5.) However, by year 8 the balance in the investment account earns almost enough interest to pay the

**Table 8.6   Carl's Flowerpot Machine (Cost $150,000)
Reduction in Tax from Taking Deduction as Soon as Possible
(Based on Example of Fast Depreciation in Chapter 4)**

1	2	3	4	5
Year	Straight-Line Depreciation on Financial Statements	Fastest Depreciation the IRS Will Allow	Extra Depreciation on Tax Return (Column 3 minus Column 2)	Reduction in Tax Due to Taking Fastest Depreciation at 48% Tax Rate
1	$ 10,000	$ 36,006	26,006	12,483
2	10,000	32,572	22,572	10,835
3	10,000	23,262	13,262	6,366
4	10,000	16,612	6,612	3,174
5	10,000	11,877	1,877	901
6	10,000	11,864	1,864	895
7	10,000	11,877	1,877	901
8	10,000	5,930	(4,070)	(1,954)
9	10,000		(10,000)	(4,800)
10	10,000		(10,000)	(4,800)
11	10,000		(10,000)	(4,800)
12	10,000		(10,000)	(4,800)
13	10,000		(10,000)	(4,800)
14	10,000		(10,000)	(4,800)
15	10,000		(10,000)	(4,800)
Totals	$150,000	$150,000		

extra tax due (because there is no more depreciation). At the end of year 15, when the flowerpot machine is worn out and he throws it away, Carl still has almost $52,000 in the tax-saving investment account.

Table 8.7   Carl's Flowerpot Machine (Cost $150,000)
Extra Cash from Taking Deduction as Soon as Possible
(Based on Example of Fast Depreciation in Chapter 4)

6	7	8	9
Year	Reduction in Tax Due to Fast Depreciation (Same as Column 5)	Interest Earned If Saving of Tax Is Put in Investment at 8% per Year	Total Cash in Investment at End of 15-Year Life of Machine
1	$12,483	$ 999	$13,482
2	10,835	1,079	25,396
3	6,366	2,032	33,794
4	3,174	2,704	39,672
5	901	3,174	43,747
6	895	3,500	48,142
7	901	3,852	52,895
8	(1,954)	4,232	55,173
9	(4,800)	4,414	54,787
10	(4,800)	4,383	54,370
11	(4,800)	4,350	53,920
12	(4,800)	4,314	53,434
13	(4,800)	4,275	52,909
14	(4,800)	4,233	52,342
15	(4,800)	4,187	51,729

Of course, Carl does not have to put that tax saving in an investment or savings account. He can probably invest it in his own business and earn a much higher return on that money.

Moral: Whenever there is an opportunity to delay the paying of tax, do so. You might even be able to delay it long enough so that the interest you earn will pay the tax!

9

Don't Ignore the Alternative Minimum Tax (AMT)

When my Uncle Ulysses first heard of this tax, he said, "Oh, that's nice. Congress is giving us a choice. We can pay a minimal tax if we don't like the regular high tax." How naive! Congress follows the advice of the IRS, and it does not make gifts as my uncle thought it had.

The "alternative" works the other way. The IRS, not we taxpayers, chooses the alternative. As you would expect, the IRS chooses that we pay the *higher* tax. (I suspect that the IRS put the misnomer of "minimum" in the name of this tax so it would slide easier through congressional approval.) This tax beast is meant to make those who successfully avoid the usual income tax pay something to Uncle Sam.

The Bad News: After you have carefully thought out a scheme to slash your tax bill, you have to run it through this AMT computation to make sure the plan will still fly.

Why, you may ask, wasn't this included in the tax computations earlier in the book? Had I done that, the explanations of what was going on in the tax calculations would have been hopelessly complicated. Also, because many aspects of financial life have an impact on this tax, the AMT will be different for each individual or corporation.

If you do find yourself struck with this tax, do not despair. Perhaps you can revise your plan so as to avoid it, or you can go ahead and pay it. The added AMT may be smaller than the regular tax you would pay if you revised your plan. There is also a possibility you may get some of the AMT tax back in future years.

In computing the effects of AMT, you should also consider the possibility that if you pay AMT, you may be able to claim a credit for some or all of the AMT tax you pay in future years. (The credit can be applied to regular income tax.) The IRS form for computing this credit is Form 8801. This form, and its instructions, can give you some insight into the computation, but I urge you to use competent professional assistance in this area.

WILL YOU HAVE THE HONOR OF PAYING THE AMT?

If you have any of the following items in your return, you do have to at least fill out Form 6251, Alternative Minimum Tax—Individuals:

1. A deduction for accelerated depreciation in excess of what your deduction would be if you computed it by the straight-line method of depreciation. (These methods are explained in Chapter 3.)
2. Income from the exercise of incentive stock options. We didn't discuss stock options, but if you are an employee of a corporation and have this benefit, you should be careful about selecting the tax years in which you exercise the options.
3. Tax-exempt interest from private activity bonds. These are tax-exempt bonds issued by a state or local government that finance a facility for a private business. Industrial development bonds would be covered by this definition.
4. Intangible drilling costs. If you have invested in oil or gas drilling investments, the exploration company will advise you of these.
5. Depletion. Depletion is similar to depreciation, but not too similar. It usually flows to individuals through a partnership that engages in mining or oil and gas drilling.
6. Circulation expenditures. (See the discussion in Chapters 3 and 8.)

7. Research and experimental expenditures. (See the discussion above and in Chapter 3.)

8. Mining exploration and development costs.

9. Amortization of pollution-control facilities.

10. Income or loss from tax-shelter farm activities.

11. Income or loss from passive business activities.

12. Income from long-term contracts figured under the percentage-of-completion method.

13. Income from installment sales of certain property. This applies only to farming and to sales that occurred in 1986 and 1987, so it would not apply to the sale of your business.

14. Interest paid on a home mortgage not used to buy, build, or substantially improve your home.

15. Investment interest expense.

16. Net-operating-loss deduction. Watch this one. When your business is young, you may be generating net operating losses.

HOW THE AMT IS COMPUTED

The short answer is: "With a computer and sophisticated tax software." If you are eager and like complicated puzzles, you can take a stab at manually filling in Form 6251, Alternative Minimum Tax—Individuals. Obtain the instructions for the form from the IRS, or even better, obtain IRS Publication 909, Alternative Minimum Tax for Individuals, which is more comprehensive than the instructions for the form. My advice, though, is to take your tax plan to your tax advisor and have him or her compute the AMT you might incur. Do this *before* you put your plan in action.

I have not laid out the computations for this tax, as the complications make anyone's attempt at explanation indecipherable. The IRS instructions are as clear as any, so use them if you must calculate it yourself. Usually, I do not recommend using the IRS instructions carte blanche, for they are skewed towards a conservative stance in interpretation of the law. However, the AMT and the related forms and instructions are essentially a mechanical reworking of what is reported on the basic tax forms. For the most part, AMT planning consists of timing (in which year you do what).

If you are a philosopher, you can ponder why the AMT law is written as it is. For instance, the AMT rules mess around with medical expenses, but before you can compute a revised medical expense for AMT purposes, you have to know what your new adjusted gross income is for AMT purposes, because the medical expense is deductible only to the extent that it exceeds 10 percent of this Alternative Tax Adjusted Gross Income (ATAGI). Why don't the rules just use the plain old medical expense you already have computed for Schedule A, Itemized Deductions? My theory: We have to keep full employment in Washington. This morass provides jobs at the IRS, law firms, and accounting firms.

To end this short but important chapter on a good note, I'll point out that after you have gone through the calculations to find an *Alternative Minimum Taxable Income (AMTI)*, you deduct an exemption amount—$45,000 if you are filing a joint return and your AMTI is not over $150,000. That is, if your AMTI is less than $45,000, you will not be subject to any AMT.

If you are subject to AMT, the rates are 26 percent on AMT up to $175,000 and 28 percent on amounts over that.

AMT—CORPORATIONS

Just in case you thought you could avoid this minimum tax quagmire by putting your business in a corporation, Congress also made corporations subject to a minimum tax. Again, this is a cookbook recomputation of what is on the regular tax return, and it needs to be computed *before* you enter your business year. Appendix D contains a copy of Form 4626, Alternative Minimum Tax—Corporations. The tax rate is 20 percent of the corporation AMT taxable income. If you want to try this yourself, you can obtain the many pages of instructions for this form from the IRS. Again, my suggestion is to have your tax advisor compute it.

Confused? So are most tax professionals, but they have the computer programs. The next chapter will help you find an advisor who fits your needs.

10

Select and Use Professional Help

The Internal Revenue Code, as published by tax services in loose-leaf form, takes up two 3-inch-thick binders. The implementing regulations, revenue rulings, revenue procedures, private letter rulings, and other pronouncements of the IRS take up a dozen or so more loose-leaf binders. How much of that can be included in a 200-page book? The highlights. I have tried to explain some IRS rules and how you may be able to tread lightly by them, but as I said in the introduction, this is not to encourage you to undertake a do-it-yourself program of aggressive tax planning. Once you have developed a tax-avoidance idea or plan, take it to a professional for fine-tuning and modification so that it complies with the latest in rulings and court cases.

But what type of professional should you use?

WHAT ARE YOUR NEEDS?

Now that after reading this book, you have come up with some creative ideas as to how to obliterate your tax bill or at least knock some big holes in it, you are going to need someone who does much more than just prepare your tax return. On the other hand, if all you have done to date is start a lawn-mower repair business in your garage, your affairs may not be complicated enough to justify using someone who will cost you hundreds of dollars. But remember this: You will need first-class help *before* you implement any sophisticated tax-avoidance plan. It's too late to plan last year when you are preparing the tax return in April of this year.

Recordkeeping Help, as in "Bookkeeping"

Some people are detail oriented and keep meticulous records. Show them the way to keep the records, and they will do it. Others of us can't get beyond the "fill in the check stub" stage and need someone who will pick up our messy notes and files and create some order out of them.

Tax Form Preparation

Again, some people can do a good job themselves, preparing a 1040 either manually or with the help of one of the inexpensive computer programs that are available. Others are befuddled by any form and easily frustrated by perplexing instructions. They need someone to fill in the forms. Also, there comes a point in the tax life of anyone who aggressively plans tax-saving maneuvers when he or she should have an experienced professional prepare the annual tax forms that report those maneuvers to the IRS. Although hiding information from the IRS can invite penalties, there are better ways and worse ways to present your picture on the tax forms and attached schedules. For instance, when someone prepares a business return, he or she would not use the word *hobby* in stating the nature of the business, even though that may have been the original source of the business.

Planning Your Tax Life

No one should do this in a vacuum. You should seek help if for no other reason than two heads are better than one. Of course, it makes sense to hire that help from someone who works with tax rules every day.

Fighting the IRS

Again, you can do it yourself, and if you don't stand to lose much money even if you lose the fight, you might as well. That is, if you can prepare yourself psychologically. For instance, if the IRS invites you to its local office to check on your deduction for business use of your car and that deduction totaled only $400, you might as well take your records and go fight your own battle. If you are in the 28 percent tax bracket and you lose the fight, it will cost you 28 percent times $400, or $112. Professional help would cost you more than that.

You might think about handling the IRS audit yourself if the audit involves your own records, if, for example, you need to prove that you really did spend $7,000 for lawn-mower carburetor parts and cleaner.[1] However, this could become a question of the reliability of your records, and the expense of a professional to argue this point might be cost-effective. If the IRS is questioning something that involves a point of law or its regulations, it is best that you are represented by someone knowledgeable in those rules. If, for example, the IRS questions whether your child's trust, to which you gave stock in your company, is a trust that will validly shift the income to the over-14 child, a professional versed in the tax rules about trusts would be a big help.

There are several levels at which you can fight the IRS, and it helps if you are aware of them when you pick a professional to help you fight.

The audit Most of us are familiar with the letter from the IRS that invites you to come to its office and show them your records. If you own a business, regardless of its legal form, you may be blessed with a field audit (IRS uses the term *examination*). In those audits, the agent would like to do his or her thing in your office, where he or she can look at all kinds of records. If your office is small and cramped, a tax professional may be able to get the site of the examination changed to his or her office, which does provide some advantage for you. Then the agent does not get to watch your company's daily activity for hours each day.

---

[1] If you really did not spend the $7,000 but only $38.92, you have lied in your tax return. You may be in bigger trouble than you think. You definitely need professional help.

Appeal of an agent's findings to his or her supervisor   This is an informal process that can take place almost immediately after the agent has completed the audit.

Appeal to the IRS Appeals Office   This office is staffed by sharp, knowledgeable employees of the IRS. Sometimes they will understand a mitigating point that the examining agent did not comprehend, so you may win your point here. Although the examining agent cannot consider the hazards of litigation and make settlements with a taxpayer, the appeals officer can make settlements.

U.S. Tax Court   This court is not part of the IRS but part of the federal court system. You can appeal to this court without first having to pay the tax that the IRS says you still owe. (The IRS calls it the *deficiency*.) Like all courts, it has extensive rules that must be followed, although it does have a simplified procedure that can be used when the amount is under $50,000. That makes it possible for taxpayers to represent themselves in litigation over small amounts.

U.S. District Court or U.S. Claims Court   This is an option that may appear to be advantageous if other court cases in the District Courts or the Claims Court seem to favor your position more than have Tax Court cases. You can also request a jury trial in a District Court. However, the deficiency has to be paid first because these courts will hear only suits for refund of taxes that the IRS wrongfully collected.

U.S. Court of Appeals   You can try to get your way here, if you didn't like what the Tax Court, the District Court, or the Claims Court did to you. This may not be worth the expense, unless the particular Court of Appeals for your area has a history of ruling in favor of the taxpayer in situations like yours.

U.S. Supreme Court   There are only so many working hours in a year for the Supreme Court justices, so the Supreme Court does not hear all the tax cases that the losers in lower courts ask it to hear. Unless your case is precedent setting, or various courts have ruled differently on the same set of financial circumstances, your case probably will not be heard. Besides, it's an expensive place to pursue your point.

Why fight the IRS in court? Won't the courts back up the IRS? In most cases, yes, the courts side with the IRS. However, individuals and businesses have won significant cases, and you could be one of those winners.

In some situations, you don't need to go to court because someone else has already fought and won the battle for you. Those are situations in which the IRS *acquiesces* to the court decision that went against the tax collectors. That is, the IRS changes its position and will follow the thinking of the court in similar situations. In other cases, the IRS does not acquiesce to the court decision. The IRS maintains that the court is wrong, and it will continue enforcing what it believes to be the correct interpretation of the law. In those *nonacquiesced* situations, you will have to take your own battle to court and hope that the court will rule against the IRS for you. Your tax attorney can advise you on your chances of winning if you do go to battle in our federal court system.

THE AVAILABLE TALENT

Let's look at what sort of help is out there in the marketplace. I have listed the types, starting with those with the least requirements in terms of education and examination to those with the highest requirements. Do not take the order as an indication of least desirable versus most desirable. They each have their function, and using the wrong category for a particular function can be expensive, even disastrous. To complicate matters, some organizations perform more than one function. Also, within each category you will find dedicated individuals who put the clients' interests first and others whom we charitably might call opportunists.

Bookkeepers

These are the people who can help the organizationally disabled among us. If your business is too small to justify the hiring of a full-time bookkeeper and you have neither the time for, nor the interest in, detail work, you will need a bookkeeping service. There is no professional exam or standard for such a service, so you will have to rely on references from other business people and professionals. Of course, you can always ask the manager of the service about the education in bookkeeping each of the employees has. Often, you can find this service, for reasonable fees, offered by someone working in his or her home.

Commercial Tax Preparation Services

Most of these organizations cater to individuals with little income other than wages, salaries, and pensions. Although they may prepare tax returns that involve very small businesses or a few rental properties, they will usually send those with more complications to an accounting firm. Also, be aware that if you have a commercial tax service prepare your business return, they are apt to take a conservative stance. For example, if there is a question as to whether your enterprise is a business or a hobby, they are likely to call it a hobby unless it meets the safe-harbor provisions. Why? They often guarantee to pay penalties that arise from the method in which the return was prepared. Obviously, they are not going to risk having to pay penalties by taking a position that the IRS may question. Although they may accompany you to an IRS audit, they generally will not represent you. That is, they cannot deal with the IRS agent unless you are present, and they can do little else than explain how your return was prepared.

Yet if you have not yet started your business, this is an economical way to have your return prepared by someone who is familiar with the tax forms and basic rules. When you are in the process of planning your less-tax life, there is no reason not to use a commercial tax service to prepare last year's return while you are engaging a more sophisticated advisor to help you plan next year.

Enrolled Agent

This is an IRS-bestowed designation on individuals who have passed a comprehensive exam on federal income tax rules.

Although there is no requirement as to education completed before one takes the exam, once designated as an enrolled agent, an individual must complete an annual schedule of courses in current tax rules. Because of the exam and continuing education requirements, you can be reasonably assured of knowledgeable tax help from an enrolled agent. Often, you will find that the manager of a bookkeeping service is also an enrolled agent, so you can avail yourself of a one-stop service for a small business.

Enrolled agents can, if you sign a power-of-attorney form, represent you before the IRS. That is, they can discuss your tax returns and the positions you have taken on them, with an IRS employee (including those from the appellate division) even if you are not present. (For some people, it is better if they are not there—particularly those who are prone to say too much in a friendly conversation with the IRS agent.)

Certified Public Accountant (CPA)

Requirements for this designation include a four-year college program that includes a heavy dose of accounting and tax courses as well as some training in business law. The biggest hurdle to being able to put CPA after one's name is the national CPA exam, which goes on for two and a half days. Although this exam is administered by the American Institute of Certified Public Accountants, the conferring of the CPA designation is done by the state where the individual resides, and the certification usually requires some experience in accounting as well as the education and exam requirements. CPAs must also adhere to a schedule of continuing education in accounting and tax rules in order to keep a license to practice. They also can represent a client before the IRS. If your financial life requires the preparation of financial statements (as for your bank) and/or you have interrelated corporations, partnerships, or similar business arrangements, you need a CPA.

Be aware that CPAs tend to specialize. Believe it or not, the body of rules for financial accounting, preparation, and auditing of financial statements is almost as extensive and often as incomprehensible as are the tax rules. To ask anyone to maintain an in-depth knowledge of both sets of rules sets up an impossible goal for anyone but a genius. Therefore, be sure to ask your prospective CPA in which field he or she specializes. In a firm of several CPAs, both types should be on hand. If you are talking to a sole practitioner, be sure he or she is tax oriented if you are going to pursue the ideas in this book.

Attorneys

These people come in many types and specialties. Those who specialize in personal-injury cases or domestic-relations law are not going to be of much help in your tax life. In fact, most non-tax-oriented attorneys will refuse to become involved in tax matters. Many tax attorneys have a dual qualification: They took undergraduate accounting courses, became CPAs, passed law school, passed the bar exam, and then earned advanced degrees in tax law. Like other professionals, they have continuing education requirements to fulfill. You will need an attorney to set up your corporation or draw up a partnership agreement, so using a tax specialist will provide someone who can also fine-tune the tax-saving plan you have developed.

If you fail to win your point with the IRS Appeals Office and pursue it in court, you should engage a tax attorney.

Best Utilization of Professionals

Try to be cost-effective. If your business is small and involves few dollars, you can use a bookkeeping service for your routine work and perhaps even tax-form preparation. (Some CPA firms also offer bookkeeping services, but check the fees. They are most likely to be more expensive than a separate bookkeeping service.)

When your financial life becomes a little more complicated, you will need a CPA. Stay in touch with him or her during the year. Keep your CPA aware of what you are doing and planning in your business. If you need legal help, he or she should tell you.

When the number of dollars involved in your enterprise becomes significant, you should expect your CPA and a tax lawyer to work together to help you dodge the tax bullets. Of course, that makes for expensive help, but if it enables you to avoid the 16-inch shells the IRS may lob at you, it's worth it.

DO NOT file forms with the IRS, handle tax audits, sign contracts (for new partners, sale of your business, and other such matters), or make other major commitments with no professional help. If you wait until you find yourself in trouble—on the road to receiving a whopper of a bill from the IRS—before you go see your accountant and lawyer, it may or may not be too late. For sure, though, it will be expensive either in terms of taxes or professional fees or both.

APPENDIX A

Tax Rate Schedules for 2000

INDIVIDUALS

Single—Schedule X			
If line 5 is: Over—	But not Over—	The Tax Is:	Of the Amount Over—
$ 0	$ 26,250	$ 0 + 15%	$ 0
26,250	63,550	3,937.50 + 28%	26,250
63,550	132,600	14,381.50 + 31%	63,550
132,600	288,350	35,787.00 + 36%	132,600
288,350	—	91,857.00 + 39.6%	288,350

Married Filing Jointly or Qualifying Widow(er)— Schedule Y-1			
If line 5 is: Over—	But not Over—	The Tax Is:	Of the Amount Over—
$ 0	$ 43,850	$ 0 + 15%	$ 0
43,850	105,950	6,577.50 + 28%	43,850
105,950	161,450	23,965.50 + 31%	105,950
161,450	288,350	41,170.50 + 36%	161,450
288,350	—	86,854.50 + 39.6%	288,350

160   APPENDIX A

Married Filing Separately—Schedule Y-2

If line 5 is: Over—	But not Over—	The Tax Is:	Of the Amount Over—
$ 0	$ 21,925	$ 0 + 15%	$ 0
21,925	52,975	3,288.75 + 28%	21,925
52,975	80,725	11,982.75 + 31%	52,975
80,725	144,175	20,585.25 + 36%	80,725
144,175	—	43,427.25 + 39.6%	144,175

Head of Household—Schedule Z

If line 5 is: Over—	But not Over—	The Tax Is:	Of the Amount Over—
$ 0	$ 35,150	$ 0 + 15%	$ 0
35,150	90,800	5,272.50 + 28%	35,150
90,800	147,050	20,854.50 + 31%	90,800
147,050	288,350	38,292.00 + 36%	147,050
288,350	—	89,160.00 + 39.6%	288,350

Personal Exemption

Most individual taxpayers can deduct a personal exemption of $2,800 for themselves and each dependent. However, high-income taxpayers cannot use some or all of this personal exemption. A taxpayer earning more than a threshold amount must reduce his or her personal exemptions by a percentage. This percentage is computed as 2 percent for each $2,500 of adjusted gross income over the threshold amount. (That's for all taxpayers except those in the "married filing separately" classification. For them, the percentage is 2 percent for each $1,250 over the threshold amount.) For 2000, these threshold amounts are:

Single	$128,950
Head of household	$161,150
Married filing jointly	$193,400
Married filing separately	$ 96,700

Table A.1   Ernie's Personal Exemption

1	Adjusted gross income	$140,000
2	Subtract threshold amount	128,950
3	Excess AGI (line 1 minus line 2)	11,050
4	Divide excess AGI by $1,250	8.8
5	Round up line 4 (always round up)	9
6	Multiply line 5 times 2%	18%
7	Amount of personal exemption(s) before reduction	$ 2,800
8	Multiply line 6 times line 7	504
9	Subtract line 8 from line 7 to compute allowable personal exemption	$ 2,296

Example: Ernie is single with no dependents, and his adjusted gross income is $125,000; he would compute his personal exemption as in Table A.1.

Standard Deduction

Single	$ 4,400
Head of household	$ 6,450
Married filing jointly	$ 7,350
Married filing separately	$ 3,675

For those who are age 65 before the end of the year, or are blind, the standard deduction is increased by these amounts:

Joint returns (for each spouse over 65)	$ 850
Head of household	1,100
Single	1,100

These amounts are doubled for those over 65 and blind.

There is no phaseout of the standard deduction.

Itemized Deductions

You can deduct whatever is the bottom line on Schedule A, unless your adjusted gross income exceeds $128,950. (This is the threshold amount for all taxpayers in 2000, except for married individuals filing separately. In that case, the threshold amount is $64,475.) The itemized deductions must then be reduced by 3 percent of the amount of adjusted gross income over the threshold amount, but not by more than 80 percent of the itemized deductions. Four classes of deductions are not affected by this reduction-of-deduction rule. They are medical expenses, investment interest expenses, casualty losses, and wagering losses to the extent of wagering gains. If you are affected by this confusing rule (that is, if your income is high enough), you can work through the calculations as for the example in Table A.2. (Erlene has an adjusted gross income of $200,000 and itemized deductions of $20,000.)

Social Security Taxes

OASDI tax   A total of 12.4 percent of compensation up to $76,200. One-half (6.2 percent) paid by employer and the other 6.2 percent paid by employee. Self-employed individuals pay 12.4 percent on first $76,200 of income from business.

Hospital insurance (Medicare) tax   A total of 2.9 percent on all compensation (no limit). One-half (1.45 percent) paid by employer and the other half paid by employee. Self-employed individuals pay 2.9 percent on all income from business.

CORPORATIONS

C Corporations

If Taxable Income Is Over	But Taxable Income Is Not Over	The Tax Is	Of the Amount Over
$ 0	$ 50,000	$ 0 + 15%	$ 0
50,000	75,000	7,500 + 25%	50,000
75,000	100,000	13,750 + 34%	75,000
100,000	335,000	22,250 + 39%	100,000
335,000	10,000,000	113,900 + 34%	335,000
10,000,000	15,000,000	3,400,000 + 35%	10,000,000
15,000,000	18,333,333	5,150,000 + 38%	15,000,000
18,333,333	—	+ 35%	0

**Table A.2   Computation of Allowable Itemized Deductions
for Erlene**

1	Total itemized deductions*		$20,000
2	Medical expense (after reduction by 7.5% of adjusted gross income)	$ 3,000	
3	Investment interest expense	4,000	
4	Casualty or theft loss (after limitations computed on Form 4684)	1,000	
5	Wagering losses to extent of wagering gains	1,000	
6	Total of lines 2, 3, 4, and 5		9,000
7	Subtract line 6 from line 1 (if negative number results, enter zero)		11,000
8	Multiply line 7 by 80%		8,800
9	Adjusted gross income	200,000	
10	Threshold amount	128,950	
11	Subtract line 10 from line 9	71,050	
12	Multiply line 11 by 3%		2,132
13	Enter smaller of line 8 or line 12		2,132
14	Subtract line 13 from line 1. This is an allowable itemized deduction.		$17,868

*This is the total computed after deduction of 7.5 percent of adjusted gross income from medical expense and 2 percent of adjusted gross income from miscellaneous expenses.

The rate increase at $15,000,000 to 38 percent and then back to 35 percent on income over $18,333,333 may look like the largest corporations are getting a 3 percent tax break. However, that is not the case. The extra 3 percent is designed to erase the benefit of the lower tax brackets. Once taxable income has reached $18,333,333, the benefit of the lower brackets has been recaptured by the IRS, and the corporation pays 35 percent on all taxable income.

(For tax rates for estate and gift taxes, see Chapter 7.)

APPENDIX B

Often Misunderstood Tax Concepts

TAX BRACKETS AND TAX RATES

" I can't make any more money because it will put me in a higher tax bracket." How often have we heard that, in the local watering hole or at any social gathering? Does this concern make sense? You decide from this example:

> Melvin is single and earns $33,450 per year. If he has no dependents and claims only the standard deduction, he pays tax as in Table B.1.
>
> Look at schedule X in Appendix A. It indicates that if Melvin makes even one dollar more of wages, his taxable income will be over $26,250, and he will be in the 28 percent bracket. That does not mean that he has to recompute the tax on his first $26,250 of

Table B.1   Melvin's 2000 Individual Income Tax Return

1	Total income	$ 33,450
2	Standard deduction	(4,400)
3	Personal exemption	(2,800)
4	Taxable income (line 1 minus both line 2 and line 3)	$ 26,250
5	Melvin's tax (2000 tax rate schedule X, for single individuals (in Appendix A) states that taxable income up to $26,250 is taxed at 15%)	$ 3,938

Table B.2   Melvin's 2000 Individual Income Tax Return Revised for $10,000 Raise

1	Total income	$ 43,450
2	Standard deduction	(4,400)
3	Personal exemption	(2,800)
4	Taxable income (line 1 minus both line 2 and line 3)	$ 36,250
5	Tax on first $26,250 of taxable income (same as in Table B.1)	$ 3,938
6	Tax on $10,000 remaining of taxable income	2,800
7	Total tax (add lines 5 and 6)	$ 6,738

taxable income. That income is still taxed at 15 percent. Only the additional money he earns is taxed at 28 percent. Let's assume Melvin receives a raise on January 1, so his earnings are now $43,450. His tax return looks like Table B.2. The additional $10,000 in income for Melvin has resulted in an increased percentage out of that $10,000. It has not increased the tax on the first $33,450 of income.

Tax deduction or tax credit?

Let's look at Melvin's tax picture in Table B.1. What if he has a tax deduction (such as moving expense) of $1,000? His tax return will look like Table B.3.

This tax, after the $1,000 deduction, is $150 less than the tax in Table B.1 ($3,938 − $3,788 = $150). The deduction has saved Melvin $150 of income tax. (You could also compute this by multiplying the deduction by his tax bracket of 15 percent.)

What if Melvin is eligible for and uses a tax credit of $1,000? Now his return from Table B.1 is changed to the picture in Table B.4.

Table B.3   Melvin's 2000 Individual Income Tax Return with Additional *Deduction* of $1,000

1	Total income	$ 33,450
2	Standard deduction	(4,400)
3	Personal exemption	(2,800)
4	Taxable income (line 1 minus both line 2 and line 3)	26,250
5	Additional *deduction*	(1,000)
6	New taxable income	$ 25,250
7	New tax (15% of line 6)	$ 3,788

Table B.4   Melvin's 2000 Individual Income Tax Return with Tax *Credit* of $1,000

1	Total income	$ 33,450
2	Standard deduction	(4,400)
3	Personal exemption	(2,800)
4	Taxable income (line 1 minus both line 2 and line 3)	$ 26,250
5	Income tax (15% of line 4)	$ 3,938
6	Subtract tax *credit* from tax	(1,000)
7	New tax	$ 2,928

To summarize, the $1,000 tax deduction has saved Melvin only $150 of tax, while the credit has saved him $1,000.

Moral: If you have a choice between a deduction and a credit of the same dollar amount, take the credit. If the dollar amounts are different, you will have to do a tax calculation as we did for Melvin to see which is more beneficial.

APPENDIX C-1

IRS Ruling on Deducting the Expense of Investigating a Business

[Reprinted below is Revenue Ruling 77-254 relative to the deductibility of expenses of investigating the possibility of entering a business, before the business is entered. (For discussion, see Chapter 3.) Typical of government pronouncements, it's pretty wordy and still leaves a lot of room for differences of opinion. Also reprinted here is Revenue Ruling 57-418. Although it dates from the 1950s, it is still effective.]

REVENUE RULING 77-254
Summary

Losses; attempted acquisition of business   An individual may deduct, in accordance with section 165(c)(2) of the Code, expenses incurred in the unsuccessful attempt to acquire a specific business, such as legal expenses incurred in drafting purchase documents. However, expenses incurred in the course of a general search for or preliminary investigation of a business, such as expenses for advertisements and travel to search for a new business, are not deductible. Rev. Rul. 57-418 amplified.

Rev. Rul. 77-254
Advice has been requested whether, under the circumstances described below, a deduction in accordance with section 165(c)(2) of the Internal Revenue Code of 1954 is allowable to a

169

taxpayer for a loss that was not compensated for by insurance or otherwise.

An individual taxpayer began to search for a business to purchase. The individual placed advertisements in several newspapers and traveled to various locations throughout the country to investigate various businesses that the individual learned were for sale. The individual commissioned audits to evaluate the potential of several of these businesses. Eventually, the individual decided to purchase a specific business and incurred expenses in an attempt to purchase this business. For example, the individual retained a law firm to draft the documents necessary for the purchase. Because of certain disagreements between the individual and the owner of the business that developed after this decision was made, the individual abandoned all attempts to acquire the business.

Section 165(a) of the Code allows as a deduction any loss sustained during the taxable year that is not compensated for by insurance or otherwise. Section 165(c) provides that in the case of individuals, the deduction is limited to (1) losses incurred in a trade or business, (2) losses incurred in any transaction entered into for profit though not connected with a trade or business, and (3) losses of property not connected with a trade or business if such losses arise from fire, storm, shipwreck or other casualty, or from theft.

Rev. Rul. 57-418, 1957-2 C.B, 143, holds that losses incurred in the search for a business or investment are deductible only when the activities are more than investigatory and the taxpayer has actually entered a transaction for profit and the project is later abandoned.

In *Seed* v. *Commissioner*, 52 T.C. 880 (1969), *acq.*, 1970-2 C.B. xxi, the United States Tax Court allowed a deduction for expenses incurred by a taxpayer during an unsuccessful attempt to secure a charter to operate a savings and loan association. The court found that the taxpayer's extensive activities in the venture qualified as a transaction entered into for profit. Following the decision in *Seed,* the court has continued to find that a taxpayer has entered a transaction for profit in cases in which the facts indicate that the taxpayer has gone beyond a general search and focused on the acquisition of a specific business or investment. *See Price* v. *Commissioner*, T.C. Memo. 1971-323; *Domenie* v. *Commissioner*, T.C. Memo. 1975-94.

In view of the decision in *Seed*, Rev. Rul. 57-418 is amplified to provide that a taxpayer will be considered to have entered a transaction for profit if, based on all the facts and circumstances, the taxpayer has gone beyond a general investigatory search for a new business or investment to focus on the acquisition of a specific business or investment.

Expenses incurred in the course of a general search for or preliminary investigation of a business or investment include those expenses related to the decisions *whether* to enter a transaction and *which* transaction to enter. Such expenses are personal and are not deductible under section 165 of the Code. Once the taxpayer has focused on the acquisition of a specific business or investment, expenses that are related to an attempt to acquire such business or investment are capital in nature and, to the extent that the expenses are allocable to an asset the cost of which is amortizable or depreciable, may be amortized as part of the asset's cost if the attempted acquisition is successful. If the attempted acquisition fails, the amount capitalized is deductible in accordance with section 165(c)(2). The taxpayer need not actually enter the business or purchase the investment in order to obtain the deduction.

Accordingly, in the present case the individual may deduct as losses incurred in a transaction entered into for profit the expenses incurred in the unsuccessful attempt to acquire a specific business. Thus, the individual's expenses in retaining a lawyer to draft the purchase documents and any other expenses incurred in the attempt to complete the purchase of the business are deductible. The expenses for advertisements, travel to search for a new business, and the cost of audits that were designed to help the individual decide whether to attempt an acquisition were investigatory expenses and are not deductible.

REVENUE RULING 57-418

The issue involved in I.T. 1505, C.B. I-2, 112 (1922), and in the decision in *Charles T. Parker* v. *Commissioner,* 1 T.C. 709, non-acquiescence C.B. 1943, 37, has been reconsidered in the light of the decisions in *Morton Frank et ux.* v. *Commissioner* 20 T.C. 511, and *Robert Lyons Hague* v. *Commissioner,* 24 B.T.A. 288.

I.T. 1505, supra, was based upon section 214(a)(5) of the Revenue Act of 1921 and Article 141, Regulations 62. Section 214(a)(5) corresponds to section 23(e)(2) of the Internal Revenue Code of 1939 and to section 165(c)(2) of the Internal Revenue Code of 1954. These sections allow deductions for losses sustained by an individual taxpayer during the taxable year and not compensated for by insurance or otherwise, if incurred in any transaction entered into for profit, though not connected with the trade or business of the taxpayer.

In I.T. 1505, supra, a deduction of the expenses incurred in sending an agent to Europe to organize an export business was disallowed as an ordinary and necessary business expense (under section 214(a)(1) of the 1921 Act). The reports of the agent were unfavorable and the idea of establishing the business was abandoned. The taxpayer's income consisted entirely of salaries and interest. While it was considered that the expenditure was not incurred in the taxpayer's trade or business, it was held that the transaction was entered into for profit, and that upon the abandonment of the enterprise any expenses incurred by the taxpayer in the course of the transaction became a loss which was deductible in the taxable year in which the enterprise was abandoned (under section 214(a)(5) of the 1921 Act).

In the *Frank* case, the taxpayers were interested in purchasing and operating a newspaper or radio station. They incurred expenses for traveling, telephone, telegraph, etc., in their search for and investigation of business properties which they could purchase and operate. Various transactions were investigated and rejected. The taxpayers contended that the expenses should be allowed as nonbusiness losses. For a loss to be sustained during the taxable year with respect to expenditures incurred in search of a prospective business or investment, it is essential that the taxpayer abandon the project which was actually entered into for profit. The phrase "entered into for profit" has been construed to mean something more than carrying on negotiations to acquire a prospective business or investment. The court held in the *Frank* case, supra, that, since the taxpayers refused to enter into transactions which they investigated, no abandonment occurred in the taxable year so as to give rise to a deductible loss.

In the *Hague* case, The United States Board of Tax Appeals denied a deduction under section 214(a)(5) of the Revenue Act of 1926 for legal fees incurred in connection with prospective investments. The Board stated that the taxpayer had not entered into these transactions but, on the contrary, stayed out of them.

The *Parker* case is distinguishable on the facts from I.T. 1505, supra, and from the *Frank* and the *Hague* cases. In the *Parker* case, the taxpayer, after investigating a mining operation owned by another individual to determine whether it might be a suitable investment for himself, contributed cash and hired several men for about 30 days to rehabilitate the mining equipment and to operate the mine temporarily to determine whether further investment was warranted. The results of the temporary operation were unsatisfactory and the project was abandoned. The taxpayer never acquired any interest nor made any other investment in the property. The court held that the taxpayer sustained a deductible loss under section 23(e)(2) of the 1939 Code in the taxable year in which the project was abandoned, because his activities in connection with the project were more than investigatory; he had actually entered into a transaction for profit which he later abandoned.

Accordingly, it is held that a loss, not compensated for by insurance or otherwise, sustained during a taxable year with respect to expenditures incurred in search of a business or investment is deductible only where the activities are more than investigatory and the taxpayer has actually entered into a transaction for profit and the project is later abandoned. The loss is allowable only in the taxable year in which the project is abandoned.

Pursuant to the authority contained in section 7805(b) of the Internal Revenue Code of 1954, the principles stated herein will neither be applied to such losses sustained before September 23, 1957, nor to such losses sustained on or after September 23, 1957, where the search for a prospective business or investment began prior to September 23, 1957, but the taxpayer never actually entered into the transaction or the business venture.

Acquiescence has been substituted for nonacquiescence in the *Parker* case. See page 6.

I.T. 1505, C.B. I-2, 112 (1922), is revoked.

APPENDIX C-2

Definition of Research and Experimental Expenditures

[As some research and development expenses can be deducted from income before a business opens, it is worth a look through the examples and other sections of this regulation. You may find that some of your anticipated expenses may qualify for this preferred tax treatment.]

IRS Regulation §1.174-2

(a) In General

(1) The term "research or experimental expenditures", as used in section 174, means expenditures incurred in connection with the taxpayer's trade or business which represent research and development costs in the experimental or laboratory sense. The term includes generally all such costs incident to development of an experimental or pilot model, a plant process, a product, a formula, an invention, or similar property, and the improvement of already existing property of the type mentioned. The term does not include expenditures such as those for the ordinary testing or inspection of materials or products for quality control or those for efficiency surveys, management studies, consumer surveys, advertising, or promotions. However, the term includes the costs of obtaining a patent, such as attorneys' fees expended in making and perfecting a patent application. On the other hand, the term does not include the cost of acquiring another's patent, model, production or process,

nor does it include expenditures paid or incurred for research in connection with historical or similar projects.

(2) The provisions of this section apply not only to costs paid or incurred by the taxpayer for research or experimentation undertaken directly by him but also to expenditures paid or incurred for research or experimentation carried on in his behalf by another person organization (such as a research institute, foundation, engineering company, or similar contractor). However, any expenditures for research or experimentation carried on in the taxpayer's behalf by another person are not expenditures to which section 174 relates, to the extent that they represent expenditures for the acquisition or improvement of land or depreciable property, used in connection with the research or experimentation, to which the taxpayer acquires rights of ownership.

(3) The application of subparagraph (2) of this paragraph may be illustrated by the following examples:

Example   (I).-A engages B to undertake research and experimental work in order to create a particular product. B will be paid annually a fixed sum plus an amount equivalent to his actual expenditures. In 1957, A pays to B in respect of the project the sum of $150,000 of which $25,000 represents an addition to B's laboratory and the balance represents charges for research and experimentation on the project. It is agreed between the parties that A will absorb the entire cost of this addition to B's laboratory which will be retained by B. A may treat the entire $150,000 as expenditures under section 174.

Example   (2).-X Corporation, a manufacturer of explosives, contracts with the Y research organization to attempt through research and experimentation the creation of a new process for making certain explosives. Because of the danger involved in such an undertaking, Y is compelled to acquire an isolated tract of land on which to conduct the research and experimentation. It is agreed that upon completion of the project Y will transfer the tract, including any improvements thereon, to X. Section 174 does not apply to the amount paid to Y representing the cost of the tract of land and improvements.

(b) Certain Expenditures with Respect to Land and Other Property

(1) Expenditures by the taxpayer for the acquisition or improvement of land, or for the acquisition or improvement of property which is subject to an allowance for depreciation under section 167 or depletion under section 6611 are not deductible under section 174, irrespective of the fact that the property or improvements may be used by the taxpayer in connection with research or experimentation. However, allowances for depreciation or depletion of property are considered as research or experimental expenditures, for purposes of section 174, to the extent that the property to which the allowances relate is used in connection with research or experimentation. If any part of the cost of acquisition or improvement of depreciable property is attributable to research or experimentation (whether made by the taxpayer or another), see subparagraphs (2), (3), and (4) of this paragraph.

(2) Expenditures for research or experimentation which result, as an end product of the research or experimentation, in depreciable property to be used in the taxpayer's trade or business may, subject to the limitations of subparagraph (4) of this paragraph, be allowable as a current expense deduction under section 174 (a). Such expenditures cannot be amortized under section 174 (b) except to the extent provided in §1.174-4(a)(4).

(3) If expenditures for research or experimentation are incurred in connection with the construction or manufacture of depreciable property by another, they are deductible under section 174(a) only if made upon the taxpayer's order and at his risk. No deduction will be allowed (i) if the taxpayer purchases another's product under a performance guarantee (whether express, implied, or imposed by local law) unless the guarantee is limited, to engineering specifications or otherwise, in such a way that economic utility is not taken into account; or (ii) for any part of the purchase price of a product in regular production. For example, if a taxpayer orders a specially-built automatic milling machine under a guarantee that the machine will be capable of producing a given number of units per hour, no portion of the expenditure is deductible since none of it is made at the taxpayer's risk. Similarly, no deductible expense is incurred if a taxpayer enters into a contract for the construction

of a new type of chemical processing plant under a turn-key contract guaranteeing a given annual production and a given consumption of raw material and fuel per unit. On the other hand, if the contract contained no guarantee of quality of production and of quantity of units in relation to consumption of raw material and fuel, and if real doubt existed as to the capabilities of the process, expenses for research or experimentation under the contract are at the taxpayer's risk and are deductible under section 174(a). However, see subparagraph (4) of this paragraph.

(4) The deductions referred to in subparagraphs (2) and (3) of this paragraph for expenditures in connection with the acquisition or production of depreciable property to be used in the taxpayer's trade or business are limited to amounts expended for research or experimentation. For the purpose of the preceding sentence, amounts expended for research or experimentation do not include the costs of the component materials of the depreciable property, the costs of labor or other elements involved in its construction and installation, or costs attributable to the acquisition of improvement of the property.

For example, a taxpayer undertakes to develop a new machine for use in his business. He expends $30,000 on the project of which $10,000 represents the actual costs of material, labor, etc., to construct the machine, and $20,000 represents research costs which are not attributable to the machine itself. Under section 174(n) the taxpayer would be permitted to deduct the $20,000 as expenses not chargeable to capital account, but the $10,000 must be charged to the asset account (the machine).

(c) Exploration Expenditures
The provisions of section 174 are not applicable to any expenditures paid or incurred for the purpose of ascertaining the existence, location, extent, or quality of any deposit of ore, oil, gas, or other mineral. See sections 615 and 263.

APPENDIX C-3

Deductibility of Computer Software Research

REVENUE PROCEDURE 69-21

Section 1, Purpose

[The purpose of this Revenue Procedure is to provide guidelines to be used in connection with the examination of federal income tax returns involving the costs of computer software.]

Sec. 2, Background

For the purpose of this Revenue Procedure, "computer software" includes all programs or routines used to cause a computer to perform a desired task or set of tasks, and the documentation required to describe and maintain those programs. Computer programs of all classes, for example, operating systems, executive systems, monitors, compilers and translators, assembly routines, and utility programs as well as application programs are included. "Computer software" does not include procedures which are external to computer operations, such as instructions to transcription operators and external control procedures.

Sec. 3, Costs of Developing Software

01. The costs of developing software (whether or not the particular software is patented or copyrighted) in many respects so closely resemble the kind of research and experimental expenditures that fall within the purview of section 174 of the Internal Revenue Code of 1954 as to warrant accounting treatment similar to that accorded such costs under that section.

Accordingly, the Internal Revenue Service will not disturb a taxpayer's treatment of costs incurred in developing software, either for his own use or to be held by him for sale or lease to others, where:

1. All of the costs properly attributable to the development of software by the taxpayer are consistently treated as current expenses and deducted in full in accordance with rules similar to those applicable under section 174 (a) of the Code; or

2. All of the costs properly attributable to the development of software by the taxpayer are consistently treated as capital expenditures that are recoverable through deductions for ratable amortization, in accordance with rules similar to those provided by section 174 (b) of the Code and the regulations thereunder, over a period of five years from the date of completion of such development or over a shorter period where such costs are attributable to the development of software that the taxpayer clearly establishes has a useful life of less than five years.

Sec. 4, Costs of Purchased Software

.01 With respect to costs of purchased software, the Service will not disturb the taxpayer's treatment of such costs if the following practices are consistently followed:

1. Where such costs are included, without being separately stated, in the cost of the hardware (computer) and such costs are treated as a part of the cost of the hardware that is capitalized and depreciated; or

2. Where such costs are separately stated, and the software is treated by the taxpayer as an intangible asset the cost of which is to be recovered by amortization deductions ratably over a period of five years or such shorter period as can be established by the taxpayer as appropriate in any particular case if the useful life of the software in his hands will be less than five years.

Sec. 5, Leased Software

Where a taxpayer leases software for use in his trade or business, the Service will not disturb a deduction allowable under the provisions of section 1.162–11 of the Income Tax Regulations, for rental.

Sec. 6, Application

.01 The costs of development of software in accordance with the above procedures will be treated as a method of accounting. Any change in the treatment of such costs is a change in method of accounting subject to the provisions of sections 446 and 481 of the Code and the regulations thereunder. .02 For taxable years ending after October 27, 1969, the date of publication of this Revenue Procedure, the Service will not disturb the taxpayer's treatment of software costs that are handled in accordance with the practices described in this Revenue Procedure. For taxable years ending prior to the date of publication of this Revenue Procedure, the Service will not disturb the taxpayer's treatment of software costs except to the extent that such treatment is markedly inconsistent with the practices described in this Revenue Procedure. For the purpose of applying the preceding sentence, the absence of any formal election similar to that required by section 174 of the Code, or the amortization of capitalized software costs over a period other than the five-year period specified in section 174 (b) of the Code, will not characterize the taxpayer's treatment of such costs as markedly inconsistent with the principles of this Revenue Procedure.

APPENDIX C-4

Self-Employed Status

[In Chapter 5 is a discussion of the advantages of being self-employed over being an employee. IRS Revenue Ruling 87-41 covers what the IRS considers the criteria for allowing someone to be considered a self-employed contractor. Although the thrust of the ruling appears to be concerned with employment taxes, the criteria are valid for any question of self-employed versus employee status.

The ruling is long and wordy, but the meat is in the 20 points the IRS will consider in deciding if you are really self-employed and in the examples.]

EXCERPT FROM REVENUE RULING 87-41

An individual is an employee for federal employment tax purposes if the individual has the status of an employee under the usual common law rules applicable in determining the employer-employee relationship. Guides for determining that status are found in the following three substantially similar sections of the Employment Tax Regulations: sections 31.3121(d)-1(c); 31.3306(i)-1; and 31.3401(c)-1.

These sections provide that generally the relationship of employer and employee exists when the person or persons for whom the services are performed have the right to control and direct the individual who performs the services, not only as to the result to be accomplished by the work but also as to the details and means by which that result is accomplished. That is, an employee is subject to the will and control of the employer not only as to what shall be done but as to how it shall be done. In this connection, it is not necessary that the employer actually direct or control the manner in which the services are performed; it is sufficient if the employer has the right to do so.

Conversely, these sections provide, in part, that individuals (such as physicians, lawyers, dentists, contractors, and sub contractors) who follow an independent trade, business, or profession, in which they offer their services to the public, generally are not employees.

Finally, if the relationship of employer and employee exists, the designation or description of the relationship by the parties as anything other than that of employer and employee is immaterial. Thus, if such a relationship exists, it is of no consequence that the employee is designated as a partner, coadventurer, agent, independent contractor, or the like. As an aid to determining whether an individual is an employee under the common law rules, twenty factors or elements have been identified as indicating whether sufficient control is present to establish an employer-employee relationship. The twenty factors have been developed based on an examination of cases and rulings considering whether an individual is an employee. The degree of importance of each factor varies depending on the occupation and the factual context in which the services are performed. The twenty factors are designed only as guides for determining whether an individual is an employee; special scrutiny is required in applying the twenty factors to assure that formalistic aspects of an arrangement designed to achieve a status do not obscure the substance of the arrangement (that is, whether the person or persons for whom the services are performed exercise sufficient control over the individual for the individual to be classified as an employee). The twenty factors are described below:

1. *Instructions.* A worker who is required to comply with other persons' instructions about when, where, and how he or she is to work is ordinarily an employee. This control factor is present if the person or persons for whom the services are performed have the *right* to require compliance with instructions. See, for example, Rev. Rul. 68-598, 1968-2 C.B. 464, and Rev. Rul. 66-381, 1966-2 C.B. 449.

2. *Training.* Training a worker by requiring an experienced employee to work with the worker, by corresponding with the

worker, by requiring the worker to attend meetings, or by using other methods, indicates that the person or persons for whom the services are performed want the services performed in a particular method or manner. See Rev. Rul. 70-630, 1970-2 C.B. 229.

3. *Integration.* Integration of the worker's services into the business operations generally shows that the worker is subject to direction and control. When the success or continuation of a business depends to an appreciable degree upon the performance of certain services, the workers who perform those services must necessarily be subject to a certain amount of control by the owner of the business. See United States v. Silk, 331 U.S. 704 (1947), 1947-2 C.B. 167.

4. *Services Rendered Personally.* If the services must be rendered personally, presumably the person or persons for whom the services are performed are interested in the methods used to accomplish the work as well as in the results. See Rev. Rul. 55-695, 1955-2 C.B. 410.

5. *Hiring, Supervising, and Paying Assistants.* If the person or persons for whom the services are performed hire, supervise, and pay assistants, that factor generally shows control over the workers on the job. However, if one worker hires, supervises, and pays the other assistants pursuant to a contract under which the worker agrees to provide materials and labor and under which the worker is responsible only for the attainment of a result, this factor indicates an independent contractor status. Compare Rev. Rul. 63-115, 1963-1 C.B. 178, with Rev. Rul. 55-593, 1955-2 C.B. 610.

6. *Continuing Relationship.* A continuing relationship between the worker and the person or persons for whom the services are performed indicates that an employer-employee relationship exists. A continuing relationship may exist where work is performed at frequently recurring although irregular intervals. See United States v. Silk.

7. *Set Hours of Work.* The establishment of set hours of work by the person or persons for whom the services are performed is a factor indicating control. See Rev. Rul. 73-591, 1973-2 C.B. 337.

8. *Full Time Required.* If the worker must devote substantially full time to the business of the person or persons for whom the services are performed, such person or persons have control

over the amount of time the worker spends working and impliedly restrict the worker from doing other gainful work. An independent contractor, on the other hand, is free to work when and for whom he or she chooses. See Rev. Rul. 56-694, 1956-2 C.B. 694.

9. *Doing Work on Employer's Premises.* If the work is performed on the premises of the person or persons for whom the services are performed, that factor suggests control over the worker, especially if the work could be done elsewhere. Rev. Rul. 5-660, 1956-2 C.B. 693. Work done off the premises of the person or persons receiving the services, such as at the office of the worker, indicates some freedom from control. However, this fact by itself does not mean that the worker is not an employee. The importance of this factor depends on the nature of the service involved and the extent to which an employer generally would require that employees perform such services on the employer's premises. Control over the place of work is indicated when the person or persons for whom the services are performed have the right to compel the worker to travel a designated route, to canvass a territory within a certain time, or to work at specific places as required. See Rev. Rul. 56-694.

10. *Order or Sequence Set.* If a worker must perform services in the order or sequence set by the person or persons for whom the services are performed, that factor shows that the worker is not free to follow the worker's own pattern of work but must follow the established routines and schedules of the person or persons for whom the services are performed. Often, because of the nature of an occupation, the person or persons for whom the services are performed do not set the order of the services or set the order infrequently. It is sufficient to show control, however, if such person or persons retain the right to do so. See Rev. Rul. 56-694.

11. *Oral or Written Reports.* A requirement that the worker submit regular or written reports to the person or persons for whom the services are performed indicates a degree of control. See Rev. Rul. 70-309, 1970-1 C.B. 199, and Rev. Rul. 68-248, 1968-1 C.B. 431.

12. *Payment by Hour, Week, Month.* Payment by the hour, week, or month generally points to an employer-employee relationship, provided that this method of payment is not just a

convenient way of paying a lump sum agreed upon as the cost of a job. Payment made by the job or on a straight commission generally indicates that the worker is an independent contractor. See Rev. Rul. 74-389, 1974-2 C.B. 330.

13. *Payment of Business and/or Traveling Expenses.* If the person or persons for whom the services are performed ordinarily pay the worker's business and/or traveling expenses, the worker is ordinarily an employee. An employer, to be able to control expenses, generally retains the right to regulate and direct the worker's business activities. See Rev. Rul. 55-144, 1955-1 C.B. 483.

14. *Furnishing of Tools and Materials.* The fact that the person or persons for whom the services are performed furnish significant tools, materials, and other equipment tends to show the existence of an employer-employee relationship. See Rev. Rul. 71-524, 1971-2 C.B. 346.

15. *Significant Investment.* If the worker invests in facilities that are used by the worker in performing services and are not typically maintained by employees (such as the maintenance of an office rented at fair value from an unrelated party), that factor tends to indicate that the worker is an independent contractor. On the other hand, lack of investment in facilities indicates dependence on the person or persons for whom the services are performed for such facilities and, accordingly, the existence of an employer-employee relationship. See Rev. Rul. 71-524. Special scrutiny is required with respect to certain types of facilities, such as home offices.

16. *Realization of Profit or Loss.* A worker who can realize a profit or suffer a loss as a result of the worker's services (in addition to the profit or loss ordinarily realized by employees) is generally an independent contractor, but the worker who cannot is an employee. See Rev. Rul. 70-309. For example, if the worker is subject to a real risk of economic loss due to significant investments or a bona fide liability for expenses, such as salary payments to unrelated employees, that factor indicates that the worker is an independent contractor. The risk that a worker will not receive payment for his or her services, however, is common to both independent contractors and employees and thus does not constitute a sufficient economic risk to support treatment as an independent contractor.

17. *Working for More Than One Firm at a Time.* If a worker performs more than de minimis services for a multiple of unrelated persons or firms at the same time, that factor generally indicates that the worker is an independent contractor. See Rev. Rul. 70-572, 1970-2 C.B. 221. However, a worker who performs services for more than one person may be an employee of each of the persons, especially where such persons are part of the same service arrangement.

18. *Making Service Available to General Public.* The fact that a worker makes his or her services available to the general public on a regular and consistent basis indicates an independent contractor relationship. See Rev. Rul. 56-660.

19. *Right to Discharge.* The right to discharge a worker is a factor indicating that the worker is an employee and the person possessing the right is an employer. An employer exercises control through the threat of dismissal, which causes the worker to obey the employer's instructions. An independent contractor, on the other hand, cannot be fired so long as the independent contractor produces a result that meets the contract specifications. Rev. Rul. 75-41, 1975-1 C.B. 323.

20. *Right to Terminate.* If the worker has the right to end his or her relationship with the person for whom the services are performed at any time he or she wishes without incurring liability, that factor indicates an employer-employee relationship. See Rev. Rul. 70-309.

Rev. Rul. 75-41 considers the employment tax status of individuals performing services for a physician's professional service corporation. The corporation is in the business of providing a variety of services to professional people and firms (subscribers), including the services of secretaries, nurses, dental hygienists, and other similarly trained personnel. The individuals who are to perform the services are recruited by the corporation, paid by the corporation, assigned to jobs, and provided with employee benefits by the corporation. Individuals who enter into contracts with the corporation agree they will not contract directly with any subscriber to which they are assigned for at least three months after cessation of their contracts with the corporation. The corporation assigns the individual to the subscriber to work on the subscriber's premises with the subscriber's equipment. Subscribers have the right to require that an individual furnished by the corporation cease providing service to them, and they have the further right to have such individual replaced by the corporation within a reasonable period of time, but the subscribers have no right to affect the contract between the individual and the corporation. The corporation retains the right to discharge the individual at any time. Rev. Rul. 75-41 concludes that the individuals are employees of the corporation for federal employment tax purposes.

Rev. Rul. 70-309 considers the employment tax status of certain individuals who perform services as oil well pumpers for a corporation under contracts that characterize such individuals as independent contractors. Even though the pumpers perform their services away from the headquarters of the corporation and are not given day-to-day directions and instructions, the ruling concludes that the pumpers are employees of the corporation because the pumpers perform their services pursuant to an arrangement that gives the corporation the right to exercise whatever control is necessary to assure proper performance of the services; the pumpers' services are both necessary and incident to the business conducted by the corporation; and the pumpers are not engaged in an independent enterprise in which they assume the usual business risks, but rather work in the course of the corporation's trade or business. See also Rev. Rul. 70-630. 1970-2 C.B. 229, which considers the employment tax status of salesclerks furnished by an employee service company to a retail store to perform temporary services for the store.

Section 530(a) of the 1978 Act, as amended by section 269(c) of the Tax Equity and Fiscal Responsibility Act of 1982, 1982-2 C.B. 462, 536, provides, for purposes of the employment taxes under subtitle C of the Code, that if a taxpayer did not treat an individual as an employee for any period, then the individual shall be deemed not to be an employee, unless the taxpayer had no reasonable basis for not treating the individual as an employee. For any period after December 31, 1978, this relief applies only if both of the following consistency rules are satisfied: (1) all federal tax returns (including information returns) required to be filed by the taxpayer with respect to the individual for the period are filed on a basis consistent with the taxpayer's treatment of the individual as not being an employee ("reporting consistency rule"), and (2) the taxpayer (and any predecessor) has not treated any individual holding a substantially similar position as an employee for purposes of the employment taxes for periods beginning after December 31, 1977 ("substantive consistency rule").

The determination of whether any individual who is treated as an employee holds a position substantially similar to the position held by an individual whom the taxpayer would otherwise be permitted to treat as other than an employee for employment tax purposes under section 530(a) of the 1978 Act requires an examination of all the facts and circumstances, including particularly the activities and functions performed by the individuals. Differences in the positions held by the respective individuals that result from the taxpayer's treatment of one individual as an employee and the other individual as other than an employee (for example, that the former individual is a participant in the taxpayer's qualified pension plan or health plan and the latter individual is not a participant in either) are to be disregarded in determining whether the individuals hold substantially similar positions.

Section 1706(a) of the 1986 Act added to section 530 of the 1978 Act a new subsection (d), which provides an exception with respect to the treatment of certain workers. Section 530(d) provides that section 530 shall not apply in the case of an individual who, pursuant to an arrangement between the taxpayer and another person, provides services for such other person as an engineer, designer, drafter, computer programmer, systems analyst, or other similarly skilled worker engaged in a similar line of work. Section 530(d) of the 1978 Act does not affect the determination of whether such workers are employees under the common law rules. Rather, it merely eliminates the employment tax relief under section 530(a) of the 1978 Act that would otherwise be available to a taxpayer with respect to those workers who are determined to be employees of the taxpayer under the usual common law rules. Section 530(d) applies to remuneration paid and services rendered after December 31, 1986.

The Conference Report on the 1986 Act discusses the effect of Section 530(d) as follows:

The Senate amendment applies whether the services of [technical service workers] are provided by the firm to only one client during the year or to more than one client, and whether or not such individuals have been designated or treated by the technical services firm as independent contractors, sole proprietors, partners, or employees of a personal service corporation controlled by such individual. The effect of the provision cannot be avoided by claims that such technical service personnel are employees of personal service corporations controlled by such personnel. For example, an engineer retained by a technical services firm to provide services to a manufacturer cannot avoid the effect of this provision by organizing a corporation that he or she controls and then claiming to provide services as an employee of that corporation.

... [T]he provision does not apply with respect to individuals who are classified, under the generally applicable common law standards, as employees of a business that is a client of the technical services firm.

2 H.R. Rep. No. 99-841 (Conf. Rep.), 99th Cong., 2d Sess. II-834 to 835 (1986).

APPENDIX C-5

Business or Hobby?

[IRS regulation §1.183-2 attempts to cover when the IRS will consider an enterprise to be a business rather than a hobby. (For a discussion of this issue, see Chapter 5.) While it is not the easiest reading, the examples in this regulation may give you some idea how the IRS thinks. Remember that there is a plethora of court cases, which may provide even better guidance, in this area. You may want your tax advisor to locate cases in which the situation is similar to your own.

These guidelines usually will apply to circumstances in which the three-out-of-five-profitable-years test has not been met. In other words, if you pass that safe-harbor test, you will not need to be too concerned with what is here. However, there are exceptions, and if you need losses to apply to other income, chances are you do not want to pass the three-of-five-years profits test.]

REGULATION §1.183-2. ACTIVITY NOT ENGAGED IN FOR PROFIT DEFINED

(a) In General
For purposes of section 183 and the regulations thereunder, the term "activity not engaged in for profit" means any activity other than one with respect to which deductions are allowable for the taxable year under section 162 or under paragraph, (1) or (2) of section 212. Deductions are allowable under section 162 for expenses of carrying on activities which constitute a trade or business of the taxpayer and under section 212 for expenses incurred in connection with activities engaged in for

the production or collection of income or for the management, conservation, or maintenance of property held for the production of income. Except as provided in section 183 and §1.183-1, no deductions are allowable for expenses incurred in connection with activities which are not engaged in for profit. Thus, for example, deductions are not allowable under section 162 or 212 for activities which are carried on primarily as a sport, hobby or for recreation. The determination whether an activity is engaged in for profit is to be made by reference to objective standards, taking into account all of the facts and circumstances of each case. Although a reasonable expectation of profit is not required, the facts and circumstances must indicate that the taxpayer entered into the activity, or continued the activity, with the objective of making a profit. In determining whether such an objective exists, it may be sufficient that there is a small chance of making a large profit. Thus it may be found that an investor in a wildcat oil well who incurs very substantial expenditures is in the venture for profit even though the expectation of a profit might be considered unreasonable. In determining whether an activity is engaged in for profit, greater weight is given to the objective facts than to the taxpayer's mere statement of his intent.

(b) Relevant Factors

In determining whether an activity is engaged in for profit, all facts and circumstances with respect to the activity are taken into account. No one factor is determinative in making this determination. In addition, it is not intended that only the factors described in this paragraph are to be taken into account in making the determination, or that a determination is to be made on the basis that the number of factors (whether or not listed in this paragraph) indicating a lack of profit objective exceeds the number of factors indicating a profit objective, or vice versa. Among the factors which should normally be taken into account are the following:

(1) *Manner in which the taxpayer carries on the activity.* The fact that the taxpayer carries on the activity in a business-like manner and maintains complete and accurate books and records may indicate that the activity is engaged in for profit. Similarly, where an activity is carried on in a manner

substantially similar to other activities of the same nature which are profitable, a profit motive may be indicated. A change of operating methods, adoption of new techniques or abandonment of unprofitable methods in a manner consistent with an intent to improve profitability may also indicate a profit motive.

(2) *The expertise of the taxpayer or his advisors.* Preparation for the activity by extensive study of its accepted business, economic, and scientific practices, or consultation with those who are expert therein, may indicate that the taxpayer has a profit motive where the taxpayer carries on the activity in accordance with such practices. Where a taxpayer has such preparation or procures such expert advice, but does not carry on the activity in accordance with such practices, a lack of intent to derive profit may be indicated unless it appears that the taxpayer is attempting to develop new or superior techniques which may result in profits from the activity.

(3) *The time and effort expended by the taxpayer in carrying on the activity.* The fact that the taxpayer devotes much of his personal time and effort to carrying on an activity, particularly if the activity does not have substantial personal or recreational aspects, may indicate an intention to derive a profit. A taxpayer's withdrawal from another occupation to devote most of his energies to the activity may also be evidence that the activity is engaged in for profit. The fact that the taxpayer devotes a limited amount of time to an activity does not necessarily indicate a lack of profit motive where the taxpayer employs competent and qualified persons to carry on such activity.

(4) *Expectation that assets used in activity may appreciate in value.* The term "profit" encompasses appreciation in the value of assets, such as land, used in the activity. Thus, the taxpayer may intend to derive a profit from the operation of the activity, and may also intend that, even if no profit from current operations is derived an overall profit will result when appreciation in the value of land used in the activity is realized since income from the activity together with the appreciation of land will exceed expenses of operation. . . .

(5) *The success of the taxpayer in carrying on other similar or dissimilar activities.* The fact that the taxpayer has engaged in similar activities in the past and converted them from unprofitable to profitable enterprises may indicate that he is

engaged in the present activity for profit, even though the activity is presently unprofitable.

(6) *The taxpayer's history of income or losses with respect to the activity.* A series of losses during the initial or start-up stage of an activity may not necessarily be an indication that the activity is not engaged in for profit. However, where losses continue to be sustained beyond the period which customarily is necessary to bring the operation to profitable status such continued losses, if not explainable, as due to customary business risks or reverses, may be indicative that the activity is not being engaged in for profit. If losses are sustained because of unforeseen or fortuitous circumstances which are beyond the control of the taxpayer, such as drought, disease, fire, theft, weather damages, other involuntary conversions, or depressed market conditions, such losses would not be an indication that the activity is not engaged in for profit. A series of years in which net income was realized would of course be strong evidence that the activity is engaged in for profit.

(7) *The amount of occasional profits, if any, which are earned.* The amount of profits in relation to the amount of losses incurred, and in relation to the amount of the taxpayer's investment and the value of the assets used in the activity, may provide useful criteria in determining the taxpayer's intent. An occasional small profit from an activity generating large losses, or from an activity in which the taxpayer has made a large investment, would not generally be determinative that the activity is engaged in for profit. However, substantial profit, though only occasional, would generally be indicative that an activity is engaged in for profit, where the investment or losses are comparatively small. Moreover, an opportunity to earn a substantial ultimate profit in a highly speculative venture is ordinarily sufficient to indicate that the activity is engaged in for profit even though losses or only occasional small profits are actually generated.

(8) *The financial status of the taxpayer.* The fact that the taxpayer does not have substantial income or capital from sources other than the activity may indicate that an activity is engaged in for profit. Substantial income from sources other than the activity (particularly if the losses from the activity generate substantial tax benefits) may indicate that the activity is not en-

gaged in for profit especially if there are personal or recreational elements involved.

(9) *Elements of personal pleasure or recreation.* The presence of personal motives in carrying on of an activity may indicate that the activity is not engaged in for profit, especially where there are recreational or personal elements involved. On the other hand, a profit motivation may be indicated where an activity lacks any appeal other than profit. It is not, however, necessary that an activity be engaged in with the exclusive intention of deriving a profit or with the intention of maximizing profits. For example, the availability of other investments which would yield a higher return, or which would be more likely to be profitable, is not evidence that an activity is not engaged in for profit. An activity will not be treated as not engaged in for profit merely because the taxpayer has purposes or motivations other than solely to make a profit. Also, the fact that the taxpayer derives personal pleasure from engaging in the activity is not sufficient to cause the activity to be classified as not engaged in for profit if the activity is in fact engaged in for profit as evidenced by other factors whether or not listed in this paragraph.

(c) Example

The provisions of this section may be illustrated by the following examples:

Example (1)   The taxpayer inherited a farm from her husband in an area which was becoming largely residential, and is now nearly all so. The farm had never made a profit before the taxpayer inherited it, and the farm has since had substantial losses in each year. The decedent from whom the taxpayer inherited the farm was a stockbroker, and he also left the taxpayer substantial stock holdings which yield large income from dividends. The taxpayer lives on an area of the farm which is set aside exclusively for living purposes. A farm manager is employed to operate the farm, but modern methods are not used in operating the farm. The taxpayer was born and raised on a farm, and expresses a strong preference for living on a farm. The taxpayer's activity of farming, based on all the facts and circumstances, could be found not to be engaged in for profit.

Example (2)   The taxpayer is a wealthy individual who is greatly interested in philosophy. During the past thirty years he has written and published at his own expense several pamphlets, and he has engaged in extensive lecturing activity, advocating and disseminating his ideas. He has made a profit from these activities in only occasional years, and the profits in those years were small in relation to the amounts of the losses in all other years. The taxpayer has very sizable income from securities (dividends and capital gains) which constitutes the principal source of his livelihood. The activity of lecturing, publishing pamphlets, and disseminating his ideas is not an activity engaged in by the taxpayer for profit.

Example (3)   The taxpayer, very successful in the business of retailing soft drinks, raises dogs and horses. He began raising a particular breed of dogs many years ago in the belief that the breed was in danger of declining, and he has raised and sold the dogs in each year since. The taxpayer recently began raising and racing thoroughbred horses. The losses from the taxpayer's dog and horse activities have increased in magnitude over the years, and he has not made a profit on these operations during any of the last fifteen years. The taxpayer generally sells the dogs only to friends, does not advertise the dogs for sale, and shows the dogs only infrequently. The taxpayer races his horses only at the "prestige" tracks at which he combines his racing activities with social and recreational activities. The horse and dog operations are conducted at a large residential property on which the taxpayer also lives, which includes substantial living quarters and attractive recreational facilities for the taxpayer and his family. Since (i) the activity of raising dogs and horses and racing the horses is of a sporting and recreational nature, (ii) the taxpayer has substantial income from his business activities of retailing soft drinks, (iii) the horse and dog operations are not conducted in a businesslike manner, and (iv) such operations have a continuous record of losses, it could be determined that the horse and dog activities of the taxpayer are not engaged in for profit.

Example (4)   The taxpayer inherited a farm of 65 acres from his parents when they died six years ago. The taxpayer moved to the farm from his house in a small nearby town, and he operates it in the same manner as his parents operated the farm before they died. The taxpayer is employed as a skilled machine operator in a nearby factory, for which he is paid approximately $8,500 per year. The farm has not been profitable for the past 15 years because of rising costs of operating farms in general, and because of the decline in the price of the produce of this farm in particular. The taxpayer consults the local agent of the State agricultural service from time-to-time, and the suggestions of the agent have generally been followed. The manner in which the farm is operated by the taxpayer is substantially similar to the manner in which farms of similar size, and which grow similar crops in the area are operated. Many of these other farms do not make profits. The taxpayer does much of the required labor around the farm himself, such as fixing fences, planting crops, etc. The activity of farming could be found, based on all the facts and circumstances, to be engaged in by the taxpayer for profit.

Example (5)   A, an independent oil and gas operator, frequently engages in the activity of searching for oil on undeveloped and unexplored land which is not near proven fields. He does so in a manner substantially similar to that of others who engage in the same activity. The chances, based on the experience of A and others who engaged in this activity, are strong that A will not find a commercially profitable oil deposit when he drills on land not established geologically to be proven oil bearing land. However, on the rare occasions that these activities do result in discovering a well, the operator generally realizes a very large return from such activity. Thus, there is a small chance that A will make a large profit from his oil exploration activity. Under these circumstances, A is engaged in the activity of oil drilling for profit.

Example (6)   C, a chemist, is employed by a large chemical company and is engaged in a wide variety of basic research projects for his employer. Although he does no work for his employer with respect to the development of new plastics, he has always been interested in such development and has outfitted a workshop in his home at his own expense which he uses to experiment in the field. He has patented several developments at his own expense but as yet has realized no income from his inventions or from such patents. C conducts his research on a regular, systematic basis, incurs fees to secure consultation on his projects from time to time, and makes extensive efforts to "market" his developments. C has devoted substantial time and expense in an effort to develop a plastic sufficiently hard, durable, and malleable that it could be used in lieu of sheet metal in many major applications, such as automobile bodies. Although there may be only a small chance that C will invent new plastics, the return from any such development would be so large that it induces C to incur the costs of his experimental work. C is sufficiently qualified by his background that there is some reasonable basis for his experimental activities. C's experimental work does not involve substantial personal or recreational aspects and is conducted in an effort to find practical applications for his work. Under these circumstances, C may be found to be engaged in the experimental activities for profit.

APPENDIX C-6

Some IRS Rules on Business Entertainment

[In Chapter 5 we discussed the ever-present problem of making sure that meals and entertainment qualify as business expenses. What follows is what the IRS says in attempting to define "directly related" and "associated with" entertainment expense. It is from IRS Publication 463, *Travel, Entertainment, and Gift Expenses.*]

DIRECTLY RELATED TEST
To meet the directly-related test for entertainment expenses (including entertainment-related meals), you must show that:

1. The main purpose of the combined business and entertainment was the active conduct of business,
2. You did engage in business with the person during the entertainment period, and
3. You had more than a general expectation of getting income or some other specific business benefit at some future time.

Business is not considered to be the main purpose when business and entertainment are combined on hunting or fishing trips, or on yachts or other pleasure boats, unless you can show otherwise. Even if you show that business was the main purpose, you generally cannot deduct the expenses for the use of an entertainment facility. . . . You must consider all the facts including the nature of the business transacted and the reasons for conducting business during the entertainment. It is not necessary to devote more time to business than to entertainment. However, if the business discussion is only incidental to the entertainment, it is not directly related. You are not required to show that business income or other business benefit actually resulted from each entertainment expense.

Clear Business Setting

If the entertainment takes place in a clear business setting and is for your business or work, the expenses are considered directly related to your business or work. The following situations are examples of entertainment in a clear business setting:

1. Entertainment in a hospitality room at a convention where business goodwill is created through the display or discussion of business products,

2. Entertainment that is mainly a price rebate on the sale of your products (such as a restaurant owner providing an occasional free meal to a loyal customer), and

3. Entertainment of a clear business nature occurring under circumstances where there is no meaningful personal or social relationship between you and the persons entertained. An example is entertainment of business and civic leaders at the opening of a new hotel or play when the purpose is to get business publicity rather than to create or maintain the goodwill of the persons entertained.

Expenses Not Considered Directly Related

Expenses generally are not considered directly related when entertainment occurs where, because of substantial distractions, there is little or no possibility of engaging in the active conduct of business. Examples are meetings at night clubs, theaters, sporting events, or essentially social gatherings. This includes cocktail parties, or meetings with a group that includes persons other than business associates at places such as cocktail lounges, country clubs, golf clubs, athletic clubs, or vacation resorts. You may prove that the entertainment is directly related by showing that you engaged in a substantial business discussion during the entertainment.

ASSOCIATED TEST

Even if your expenses do not meet the directly-related test, they may meet the associated test. To meet the associated test for entertainment expenses (including entertainment-related meals), you must show that the entertainment is associated with your trade or business and that it directly precedes or follows a substantial business discussion (defined below).

Generally, any ordinary and necessary expense is associated with the active conduct of your trade or business if you can show that you had a clear business purpose for having the expense. The purpose may be to get new business or to encourage the continuation of an existing business relationship. However, if part of the entertainment expense is for persons not closely connected with your guests who attended the substantial business discussion, that part of the expense would not qualify for the associated test.

Substantial Business Discussion

Whether a business discussion is substantial depends on all the facts of each case. You must show that you or your representative actively engaged in a discussion, meeting, negotiation, or other business transaction to get income or some other specific business benefit. You may be able to deduct goodwill entertainment.

The meeting does not have to be for any specified length of time, but you must show that the business discussion was substantial in relation to the meal or entertainment. It is not necessary that you devote more time to business than to entertainment. You do not have to discuss business during the meal or entertainment.

Meetings at Conventions

You are considered to have a substantial business discussion if you attend meetings at a convention or similar event, or at a trade or business meeting sponsored and conducted by a business or professional organization. However, you must attend the convention or meeting to further your trade or business. In addition, the organization that sponsors the convention or meeting must schedule a program of business activities that is the main activity of the convention or meeting.

Directly Before or After Business Discussion

Entertainment that is held on the same day as the business discussion is considered to be held directly before or after the business discussion. However, if the entertainment and the business discussion are not held on the same day, you must consider the facts of each case to see if the associated test is met. Among the facts to consider are the place, date, and duration of the business discussion.

Also, if you or your business associates are from out of town, you must consider the dates of arrival and departure, and the reasons the entertainment and the discussion did not take place on the same day.

Example   A group of business associates comes from out of town to your place of business to hold a substantial business discussion. If you entertain those business guests and their spouses on the evening before the business discussion, or on the evening of the day following the business discussion, the entertainment generally is considered to be held directly before or after the discussion. The expense meets the associated test.

APPENDIX C-7

Low Tax on Multiple Corporations

[These regulations outline situations when several somewhat related C corporations can take advantage of being taxed at only 15 percent. (That can happen if they can avoid being classified as a controlled group of corporations, either as a parent-subsidiary or brother-sister setup.) Much of the regulation is barely, if at all, comprehensible, but the examples are helpful. If you try to cut taxes by the brother-sister C corporation route, you also need to be aware that the rules change if the stockholders are themselves related. (Setting up several corporations and transferring some of the stock to your spouse and children usually will not work, but there are exceptions.)

The section of Regulation §1.1563-1 that is reprinted here defines what is meant by "controlled corporation" in those situations that most business people might run into. Part of Regulation §1.1563-3 is also reprinted. The part included here sets out the situations in which family members might own stock in some of the same corporations without those corporations being considered controlled corporations. (Being a group of "controlled" corporations is not good, for it means only *one* lot of $50,000 will be taxed at only 15 percent. If they are not "controlled," *each* corporation is favored with a tax of only 15 percent on the first $50,000 of taxable income.)

If nothing else, perusing this esoteric material will reveal that it is possible to be taxed on more than $50,000 of corporate income at only 15 percent. Also, it should convince you that careful planning of multiple corporations, *with professional help*, can save you many dollars. Especially, if other individuals have ownership interests in your business, you may be in a

205

position to plan around the restrictions that are in these regulations and pay only 15 percent tax on hundreds of thousands of corporate income dollars.

(See Chapter 7 for discussion of the multiple corporation concept.)]

IRS REGULATION §1.1563-1. DEFINITION OF CONTROLLED GROUP OF CORPORATIONS AND COMPONENT MEMBERS

(a) Controlled Group of Corporations

(1) In general. For purposes of sections 1561 through 1563 and the regulations thereunder, the term "controlled group of corporations" means any group of corporations which is either a "parent-subsidiary controlled group" (as defined in subparagraph (2) of this paragraph), a "brother-sister controlled group" (as defined in subparagraph (3) of this paragraph), a "combined group" (as defined in subparagraph (4) of this paragraph), or an "insurance group" (as defined in subparagraph (5) of this paragraph). For the exclusion of certain stock for purposes of applying the definitions contained in this paragraph, see section 1563(c) and §1.1563-2.

(2) *Parent-subsidiary controlled group—*

(i)   The term "parent-subsidiary controlled group" means one or more chains of corporations connected through stock ownership with a common parent corporation if—

(a) Stock possessing at least 80 percent of the total combined voting power of all classes of stock entitled to vote or at least 80 percent of the total value of shares of all classes of stock of each of the corporations, except the common parent corporation, is owned (directly and with the application of paragraph (b)(1) of §1.1563-3, relating to options) by one or more of the other corporations; and

(b) The common parent corporation owns (directly and with the application of paragraph (b)(1) of §1.1563-3, relating to options) stock possessing at least 80 per-

cent of the total combined voting power of all classes
of stock entitled to vote or at least 80 percent of the
total value of shares of all classes of stock of at least
one of the other corporations excluding, in computing such voting power or value, stock owned directly
by such other corporations.

(ii) The definition of a parent-subsidiary controlled group
of corporations may be illustrated by the following
examples:

Example (1). P Corporation owns stock possessing 80 percent of the total combined voting power of all classes of stock
entitled to vote of S Corporation. P is the common parent of a
parent-subsidiary controlled group consisting of member corporations P and S.

Example (2). Assume the same facts as in example (1). Assume further that S owns stock possessing 80 percent of the total
value of shares of all classes of stock of T Corporation. P is the
common parent of a parent-subsidiary controlled group consisting of member corporations P, S, and T. The result would be
the same if P, rather than S, owned the T stock.

Example (3). L Corporation owns 80 percent of the only class
of stock of M Corporation and M in turn owns 40 percent of the
only class of stock of O Corporation. L also owns 80 percent of
the only class of stock of N Corporation and N in turn, owns 40
percent of the only class of stock of O. L is the common parent
of a parent-subsidiary controlled group consisting of member
corporations L, M, N, and O.

Example (4). X Corporation owns 75 percent of the only class
of stock of Y and Z Corporations; Y owns all the remaining stock
of Z; and Z owns all the remaining stock of Y. Since inter-
company stockholdings are excluded (that is, are not treated as
outstanding) for purposes of determining whether X owns stock
possessing at least 80 percent of the voting power or value of at
least one of the other corporations, X is treated as the owner of
stock possessing 100 percent of the voting power and value of

Y and of Z for purposes of subdivision (i)(b) of this subparagraph. Also, stock possessing 100 percent of the voting power and value of Y and Z is owned by the other corporations in the group within the meaning of subdivision (i)(a) of this subparagraph. (X and Y together own stock possessing 100 percent of the voting power and value of Z, and X and Z together own stock possessing 100 percent of the voting power and value of Y.) Therefore, X is the common parent of a parent-subsidiary controlled group of corporations consisting of member corporations X, Y, and Z.

(3) *Brother-sister controlled group*

(i) The term "brother-sister controlled group" means two or more corporations if the same five or fewer persons who are individuals, estates, or trusts own (directly and with the application of the rules contained in paragraph (b) of §1-1563-3), stock possessing—

(a) At least 80 percent of the total combined voting power of all classes of stock entitled to vote or at least 80 percent of the total value of shares of all classes of the stock of each corporation; and

(b) More than 50 percent of the total combined voting power of all classes of stock entitled to vote or more than 50 percent of the total value of shares of all classes of stock of each corporation, taking into account the stock ownership of each such person only to the extent such stock ownership is identical with respect to each such corporation.

The five or fewer persons whose stock ownership is considered for purposes of the 80 percent requirement must be the same persons whose stock ownership is considered for purposes of the more-than-50 percent requirement.

(ii) The principles of this subparagraph may be illustrated by the following examples:

Example (1). The outstanding stock of corporations P, Q, R, S, and T, which have only one class of stock outstanding, is owned by the following unrelated individuals:

Individuals	Corporations					Identical Ownership
	P (%)	Q (%)	R (%)	S (%)	T (%)	
A	55	51	55	55	55	51
B	45	49	-	-	-	(45 in P and Q)
C	-	-	45	-	-	-
D	-	-	-	45	-	-
E	-	-	-	-	45	-
Total	100	100	100	100	100	

Corporations P and Q are members of a brother-sister controlled group of corporations. Although the more-than-50 percent identical ownership requirement is met for all 5 corporations, corporations R, S, and T are not members because at least 80 percent of the stock of each of those corporations is not owned by the same 5 or fewer persons whose stock ownership is considered for purposes of the more-than-50 percent identical ownership requirement.

Example (2).   The outstanding stock of corporations U and V, which have only one class of stock outstanding, is owned by the following unrelated individuals:

Individuals	Corporations	
	U (%)	V (%)
A	12	12
B	12	12
C	12	12
D	12	12
E	13	13
F	13	13

	Corporations	
Individuals	U (%)	V (%)
G	13	13
H	13	13
Totals	100	100

Any group of five of the shareholders will own more than 50 percent of the stock in each corporation, in identical holdings. However, U and V are not members of brother-sister controlled group because at least 80 percent of the stock of each corporation is not owned by the same five or fewer persons.

Example (3). Corporations X and Y each have two classes of stock outstanding, voting common and non-voting common. (None of this stock is excluded from the definition of stock under section 1563(c).) Unrelated individuals A and B own the following percentages of the class of stock entitled to vote (voting) and of the total value of shares of all classes of stock (value) in each of corporations X and Y:

	Corporations	
Individuals	X	Y
A	100% voting 60% value	75% voting 60% value
B	0% voting 10% value	25% voting 10% value

No other shareholder of Y owns (or is considered to own) any stock in Y. X and Y are a brother-sister controlled group of corporations. The group meets the more-than-50 percent ownership requirements because A and B own more than 50 percent of the total value of shares of all classes of stock of X and Y in identical holdings. (The group also meets the more-than-50 percent ownership requirement because of A's voting stock ownership.) The group meets the 80 percent requirement because A and B own at least 80 percent of the total combined voting power of all classes of stock entitled to vote.

Example (4).   Assume the same facts as in example (3) except that the value of the stock owned by A and B is not more than 50 percent of the total value of shares of all classes of stock of each corporation in identical holdings. X and Y are not a brother-sister controlled group of corporations. The group meets the more-than-50 percent ownership requirement because A owns more than 50 percent of the total combined voting power of the voting stock of each corporation. For purposes of the 80 percent requirement, B's voting stock in Y cannot be combined with A's voting stock in Y since B, who does not own any voting stock in X, is not a person whose ownership is considered for purposes of the more-than-50 percent requirement. Because no other shareholder owns stock in both X and Y, these other shareholders' stock ownership is not counted towards meeting either the more-than-50 percent ownership requirement or the 80 percent ownership requirement.

(iii) [Paragraph omitted]

(4) *Combined group.*

(i)   The term "combined group" means any group of three or more corporations, if—

(a) Each such corporation is a member of either a parent-subsidiary controlled group of corporations or a brother-sister controlled group of corporations, and

(b) At least one of such corporations is the common parent of a parent-subsidiary controlled group and also is a member of a brother-sister controlled group.

(ii) The definition of a combined group of corporations may be illustrated by the following examples:

Example (1).   Smith, an individual, owns stock possessing 80 percent of the total combined voting power of all classes of the stock of corporations X and Y. Y, in turn, owns stock possessing 80 percent of the total combined voting power of all classes of the stock of corporation Z. Since—

(a) X, Y, and Z are each members of either a parent-subsidiary or brother-sister controlled group of corporations, and
(b) Y is the common parent of a parent-subsidiary controlled group of corporations consisting of Y and Z, and also is a member of a brother-sister controlled group of corporations consisting of X and Y,

X, Y, and Z are members of the same combined group.

Example (2).   Assume the same facts as in example (1), and further assume that corporation X owns 80 percent of the total value of shares of all classes of stock of corporation T. X, Y, Z, and T are members of the same combined group.
[The regulation continues with a discussion of controlled insurance groups, overlapping corporations, and other specialized rules.]

IRS REGULATION §1.1563-3. RULES FOR DETERMINING STOCK OWNERSHIP
[Excerpt from the full regulation that includes complicated rules on attribution of ownership from stock owned by partnerships and corporations.]

(5) *Spouse*

(i)   Except as provided in subdivision (ii) of this subparagraph, an individual shall be considered to own the stock owned, directly or indirectly, by or for his spouse other than a spouse who is legally separated from the individual under a decree of divorce whether interlocutory or final, or a decree of separate maintenance.

(ii)   An individual shall not be considered to own stock in a corporation owned, directly or indirectly, by or for his spouse on any day of a taxable year of such corporation provided that each of the following conditions are satisfied with respect to such taxable year:

(a) Such individual does not, at any time during such taxable year, own directly any stock in such corporation.

(b) Such individual is not a member of the board of directors or an employee of such corporation and does not participate in the management of such corporation at any time during such taxable year.

(c) Not more than 50 percent of such corporation's gross income for taxable year was derived from royalties, rents, dividends, interest, and annuities.

(d) Such stock in such corporation is not, at any time during such taxable year subject to conditions which substantially restrict or limit the spouse's right to dispose of such stock and which run in favor of the individual or his children who have not attained the age of 21 years. The principles of paragraph (b)(2)(iii) of 1.1563-2 shall apply in determining whether a condition is a condition described in the preceding sentence.

(iii) For purposes of subdivision (ii)(c) of this subparagraph, the gross income of a corporation for a taxable year shall be determined under section 61 and the regulations thereunder. The terms "royalties", "rents", "dividends", "interest", and "annuities" shall have the same meanings such terms are given for purposes of section 1244(c). See paragraph (e)(I)(ii), (iii), (iv), (v), and (vi) of §1.1244(c)-1.

(6) Children, grandchildren, parents, and grandparents

(i) An individual shall be considered to own the stock owned, directly or indirectly, by or for his children who have not attained the age of 21 years, and, if the individual has not attained the age of 21 years, the stock owned, directly or indirectly, by or for his parents.

(ii) If an individual owns (directly, and with the application of the rules of this paragraph but without regard to this subdivision) stock possessing more than 50 percent of the total combined voting power of all classes of stock entitled to vote or more than 50 percent of the total value of shares of all classes of stock in a corporation, then such individual shall be considered to own the stock in such corporation owned, directly or indirectly, by or for his parents, grandparents, grandchildren, and children who have attained the age of 21 years. In determining whether the stock owned by an individual possesses the requisite percentage of the total combined voting power of all classes of stock entitled to vote of a corporation, see paragraph (a)(6) of §1.1563-1.

(iii) For purposes of section 1563, and § §1.1563-1 through 1.1563-4, a legally adopted child of an individual shall be treated as a child of such individual by blood.

(iv) The provisions of this subparagraph may be illustrated by the following example:

Example-(a) *Facts.*   Individual F owns directly 40 shares of the 100 shares of the only class of stock of Z Corporation. His son, M (20 years of age), owns directly 30 shares of such stock, and his son, A (30 years of age), owns directly 20 shares of such stock. The remaining 10 shares of the Z stock are owned by an unrelated person.

(b) F's ownership. Individual F owns 40 shares of the Z stock directly and is considered to own the 30 shares of Z stock owned directly by M. Since, for purposes of the more-than-50-percent stock ownership test contained in subdivision (ii) of this subparagraph, F is treated as owning 70 shares or 70 percent of the total voting power and value of the Z stock, he is also considered as owning the 20 shares owned by his adult son, A. Accordingly, F is considered as owning a total of 90 shares of the Z stock.

(c) M's ownership. Minor son, M, owns 30 shares of the Z stock directly, and is considered to own the 40 shares of Z stock owned directly by his father, F. However, M is not considered to own the 20 shares of Z stock owned directly by his brother, A, and constructively by F, because stock constructively owned by F by reason of family attribution is not considered as owned by him for purposes of making another member of his family

the constructive owner of such stock. See paragraph (c)(2) of this section. Accordingly, M owns and is considered as owning a total of 70 shares of the Z stock.

(d) A's ownership. Adult son, A, owns 20 shares of the Z stock directly. Since, for purposes of the more-than-50-percent stock ownership test contained in subdivision (ii) of this subparagraph, A is treated as owning only the Z stock which he owns directly, he does not satisfy the condition precedent for the attribution of Z stock from his father. Accordingly, A is treated as owning only the 20 shares of Z stock which he owns directly.

APPENDIX D

Federal Tax Forms

The following pages contain copies of tax forms that have been mentioned, or are pertinent to, subjects covered in this book. They may help you envision what is entailed in the tax reporting of a new business or a new form for your present business. The forms are, in order:

Schedule C   Profit or Loss From Business
(Sole Proprietorship)
(This schedule becomes part of Form 1040, U.S. Individual Income Tax Return.)

Form 1065   U.S. Partnership Return of Income

Form 1120   U.S. Corporation Income Tax Return
(For C corporations.)

Form 1120S   U.S. Income Tax Return for an S Corporation

Form 4562   Depreciation and Amortization
(This form is used with any other form on which you can deduct depreciation.)

Form 8829   Expenses for Business Use of Your Home
(This form supports the deduction on a Schedule C, line 30.)

Form 6251   Alternative Minimum Tax—Individuals
(This is attached to Form 1040.)

Form 8832   Entity Classification Election

Form 6765   Credit for Increasing Research Activities, with Instructions

SS-8   Determination of Employee Work Status for Purposes of Federal Employment Taxes and Income Tax Withholding
(You *may* file this form to obtain a ruling as to whether you can be considered a self-employed contractor instead of an employee. It is not necessary to file this form if you are confident that you do qualify as self-employed.)

| SCHEDULE C
(Form 1040)

Department of the Treasury
Internal Revenue Service (99) | **Profit or Loss From Business**
(Sole Proprietorship)
▶ Partnerships, joint ventures, etc., must file Form 1065 or Form 1065-B.
▶ Attach to Form 1040 or Form 1041. ▶ See Instructions for Schedule C (Form 1040). | OMB No 1545-0074
2000
Attachment
Sequence No. 09 |

Name of proprietor | Social security number (SSN)

| A | Principal business or profession, including product or service (see page C-1 of the instructions) | B Enter code from pages C-7 & 8 ▶ |

| C | Business name. If no separate business name, leave blank. | D Employer ID number (EIN), if any |

E   Business address (including suite or room no.) ▶ ....
     City, town or post office, state, and ZIP code

F   Accounting method: **(1)** ☐ Cash   **(2)** ☐ Accrual   **(3)** ☐ Other (specify) ▶ ....

G   Did you "materially participate" in the operation of this business during 2000? If "No," see page C-2 for limit on losses   ☐ Yes ☐ No

H   If you started or acquired this business during 2000, check here . . . . ▶ ☐

Part I Income

1	Gross receipts or sales. **Caution.** If this income was reported to you on Form W-2 and the "Statutory employee" box on that form was checked, see page C-2 and check here . . . . ▶ ☐	1	
2	Returns and allowances	2	
3	Subtract line 2 from line 1	3	
4	Cost of goods sold (from line 42 on page 2)	4	
5	**Gross profit.** Subtract line 4 from line 3	5	
6	Other income, including Federal and state gasoline or fuel tax credit or refund (see page C-2) . . .	6	
7	**Gross income.** Add lines 5 and 6 . . . . ▶	7	

Part II Expenses. Enter expenses for business use of your home **only** on line 30.

8	Advertising	8		19	Pension and profit-sharing plans	19	
9	Bad debts from sales or services (see page C-3) . .	9		20	Rent or lease (see page C-4):		
				a	Vehicles, machinery, and equipment .	20a	
10	Car and truck expenses (see page C-3)	10		b	Other business property . .	20b	
11	Commissions and fees . .	11		21	Repairs and maintenance . .	21	
12	Depletion	12		22	Supplies (not included in Part III) .	22	
13	Depreciation and section 179 expense deduction (not included in Part III) (see page C-3) . .	13		23	Taxes and licenses	23	
				24	Travel, meals, and entertainment:		
				a	Travel	24a	
14	Employee benefit programs (other than on line 19) . . .	14		b	Meals and entertainment		
15	Insurance (other than health) .	15		c	Enter nondeductible amount included on line 24b (see page C-5) .		
16	Interest:			d	Subtract line 24c from line 24b .	24d	
a	Mortgage (paid to banks, etc) .	16a		25	Utilities	25	
b	Other	16b		26	Wages (less employment credits) .	26	
17	Legal and professional services	17		27	Other expenses (from line 48 on page 2)	27	
18	Office expense	18					

28	**Total expenses** before expenses for business use of home. Add lines 8 through 27 in columns . . ▶	28	
29	Tentative profit (loss). Subtract line 28 from line 7	29	
30	Expenses for business use of your home. Attach **Form 8829**	30	
31	**Net profit or (loss).** Subtract line 30 from line 29. • If a profit, enter on **Form 1040, line 12,** and also on **Schedule SE, line 2** (statutory employees. see page C-5). Estates and trusts, enter on Form 1041, line 3. • If a loss, you **must** go to line 32.	31	
32	If you have a loss, check the box that describes your investment in this activity (see page C-5). • If you checked 32a, enter the loss on **Form 1040, line 12,** and **also** on **Schedule SE, line 2** (statutory employees, see page C-5). Estates and trusts, enter on Form 1041, line 3. • If you checked 32b, you **must** attach **Form 6198.**	32a ☐ All investment is at risk. 32b ☐ Some investment is not at risk.	

For Paperwork Reduction Act Notice, see Form 1040 instructions.   Cat No. 11334P   Schedule C (Form 1040) 2000

220 APPENDIX D

Part III   **Cost of Goods Sold** (see page C-6)

33	Method(s) used to value closing inventory: **a** ☐ Cost **b** ☐ Lower of cost or market **c** ☐ Other (attach explanation)	
34	Was there any change in determining quantities, costs, or valuations between opening and closing inventory? If "Yes," attach explanation . . . . ☐ Yes ☐ No	
35	Inventory at beginning of year. If different from last year's closing inventory, attach explanation . . .	**35**
36	Purchases less cost of items withdrawn for personal use	**36**
37	Cost of labor. Do not include any amounts paid to yourself	**37**
38	Materials and supplies	**38**
39	Other costs	**39**
40	Add lines 35 through 39	**40**
41	Inventory at end of year	**41**
42	**Cost of goods sold.** Subtract line 41 from line 40. Enter the result here and on page 1, line 4 . . .	**42**

Part IV   **Information on Your Vehicle.** Complete this part **only** if you are claiming car or truck expenses on line 10 and are not required to file Form 4562 for this business. See the instructions for line 13 on page C-3 to find out if you must file.

43   When did you place your vehicle in service for business purposes? (month, day, year) ▶ ..../......./...... .

44   Of the total number of miles you drove your vehicle during 2000, enter the number of miles you used your vehicle for:

a   Business ....   **b** Commuting ....   **c** Other ....

45   Do you (or your spouse) have another vehicle available for personal use? . . . . ☐ Yes   ☐ No

46   Was your vehicle available for use during off-duty hours? . . . . ☐ Yes   ☐ No

47a   Do you have evidence to support your deduction? . . . . ☐ Yes   ☐ No

b   If "Yes," is the evidence written? . . . . ☐ Yes   ☐ No

Part V   **Other Expenses.** List below business expenses not included on lines 8–26 or line 30.

....	
....	
....	
....	
....	
....	
....	
....	

48	**Total other expenses.** Enter here and on page 1, line 27	**48**

Form **1065**		**U.S. Return of Partnership Income**		OMB No. 1545-0099
Department of the Treasury Internal Revenue Service		For calendar year 2000, or tax year beginning .... , 2000, and ending .... , 20..... . ▶ **See separate instructions.**		**2000**

A Principal business activity	Use the IRS label. Other- wise, print or type.	Name of partnership	D Employer identification number
B Principal product or service		Number, street, and room or suite no. If a P.O. box, see page 13 of the instructions	E Date business started
C Business code number		City or town, state, and ZIP code	F Total assets (see page 13 of the instructions) $

G Check applicable boxes: (1) ☐ Initial return (2) ☐ Final return (3) ☐ Change in address (4) ☐ Amended return
H Check accounting method: (1) ☐ Cash (2) ☐ Accrual (3) ☐ Other (specify) ▶ ....
I Number of Schedules K-1. Attach one for each person who was a partner at any time during the tax year ▶ ....

Caution: *Include only trade or business income and expenses on lines 1a through 22 below. See the instructions for more information.*

Income

1a Gross receipts or sales	**1a**	
b Less returns and allowances.	**1b**	**1c**
2 Cost of goods sold (Schedule A, line 8)		**2**
3 Gross profit. Subtract line 2 from line 1c		**3**
4 Ordinary income (loss) from other partnerships, estates, and trusts *(attach schedule)*. . .		**4**
5 Net farm profit (loss) *(attach Schedule F (Form 1040))*		**5**
6 Net gain (loss) from Form 4797, Part II, line 18.		**6**
7 Other income (loss) *(attach schedule)*		**7**
8 **Total income (loss).** Combine lines 3 through 7		**8**

Deductions (see page 14 of the instructions for limitations)

9 Salaries and wages (other than to partners) (less employment credits)		**9**
10 Guaranteed payments to partners		**10**
11 Repairs and maintenance		**11**
12 Bad debts		**12**
13 Rent		**13**
14 Taxes and licenses		**14**
15 Interest		**15**
16a Depreciation (if required, attach Form 4562)	**16a**	
b Less depreciation reported on Schedule A and elsewhere on return	**16b**	**16c**
17 Depletion **(Do not deduct oil and gas depletion.)**		**17**
18 Retirement plans, etc.		**18**
19 Employee benefit programs		**19**
20 Other deductions *(attach schedule)*		**20**
21 **Total deductions.** Add the amounts shown in the far right column for lines 9 through 20 .		**21**

22 **Ordinary income (loss)** from trade or business activities. Subtract line 21 from line 8 . .		**22**

Sign Here

Under penalties of perjury, I declare that I have examined this return, including accompanying schedules and statements, and to the best of my knowledge and belief, it is true, correct, and complete. Declaration of preparer (other than general partner or limited liability company member) is based on all information of which preparer has any knowledge

▶ _____ ▶ _____
Signature of general partner or limited liability company member   Date

Paid Preparer's Use Only

Preparer's signature ▶		Date	Check if self-employed ▶ ☐	Preparer's SSN or PTIN
Firm's name (or yours if self-employed), address, and ZIP code ▶			EIN ▶	
			Phone no. ( )	

For Paperwork Reduction Act Notice, see separate instructions.   Cat No. 11390Z   Form **1065** (2000)

Form 1065 (2000)   Page **2**

Schedule A   **Cost of Goods Sold** (see page 17 of the instructions)

1	Inventory at beginning of year	**1**
2	Purchases less cost of items withdrawn for personal use	**2**
3	Cost of labor	**3**
4	Additional section 263A costs *(attach schedule)*	**4**
5	Other costs *(attach schedule)*	**5**
6	**Total.** Add lines 1 through 5	**6**
7	Inventory at end of year	**7**
8	**Cost of goods sold.** Subtract line 7 from line 6. Enter here and on page 1, line 2	**8**

9a Check all methods used for valuing closing inventory:
    (i) ☐ Cost as described in Regulations section 1.471-3
    (ii) ☐ Lower of cost or market as described in Regulations section 1.471-4
    (iii) ☐ Other (specify method used and attach explanation) ▶ ....
  b Check this box if there was a writedown of "subnormal" goods as described in Regulations section 1.471-2(c). . . . ▶ ☐
  c Check this box if the LIFO inventory method was adopted this tax year for any goods *(if checked, attach Form 970)* . . ▶ ☐
  d Do the rules of section 263A (for property produced or acquired for resale) apply to the partnership? . . ☐ **Yes** ☐ **No**
  e Was there any change in determining quantities, cost, or valuations between opening and closing inventory? ☐ **Yes** ☐ **No**
    If "Yes," attach explanation.

Schedule B   **Other Information**

		Yes	No
1	What type of entity is filing this return? Check the applicable box:		

  a ☐ Domestic general partnership   **b** ☐ Domestic limited partnership
  c ☐ Domestic limited liability company   **d** ☐ Domestic limited liability partnership
  e ☐ Foreign partnership   **f** ☐ Other ▶ ....

2 Are any partners in this partnership also partnerships? . . . .

3 During the partnership's tax year, did the partnership own any interest in another partnership or in any foreign entity that was disregarded as an entity separate from its owner under Regulations sections 301.7701-2 and 301.7701-3? If yes, see instructions for required attachment . . . .

4 Is this partnership subject to the consolidated audit procedures of sections 6221 through 6233? If "Yes," see **Designation of Tax Matters Partner** below . . . .

5 Does this partnership meet **all three** of the following requirements?
  a The partnership's total receipts for the tax year were less than $250,000;
  b The partnership's total assets at the end of the tax year were less than $600,000; **and**
  c Schedules K-1 are filed with the return and furnished to the partners on or before the due date (including extensions) for the partnership return.
  If "Yes," the partnership is not required to complete Schedules L, M-1, and M-2; Item F on page 1 of Form 1065; or Item J on Schedule K-1 . . . .

6 Does this partnership have any foreign partners? . . . .

7 Is this partnership a publicly traded partnership as defined in section 469(k)(2)? . . . .

8 Has this partnership filed, or is it required to file, **Form 8264**, Application for Registration of a Tax Shelter? . .

9 At any time during calendar year 2000, did the partnership have an interest in or a signature or other authority over a financial account in a foreign country (such as a bank account, securities account, or other financial account)? See page 19 of the instructions for exceptions and filing requirements for Form TD F 90-22.1. If "Yes," enter the name of the foreign country. ▶ ....

10 During the tax year, did the partnership receive a distribution from, or was it the grantor of, or transferor to, a foreign trust? If "Yes," the partnership may have to file Form 3520. See page 19 of the instructions . . .

11 Was there a distribution of property or a transfer (e.g., by sale or death) of a partnership interest during the tax year? If "Yes," you may elect to adjust the basis of the partnership's assets under section 754 by attaching the statement described under **Elections Made By the Partnership** on page 7 of the instructions . . . . .

12 Enter the number of Forms 8865 attached to this return . . . . ▶ ....

Designation of Tax Matters Partner (see page 19 of the instructions)
Enter below the general partner designated as the tax matters partner (TMP) for the tax year of this return:

Name of designated TMP ▶	Identifying number of TMP ▶
Address of designated TMP ▶	

Form **1065** (2000)

Form 1065 (2000)   Page **3**

Schedule K	Partners' Shares of Income, Credits, Deductions, etc.		
	(a) Distributive share items		**(b) Total amount**

			(a) Distributive share items		(b) Total amount
Income (Loss)	1	Ordinary income (loss) from trade or business activities (page 1, line 22)	1	
	2	Net income (loss) from rental real estate activities *(attach Form 8825)*	2	
	3a	Gross income from other rental activities	3a	
	b	Expenses from other rental activities *(attach schedule)*	3b	
	c	Net income (loss) from other rental activities. Subtract line 3b from line 3a	3c	
	4	Portfolio income (loss): a Interest income	4a	
	b	Ordinary dividends	4b	
	c	Royalty income	4c	
	d	Net short-term capital gain (loss) *(attach Schedule D (Form 1065))*	4d	
	e	Net long-term capital gain (loss) *(attach Schedule D (Form 1065))*:		
		(1) 28% rate gain (loss) ▶ . . . . (2) Total for year . . . . . . ▶	4e(2)	
	f	Other portfolio income (loss) *(attach schedule)*	4f	
	5	Guaranteed payments to partners	5	
	6	Net section 1231 gain (loss) (other than due to casualty or theft) *(attach Form 4797)* . . .	6	
	7	Other income (loss) *(attach schedule)*	7	
Deductions	8	Charitable contributions *(attach schedule)*	8	
	9	Section 179 expense deduction *(attach Form 4562)*	9	
	10	Deductions related to portfolio income (itemize)	10	
	11	Other deductions *(attach schedule)*	11	
Credits	12a	Low-income housing credit:		
		(1) From partnerships to which section 42(j)(5) applies for property placed in service before 1990 .	12a(1)	
		(2) Other than on line 12a(1) for property placed in service before 1990	12a(2)	
		(3) From partnerships to which section 42(j)(5) applies for property placed in service after 1989	12a(3)	
		(4) Other than on line 12a(3) for property placed in service after 1989	12a(4)	
	b	Qualified rehabilitation expenditures related to rental real estate activities *(attach Form 3468)*	12b	
	c	Credits (other than credits shown on lines 12a and 12b) related to rental real estate activities	12c	
	d	Credits related to other rental activities	12d	
	13	Other credits	13	
Invest-ment Interest	14a	Interest expense on investment debts	14a	
	b	(1) Investment income included on lines 4a, 4b, 4c, and 4f above	14b(1)	
		(2) Investment expenses included on line 10 above.	14b(2)	
Self-Employ-ment	15a	Net earnings (loss) from self-employment	15a	
	b	Gross farming or fishing income	15b	
	c	Gross nonfarm income	15c	
Adjustments and Tax Preference Items	16a	Depreciation adjustment on property placed in service after 1986	16a	
	b	Adjusted gain or loss	16b	
	c	Depletion (other than oil and gas)	16c	
	d	(1) Gross income from oil, gas, and geothermal properties	16d(1)	
		(2) Deductions allocable to oil, gas, and geothermal properties	16d(2)	
	e	Other adjustments and tax preference items *(attach schedule)*	16e	
Foreign Taxes	17a	Name of foreign country or U.S. possession ▶		
	b	Gross income sourced at partner level	17b	
	c	Foreign gross income sourced at partnership level:		
		(1) Passive ▶ . . . . (2) Listed categories *(attach schedule)* ▶ . . . . (3) General limitation ▶	17c(3)	
	d	Deductions allocated and apportioned at partner level:		
		(1) Interest expense ▶ . . . . (2) Other ▶	17d(2)	
	e	Deductions allocated and apportioned at partnership level to foreign source income:		
		(1) Passive ▶ . . . . (2) Listed categories *(attach schedule)* ▶ . . . . (3) General limitation ▶	17e(3)	
	f	Total foreign taxes (check one): ▶ Paid ☐ Accrued ☐	17f	
	g	Reduction in taxes available for credit and gross income from all sources *(attach schedule)* .	17g	
Other	18	Section 59(e)(2) expenditures: a Type ▶ . . . . b Amount ▶	18b	
	19	Tax-exempt interest income	19	
	20	Other tax-exempt income	20	
	21	Nondeductible expenses	21	
	22	Distributions of money (cash and marketable securities)	22	
	23	Distributions of property other than money	23	
	24	Other items and amounts required to be reported separately to partners *(attach schedule)*		

Form **1065** (2000)

Form 1065 (2000)   Page 4

Analysis of Net Income (Loss)

1 Net income (loss). Combine Schedule K, lines 1 through 7 in column (b). From the result, subtract the sum of Schedule K, lines 8 through 11, 14a, 17f, and 18b					**1**	

2 Analysis by partner type:	(i) Corporate	(ii) Individual (active)	(iii) Individual (passive)	(iv) Partnership	(v) Exempt organization	(vi) Nominee/Other
a General partners						
b Limited partners						

Schedule L — Balance Sheets per Books (Not required if Question 5 on Schedule B is answered "Yes.")

Assets	Beginning of tax year		End of tax year	
	(a)	(b)	(c)	(d)
1 Cash				
2a Trade notes and accounts receivable . . .				
b Less allowance for bad debts				
3 Inventories				
4 U.S. government obligations				
5 Tax-exempt securities				
6 Other current assets (attach schedule) . . .				
7 Mortgage and real estate loans				
8 Other investments (attach schedule) . . .				
9a Buildings and other depreciable assets . . .				
b Less accumulated depreciation				
10a Depletable assets				
b Less accumulated depletion				
11 Land (net of any amortization)				
12a Intangible assets (amortizable only). . . .				
b Less accumulated amortization				
13 Other assets (attach schedule)				
14 Total assets				
Liabilities and Capital				
15 Accounts payable				
16 Mortgages, notes, bonds payable in less than 1 year .				
17 Other current liabilities (attach schedule) . . .				
18 All nonrecourse loans				
19 Mortgages, notes, bonds payable in 1 year or more .				
20 Other liabilities (attach schedule)				
21 Partners' capital accounts				
22 Total liabilities and capital				

Schedule M-1 — Reconciliation of Income (Loss) per Books With Income (Loss) per Return
(Not required if Question 5 on Schedule B is answered "Yes." See page 30 of the instructions.)

1 Net income (loss) per books		**6** Income recorded on books this year not included on Schedule K, lines 1 through 7 (itemize):	
2 Income included on Schedule K, lines 1 through 4, 6, and 7, not recorded on books this year (itemize):		**a** Tax-exempt interest $	
3 Guaranteed payments (other than health insurance)		**7** Deductions included on Schedule K, lines 1 through 11, 14a, 17f, and 18b, not charged against book income this year (itemize):	
4 Expenses recorded on books this year not included on Schedule K, lines 1 through 11, 14a, 17f, and 18b (itemize):		**a** Depreciation $	
a Depreciation $		....	
b Travel and entertainment $		**8** Add lines 6 and 7	
....		**9** Income (loss) (Analysis of Net Income (Loss), line 1) Subtract line 8 from line 5 . . .	
5 Add lines 1 through 4			

Schedule M-2 — Analysis of Partners' Capital Accounts (Not required if Question 5 on Schedule B is answered "Yes.")

1 Balance at beginning of year		**6** Distributions: **a** Cash	
2 Capital contributed during year		**b** Property	
3 Net income (loss) per books		**7** Other decreases (itemize):	
4 Other increases (itemize):		....	
....		**8** Add lines 6 and 7	
5 Add lines 1 through 4		**9** Balance at end of year. Subtract line 8 from line 5	

⊕   Form **1065** (2000)

Form **1120**		U.S. Corporation Income Tax Return		OMB No 1545-0123

Department of the Treasury
Internal Revenue Service

For calendar year 2000 or tax year beginning .... , 2000, ending .... , 20....
► Instructions are separate. See page 1 for Paperwork Reduction Act Notice.

2000

A Check if a:
1 Consolidated return (attach Form 851) ☐
2 Personal holding co (attach Sch PH) ☐
3 Personal service corp. (as defined in Temporary Rqgs. sec. 1.441-4T— see instructions) ☐

Use IRS label. Other-wise, print or type.

Name

Number, street, and room or suite no. (If a P.O. box, see page 7 of instructions.)

City or town, state, and ZIP code

B Employer identification number

C Date incorporated

D Total assets (see page 8 of instructions)

E Check applicable boxes   (1) ☐ Initial return   (2) ☐ Final return   (3) ☐ Change of address $

Income

1a	Gross receipts or sales	b Less returns and allowances	c Bal ►	1c	
2	Cost of goods sold (Schedule A, line 8)			2	
3	Gross profit. Subtract line 2 from line 1c			3	
4	Dividends (Schedule C, line 19)			4	
5	Interest			5	
6	Gross rents			6	
7	Gross royalties			7	
8	Capital gain net income (attach Schedule D (Form 1120))			8	
9	Net gain or (loss) from Form 4797, Part II, line 18 (attach Form 4797)			9	
10	Other income (see page 8 of instructions—attach schedule)			10	
11	**Total income.** Add lines 3 through 10		►	11	

Deductions (See instructions for limitations on deductions.)

12	Compensation of officers (Schedule E, line 4)		12	
13	Salaries and wages (less employment credits)		13	
14	Repairs and maintenance		14	
15	Bad debts		15	
16	Rents		16	
17	Taxes and licenses		17	
18	Interest		18	
19	Charitable contributions (see page 11 of instructions for 10% limitation)		19	
20	Depreciation (attach Form 4562)	20		
21	Less depreciation claimed on Schedule A and elsewhere on return	21a	21b	
22	Depletion		22	
23	Advertising		23	
24	Pension, profit-sharing, etc., plans		24	
25	Employee benefit programs		25	
26	Other deductions (attach schedule)		26	
27	**Total deductions.** Add lines 12 through 26	►	27	
28	Taxable income before net operating loss deduction and special deductions. Subtract line 27 from line 11		28	
29	**Less:** a Net operating loss (NOL) deduction (see page 13 of instructions)	29a		
	b Special deductions (Schedule C, line 20)	29b	29c	

Tax and Payments

30	**Taxable income.** Subtract line 29c from line 28			30	
31	**Total tax** (Schedule J, line 11)			31	
32	Payments: a 1999 overpayment credited to 2000	32a			
b	2000 estimated tax payments	32b			
c	Less 2000 refund applied for on Form 4466	32c (	) d Bal ►	32d	
e	Tax deposited with Form 7004			32e	
f	Credit for tax paid on undistributed capital gains (attach Form 2439)		32f		
g	Credit for Federal tax on fuels (attach Form 4136). See instructions		32g	32h	
33	Estimated tax penalty (see page 14 of instructions). Check if Form 2220 is attached ► ☐			33	
34	**Tax due.** If line 32h is smaller than the total of lines 31 and 33, enter amount owed			34	
35	**Overpayment.** If line 32h is larger than the total of lines 31 and 33, enter amount overpaid			35	
36	Enter amount of line 35 you want: **Credited to 2001 estimated tax** ►	Refunded ►		36	

Sign Here

Under penalties of perjury, I declare that I have examined this return, including accompanying schedules and statements, and to the best of my knowledge and belief, it is true, correct, and complete. Declaration of preparer (other than taxpayer) is based on all information of which preparer has any knowledge

► Signature of officer   Date   ► Title

Paid Preparer's Use Only

Preparer's signature ►		Date	Check if self-employed ☐	Preparer's SSN or PTIN
Firm's name (or yours if self-employed), address, and ZIP code ►			EIN	
			Phone no ( )	

Cat No 11450Q   Form **1120** (2000)

Form 1120 (2000)   Page **2**

Schedule A — Cost of Goods Sold (See page 14 of instructions.)

1	Inventory at beginning of year	1	
2	Purchases	2	
3	Cost of labor	3	
4	Additional section 263A costs (attach schedule)	4	
5	Other costs (attach schedule)	5	
6	**Total.** Add lines 1 through 5	6	
7	Inventory at end of year	7	
8	**Cost of goods sold.** Subtract line 7 from line 6. Enter here and on line 2, page 1	8	

9a Check all methods used for valuing closing inventory:
    (i) ☐ Cost as described in Regulations section 1.471-3
    (ii) ☐ Lower of cost or market as described in Regulations section 1.471-4
    (iii) ☐ Other (Specify method used and attach explanation.) ▶ _____
  b Check if there was a writedown of subnormal goods as described in Regulations section 1.471-2(c) . . . . ▶ ☐
  c Check if the LIFO inventory method was adopted this tax year for any goods (if checked, attach Form 970) . . . . . ▶ ☐
  d If the LIFO inventory method was used for this tax year, enter percentage (or amounts) of closing inventory computed under LIFO . . . . | 9d |
  e If property is produced or acquired for resale, do the rules of section 263A apply to the corporation? . . . . . ☐ Yes ☐ No
  f Was there any change in determining quantities, cost, or valuations between opening and closing inventory? If "Yes," attach explanation . . . . ☐ Yes ☐ No

Schedule C — Dividends and Special Deductions (See page 15 of instructions.)

		(a) Dividends received	(b) %	(c) Special deductions (a) × (b)
1	Dividends from less-than-20%-owned domestic corporations that are subject to the 70% deduction (other than debt-financed stock)		70	
2	Dividends from 20%-or-more-owned domestic corporations that are subject to the 80% deduction (other than debt-financed stock)		80	
3	Dividends on debt-financed stock of domestic and foreign corporations (section 246A)		see instructions	
4	Dividends on certain preferred stock of less-than-20%-owned public utilities		42	
5	Dividends on certain preferred stock of 20%-or-more-owned public utilities		48	
6	Dividends from less-than-20%-owned foreign corporations and certain FSCs that are subject to the 70% deduction		70	
7	Dividends from 20%-or-more-owned foreign corporations and certain FSCs that are subject to the 80% deduction		80	
8	Dividends from wholly owned foreign subsidiaries subject to the 100% deduction (section 245(b))		100	
9	**Total.** Add lines 1 through 8. See page 16 of instructions for limitation	//////	//////	
10	Dividends from domestic corporations received by a small business investment company operating under the Small Business Investment Act of 1958		100	
11	Dividends from certain FSCs that are subject to the 100% deduction (section 245(c)(1))		100	
12	Dividends from affiliated group members subject to the 100% deduction (section 243(a)(3))		100	
13	Other dividends from foreign corporations not included on lines 3, 6, 7, 8, or 11		//////	
14	Income from controlled foreign corporations under subpart F (attach Form(s) 5471)		//////	
15	Foreign dividend gross-up (section 78)		//////	
16	IC-DISC and former DISC dividends not included on lines 1, 2, or 3 (section 246(d))		//////	
17	Other dividends		//////	
18	Deduction for dividends paid on certain preferred stock of public utilities	//////	//////	
19	**Total dividends.** Add lines 1 through 17. Enter here and on line 4, page 1 . . ▶		//////	
20	**Total special deductions.** Add lines 9, 10, 11, 12, and 18. Enter here and on line 29b, page 1 . . . . . . ▶			

Schedule E — Compensation of Officers (See instructions for line 12, page 1.)

Note: *Complete Schedule E only if total receipts (line 1a plus lines 4 through 10 on page 1, Form 1120) are $500,000 or more.*

	(a) Name of officer	(b) Social security number	(c) Percent of time devoted to business	Percent of corporation stock owned (d) Common	(e) Preferred	(f) Amount of compensation
1			%	%	%	
			%	%	%	
			%	%	%	
			%	%	%	
			%	%	%	

2	Total compensation of officers	
3	Compensation of officers claimed on Schedule A and elsewhere on return	
4	Subtract line 3 from line 2. Enter the result here and on line 12, page 1	

Form **1120** (2000)

Form 1120 (2000)

Schedule J   Tax Computation (See page 17 of instructions.)

1 Check if the corporation is a member of a controlled group (see sections 1561 and 1563) . . . . . ▶ ☐
   Important: Members of a controlled group, see instructions on page 17.

2a If the box on line 1 is checked, enter the corporation's share of the $50,000, $25,000, and $9,925,000 taxable income brackets (in that order):

   (1) ⌊ $ _____ ⌋   (2) ⌊ $ _____ ⌋   (3) ⌊ $ _____ ⌋

  b Enter the corporation's share of: **(1)** Additional 5% tax (not more than $11,750) ⌊ $ _____ ⌋

   (2) Additional 3% tax (not more than $100,000) ⌊ $ _____ ⌋

3 Income tax. Check if a qualified personal service corporation under section 448(d)(2) (see page 17) . ▶ ☐ | **3** |

4 Alternative minimum tax (attach Form 4626) . . . . | **4** |

5 Add lines 3 and 4 . . . . | **5** |

6a Foreign tax credit (attach Form 1118) . . . . | **6a** |

  b Possessions tax credit (attach Form 5735) . . . . | **6b** |

  c Check: ☐ Nonconventional source fuel credit ☐ QEV credit (attach Form 8834) | **6c** |

  d General business credit. Enter here and check which forms are attached: ☐ 3800
   ☐ 3468 ☐ 5884 ☐ 6478 ☐ 6765 ☐ 8586 ☐ 8830 ☐ 8826
   ☐ 8835 ☐ 8844 ☐ 8845 ☐ 8846 ☐ 8820 ☐ 8847 ☐ 8861 | **6d** |

  e Credit for prior year minimum tax (attach Form 8827) . . . . | **6e** |

  f Qualified zone academy bond credit (attach Form 8860) . . . . | **6f** |

7 **Total credits.** Add lines 6a through 6f . . . . | **7** |

8 Subtract line 7 from line 5 . . . . | **8** |

9 Personal holding company tax (attach Schedule PH (Form 1120)) . . . . | **9** |

10 Recapture taxes. Check if from: ☐ Form 4255 ☐ Form 8611 . . . . | **10** |

11 **Total tax.** Add lines 8 through 10. Enter here and on line 31, page 1 . . . . | **11** |

Schedule K   Other Information (See page 19 of instructions.)

	Yes	No			Yes	No

1 Check method of accounting: **a** ☐ Cash
  b ☐ Accrual **c** ☐ Other (specify) ▶ ....

2 See page 21 of the instructions and enter the:
  a Business activity code no. ▶ ....
  b Business activity ▶ ....
  c Product or service ▶ ....

3 At the end of the tax year, did the corporation own, directly or indirectly, 50% or more of the voting stock of a domestic corporation? (For rules of attribution, see section 267(c).) . . . .
  If "Yes," attach a schedule showing: **(a)** name and employer identification number (EIN), **(b)** percentage owned, and **(c)** taxable income or (loss) before NOL and special deductions of such corporation for the tax year ending with or within your tax year.

4 Is the corporation a subsidiary in an affiliated group or a parent-subsidiary controlled group? . . . . .
  If "Yes," enter name and EIN of the parent corporation ▶ ....
  ....

5 At the end of the tax year, did any individual, partnership, corporation, estate, or trust own, directly or indirectly, 50% or more of the corporation's voting stock? (For rules of attribution, see section 267(c).) . . . . . .
  If "Yes," attach a schedule showing name and identifying number. (Do not include any information already entered in **4** above.) Enter percentage owned ▶..............

6 During this tax year, did the corporation pay dividends (other than stock dividends and distributions in exchange for stock) in excess of the corporation's current and accumulated earnings and profits? (See sections 301 and 316.). . . . .

If "Yes," file **Form 5452,** Corporate Report of Nondividend Distributions.
If this is a consolidated return, answer here for the parent corporation and on **Form 851,** Affiliations Schedule, for each subsidiary.

7 At any time during the tax year, did one foreign person own, directly or indirectly, at least 25% of **(a)** the total voting power of all classes of stock of the corporation entitled to vote or **(b)** the total value of all classes of stock of the corporation?. . . . .
  If "Yes,"
  a Enter percentage owned ▶...........................
  b Enter owner's country ▶...........................
  c The corporation may have to file **Form 5472,** Information Return of a 25% Foreign-Owned U.S. Corporation or a Foreign Corporation Engaged in a U.S. Trade or Business. Enter number of Forms 5472 attached ▶...........

8 Check this box if the corporation issued publicly offered debt instruments with original issue discount . . ▶ ☐
  If checked, the corporation may have to file **Form 8281,** Information Return for Publicly Offered Original Issue Discount Instruments.

9 Enter the amount of tax-exempt interest received or accrued during the tax year ▶ $ ....

10 Enter the number of shareholders at the end of the tax year (if 75 or fewer) ▶ ....

11 If the corporation has an NOL for the tax year and is electing to forego the carryback period, check here ▶ ☐

12 Enter the available NOL carryover from prior tax years (Do not reduce it by any deduction on line 29a.) ▶ $ ....

Note: If the corporation, at any time during the tax year, had assets or operated a business in a foreign country or U.S. possession, it may be required to attach **Schedule N (Form 1120),** Foreign Operations of U.S. Corporations, to this return. See Schedule N for details.

Form **1120** (2000)

Form 1120 (2000)   Page **4**

Schedule L	Balance Sheets per Books	Beginning of tax year		End of tax year	
	Assets	(a)	(b)	(c)	(d)
1	Cash				
2a	Trade notes and accounts receivable . . .				
b	Less allowance for bad debts	( )		( )	
3	Inventories				
4	U.S. government obligations				
5	Tax-exempt securities (see instructions) . .				
6	Other current assets (attach schedule) . .				
7	Loans to shareholders				
8	Mortgage and real estate loans				
9	Other investments (attach schedule) . . .				
10a	Buildings and other depreciable assets . .				
b	Less accumulated depreciation	( )		( )	
11a	Depletable assets				
b	Less accumulated depletion	( )		( )	
12	Land (net of any amortization)				
13a	Intangible assets (amortizable only) . . .				
b	Less accumulated amortization	( )		( )	
14	Other assets (attach schedule)				
15	Total assets				
	Liabilities and Shareholders' Equity				
16	Accounts payable				
17	Mortgages, notes, bonds payable in less than 1 year				
18	Other current liabilities (attach schedule) . .				
19	Loans from shareholders				
20	Mortgages, notes, bonds payable in 1 year or more				
21	Other liabilities (attach schedule) . . .				
22	Capital stock: a Preferred stock . . .				
	b Common stock . . .				
23	Additional paid-in capital				
24	Retained earnings—Appropriated (attach schedule)				
25	Retained earnings—Unappropriated . . .				
26	Adjustments to shareholders' equity (attach schedule)				
27	Less cost of treasury stock		( )		( )
28	Total liabilities and shareholders' equity . .				

Note: *The corporation is not required to complete Schedules M-1 and M-2 if the total assets on line 15, col. (d) of Schedule L are less than $25,000.*

Schedule M-1	Reconciliation of Income (Loss) per Books With Income per Return (See page 20 of instructions.)

1	Net income (loss) per books		7	Income recorded on books this year not	
2	Federal income tax			included on this return (itemize):	
3	Excess of capital losses over capital gains .			Tax-exempt interest $	
4	Income subject to tax not recorded on books			. . . .	
	this year (itemize):		8	Deductions on this return not charged	
	. . . .			against book income this year (itemize):	
5	Expenses recorded on books this year not		a	Depreciation . . . . . $	
	deducted on this return (itemize):		b	Contributions carryover $	
a	Depreciation . . . . $			. . . .	
b	Contributions carryover $			. . . .	
c	Travel and entertainment $			. . . .	
	. . . .		9	Add lines 7 and 8	
6	Add lines 1 through 5		10	Income (line 28, page 1)—line 6 less line 9	

Schedule M-2	Analysis of Unappropriated Retained Earnings per Books (Line 25, Schedule L)

1	Balance at beginning of year		5	Distributions: a Cash	
2	Net income (loss) per books			b Stock	
3	Other increases (itemize):			c Property	
	. . . .		6	Other decreases (itemize):	
	. . . .		7	Add lines 5 and 6	
4	Add lines 1, 2, and 3		8	Balance at end of year (line 4 less line 7)	

✱

Form **1120** (2000)

Form **1120S**	**U.S. Income Tax Return for an S Corporation**	OMB No. 1545-0130
Department of the Treasury Internal Revenue Service	▶ Do not file this form unless the corporation has timely filed Form 2553 to elect to be an S corporation. ▶ See separate instructions.	**2000**

For calendar year 2000, or tax year beginning _____ , 2000, and ending _____ , 20 _____

A Effective date of election as an S corporation	Use IRS label. Other-wise, print or type.	Name	C Employer identification number
B Business code no. (see pages 29–31)		Number, street, and room or suite no. (If a P.O. box, see page 11 of the instructions.)	D Date incorporated
		City or town, state, and ZIP code	E Total assets (see page 11) $

F Check applicable boxes: (1) ☐ Initial return (2) ☐ Final return (3) ☐ Change in address (4) ☐ Amended return

G Enter number of shareholders in the corporation at end of the tax year . . . . ▶

Caution: *Include only trade or business income and expenses on lines 1a through 21. See page 11 of the instructions for more information.*

Income

1a	Gross receipts or sales			b Less returns and allowances			c Bal ▶	1c	
2	Cost of goods sold (Schedule A, line 8)							2	
3	Gross profit. Subtract line 2 from line 1c							3	
4	Net gain (loss) from Form 4797, Part II, line 18 *(attach Form 4797)*							4	
5	Other income (loss) *(attach schedule)*.							5	
6	**Total income (loss)**. Combine lines 3 through 5 . . . . ▶							6	

Deductions (see page 12 of the instructions for limitations)

7	Compensation of officers	7	
8	Salaries and wages (less employment credits)	8	
9	Repairs and maintenance	9	
10	Bad debts	10	
11	Rents.	11	
12	Taxes and licenses	12	
13	Interest	13	
14a	Depreciation *(if required, attach Form 4562)*	14a		
b	Depreciation claimed on Schedule A and elsewhere on return . .	14b		
c	Subtract line 14b from line 14a	14c	
15	Depletion (**Do not deduct oil and gas depletion.**)	15	
16	Advertising	16	
17	Pension, profit-sharing, etc., plans	17	
18	Employee benefit programs.	18	
19	Other deductions *(attach schedule)*	19	
20	**Total deductions**. Add the amounts shown in the far right column for lines 7 through 19 . ▶	20	

21	Ordinary income (loss) from trade or business activities. Subtract line 20 from line 6. . . .	21	

Tax and Payments

22	Tax: a Excess net passive income tax *(attach schedule)* . . .	22a		
b	Tax from Schedule D (Form 1120S)	22b		
c	Add lines 22a and 22b (see page 15 of the instructions for additional taxes)		22c	
23	Payments: a 2000 estimated tax payments and amount applied from 1999 return	23a		
b	Tax deposited with Form 7004.	23b		
c	Credit for Federal tax paid on fuels *(attach Form 4136)*	23c		
d	Add lines 23a through 23c		23d	
24	Estimated tax penalty. Check if Form 2220 is attached . . . . ▶☐		24	
25	**Tax due.** If the total of lines 22c and 24 is larger than line 23d, enter amount owed. See page 4 of the instructions for depository method of payment . . . . ▶		25	
26	**Overpayment.** If line 23d is larger than the total of lines 22c and 24, enter amount overpaid ▶		26	
27	Enter amount of line 26 you want: **Credited to 2001 estimated tax** ▶ | **Refunded** ▶		27	

Sign Here

Under penalties of perjury, I declare that I have examined this return, including accompanying schedules and statements, and to the best of my knowledge and belief, it is true, correct, and complete. Declaration of preparer (other than taxpayer) is based on all information of which preparer has any knowledge.

▶ _____ _____ ▶ _____
Signature of officer   Date   Title

Paid Preparer's Use Only

Preparer's signature ▶		Date		Check if self-employed ☐	Preparer's SSN or PTIN
Firm's name (or yours if self-employed), address, and ZIP code	▶			EIN	
				Phone no. ( )	

For Paperwork Reduction Act Notice, see the separate instructions.   Cat. No. 11510H   Form **1120S** (2000)

230 APPENDIX D

Form 1120S (2000)   Page **2**

Schedule A   Cost of Goods Sold (see page 16 of the instructions)

1	Inventory at beginning of year	1
2	Purchases	2
3	Cost of labor	3
4	Additional section 263A costs (attach schedule)	4
5	Other costs (attach schedule)	5
6	**Total.** Add lines 1 through 5	6
7	Inventory at end of year	7
8	**Cost of goods sold.** Subtract line 7 from line 6. Enter here and on page 1, line 2	8

9a   Check all methods used for valuing closing inventory:
    (i) ☐ Cost as described in Regulations section 1.471-3
    (ii) ☐ Lower of cost or market as described in Regulations section 1.471-4
    (iii) ☐ Other (specify method used and attach explanation) ▶ ....
  b   Check if there was a writedown of "subnormal" goods as described in Regulations section 1.471-2(c) . . . . ▶ ☐
  c   Check if the LIFO inventory method was adopted this tax year for any goods (if checked, attach Form 970) . . . . . ▶ ☐
  d   If the LIFO inventory method was used for this tax year, enter percentage (or amounts) of closing
      inventory computed under LIFO . . . . |9d|
  e   Do the rules of section 263A (for property produced or acquired for resale) apply to the corporation? . . . . . ☐ Yes ☐ No
  f   Was there any change in determining quantities, cost, or valuations between opening and closing inventory?. . . ☐ Yes ☐ No
      If "Yes," attach explanation.

Schedule B   Other Information   Yes   No

1   Check method of accounting: **(a)** ☐ Cash   **(b)** ☐ Accrual   **(c)** ☐ Other (specify) ▶.............................
2   Refer to the list on pages 29 through 31 of the instructions and state the corporation's principal:
    (a) Business activity ▶ .... **(b)** Product or service ▶ ....
3   Did the corporation at the end of the tax year own, directly or indirectly, 50% or more of the voting stock of a domestic
    corporation? (For rules of attribution, see section 267(c).) If "Yes," attach a schedule showing: **(a)** name, address, and
    employer identification number and **(b)** percentage owned. . . . .
4   Was the corporation a member of a controlled group subject to the provisions of section 1561? . . . .
5   Check this box if the corporation has filed or is required to file **Form 8264**, Application for Registration of a Tax
    Shelter . . . . ▶ ☐
6   Check this box if the corporation issued publicly offered debt instruments with original issue discount . . . ▶ ☐
    If so, the corporation may have to file **Form 8281**, Information Return for Publicly Offered Original Issue Discount
    Instruments.
7   If the corporation: **(a)** filed its election to be an S corporation after 1986, **(b)** was a C corporation before it elected to
    be an S corporation **or** the corporation acquired an asset with a basis determined by reference to its basis (or the
    basis of any other property) in the hands of a C corporation, and **(c)** has net unrealized built-in gain (defined in section
    1374(d)(1)) in excess of the net recognized built-in gain from prior years, enter the net unrealized built-in gain reduced
    by net recognized built-in gain from prior years (see page 17 of the instructions) . . . . . ▶ $ ....
8   Check this box if the corporation had accumulated earnings and profits at the close of the tax year (see
    page 18 of the instructions) . . . . ▶ ☐

Note: If the corporation had assets or operated a business in a foreign country or U.S. possession, it may be required to attach
Schedule N (Form 1120), Foreign Operations of U.S. Corporations, to this return. See Schedule N for details.

Schedule K   Shareholders' Shares of Income, Credits, Deductions, etc.

	(a) Pro rata share items			(b) Total amount
	1 Ordinary income (loss) from trade or business activities (page 1, line 21)		1	
	2 Net income (loss) from rental real estate activities (attach Form 8825)		2	
	3a Gross income from other rental activities	3a		
	b Expenses from other rental activities (attach schedule) . .	3b		
	c Net income (loss) from other rental activities. Subtract line 3b from line 3a		3c	
Income (Loss)	4 Portfolio income (loss):			
	a Interest income		4a	
	b Ordinary dividends		4b	
	c Royalty income		4c	
	d Net short-term capital gain (loss) (attach Schedule D (Form 1120S)).		4d	
	e Net long-term capital gain (loss) (attach Schedule D (Form 1120S)):			
	(1) 28% rate gain (loss) ▶ .... (2) Total for year ▶		4e(2)	
	f Other portfolio income (loss) (attach schedule)		4f	
	5 Net section 1231 gain (loss) (other than due to casualty or theft) (attach Form 4797) . .		5	
	6 Other income (loss) (attach schedule)		6	

Form **1120S** (2000)

Form 1120S (2000)   Page **3**

Schedule K   Shareholders' Shares of Income, Credits, Deductions, etc. *(continued)*

		(a) Pro rata share items		(b) Total amount
Deductions	7	Charitable contributions *(attach schedule)*	7	
	8	Section 179 expense deduction *(attach Form 4562)*	8	
	9	Deductions related to portfolio income (loss) (itemize)	9	
	10	Other deductions *(attach schedule)*	10	
Investment Interest	11a	Interest expense on investment debts	11a	
	b (1)	Investment income included on lines 4a, 4b, 4c, and 4f above	11b(1)	
	(2)	Investment expenses included on line 9 above	11b(2)	
Credits	12a	Credit for alcohol used as a fuel *(attach Form 6478)*	12a	
	b	Low-income housing credit:		
	(1)	From partnerships to which section 42(j)(5) applies for property placed in service before 1990	12b(1)	
	(2)	Other than on line 12b(1) for property placed in service before 1990	12b(2)	
	(3)	From partnerships to which section 42(j)(5) applies for property placed in service after 1989	12b(3)	
	(4)	Other than on line 12b(3) for property placed in service after 1989	12b(4)	
	c	Qualified rehabilitation expenditures related to rental real estate activities *(attach Form 3468)* .	12c	
	d	Credits (other than credits shown on lines 12b and 12c) related to rental real estate activities	12d	
	e	Credits related to other rental activities	12e	
	13	Other credits	13	
Adjustments and Tax Preference Items	14a	Depreciation adjustment on property placed in service after 1986	14a	
	b	Adjusted gain or loss	14b	
	c	Depletion (other than oil and gas)	14c	
	d (1)	Gross income from oil, gas, or geothermal properties	14d(1)	
	(2)	Deductions allocable to oil, gas, or geothermal properties	14d(2)	
	e	Other adjustments and tax preference items *(attach schedule)*	14e	
Foreign Taxes	15a	Name of foreign country or U.S. possession ▶		
	b	Gross income sourced at shareholder level	15b	
	c	Foreign gross income sourced at corporate level:		
	(1)	Passive	15c(1)	
	(2)	Listed categories *(attach schedule)*	15c(2)	
	(3)	General limitation	15c(3)	
	d	Deductions allocated and apportioned at shareholder level:		
	(1)	Interest expense	15d(1)	
	(2)	Other	15d(2)	
	e	Deductions allocated and apportioned at corporate level to foreign source income:		
	(1)	Passive	15e(1)	
	(2)	Listed categories *(attach schedule)*	15e(2)	
	(3)	General limitation	15e(3)	
	f	Total foreign taxes (check one): ▶ ☐ Paid ☐ Accrued	15f	
	g	Reduction in taxes available for credit and gross income from all sources *(attach schedule)*	15g	
Other	16	Section 59(e)(2) expenditures: a Type ▶ .... b Amount ▶	16b	
	17	Tax-exempt interest income	17	
	18	Other tax-exempt income	18	
	19	Nondeductible expenses	19	
	20	Total property distributions (including cash) other than dividends reported on line 22 below	20	
	21	Other items and amounts required to be reported separately to shareholders *(attach schedule)*		
	22	Total dividend distributions paid from accumulated earnings and profits	22	
	23	**Income (loss).** (Required only if Schedule M-1 must be completed.) Combine lines 1 through 6 in column (b). From the result, subtract the sum of lines 7 through 11a, 15f, and 16b .	23	

Form **1120S** (2000)

Form 1120S (2000)   Page **4**

Schedule L — Balance Sheets per Books

Assets	Beginning of tax year (a)	(b)	End of tax year (c)	(d)
1 Cash				
2a Trade notes and accounts receivable . . .				
b Less allowance for bad debts				
3 Inventories				
4 U.S. Government obligations				
5 Tax-exempt securities				
6 Other current assets (attach schedule) . .				
7 Loans to shareholders				
8 Mortgage and real estate loans				
9 Other investments (attach schedule) . . .				
10a Buildings and other depreciable assets . .				
b Less accumulated depreciation				
11a Depletable assets				
b Less accumulated depletion.				
12 Land (net of any amortization)				
13a Intangible assets (amortizable only) . . .				
b Less accumulated amortization.				
14 Other assets (attach schedule)				
15 Total assets				
Liabilities and Shareholders' Equity				
16 Accounts payable				
17 Mortgages, notes, bonds payable in less than 1 year				
18 Other current liabilities (attach schedule) . .				
19 Loans from shareholders.				
20 Mortgages, notes, bonds payable in 1 year or more				
21 Other liabilities (attach schedule)				
22 Capital stock				
23 Additional paid-in capital.				
24 Retained earnings				
25 Adjustments to shareholders' equity (attach schedule)				
26 Less cost of treasury stock		( )		( )
27 Total liabilities and shareholders' equity . .				

Schedule M-1 — Reconciliation of Income (Loss) per Books With Income (Loss) per Return (You are not required to complete this schedule if the total assets on line 15, column (d), of Schedule L are less than $25,000.)

1 Net income (loss) per books.		**5** Income recorded on books this year not included on Schedule K, lines 1 through 6 (itemize):	
2 Income included on Schedule K, lines 1 through 6, not recorded on books this year (itemize):		**a** Tax-exempt interest $	
....		**6** Deductions included on Schedule K, lines 1 through 11a, 15f, and 16b, not charged against book income this year (itemize):	
3 Expenses recorded on books this year not included on Schedule K, lines 1 through 11a, 15f, and 16b (itemize):		**a** Depreciation $	
a Depreciation $		....	
b Travel and entertainment $		**7** Add lines 5 and 6.	
....		**8** Income (loss) (Schedule K, line 23). Line 4 less line 7	
4 Add lines 1 through 3.			

Schedule M-2 — Analysis of Accumulated Adjustments Account, Other Adjustments Account, and Shareholders' Undistributed Taxable Income Previously Taxed (see page 27 of the instructions)

	(a) Accumulated adjustments account	(b) Other adjustments account	(c) Shareholders' undistributed taxable income previously taxed
1 Balance at beginning of tax year			
2 Ordinary income from page 1, line 21. . .			
3 Other additions.			
4 Loss from page 1, line 21	( )		
5 Other reductions	( )	( )	
6 Combine lines 1 through 5			
7 Distributions other than dividend distributions. .			
8 Balance at end of tax year. Subtract line 7 from line 6			

Form **1120S** (2000)

Form **4562**	**Depreciation and Amortization**	OMB No. 1545-0172
Department of the Treasury Internal Revenue Service (99)	**(Including Information on Listed Property)** ▶ See separate instructions. ▶ Attach this form to your return.	**2000** Attachment Sequence No. **67**
Name(s) shown on return	Business or activity to which this form relates	Identifying number

Part I   Election To Expense Certain Tangible Property (Section 179)
Note: *If you have any "listed property," complete Part V before you complete Part I.*

1	Maximum dollar limitation. If an enterprise zone business, see page 2 of the instructions . .	**1**	$20,000
2	Total cost of section 179 property placed in service. See page 2 of the instructions	**2**	
3	Threshold cost of section 179 property before reduction in limitation	**3**	$200,000
4	Reduction in limitation. Subtract line 3 from line 2. If zero or less, enter -0-	**4**	
5	Dollar limitation for tax year. Subtract line 4 from line 1. If zero or less, enter -0-. If married filing separately, see page 2 of the instructions	**5**	

(a) Description of property	(b) Cost (business use only)	(c) Elected cost	
6			

7	Listed property. Enter amount from line 27.	**7**	
8	Total elected cost of section 179 property. Add amounts in column (c), lines 6 and 7 . . .	**8**	
9	Tentative deduction. Enter the smaller of line 5 or line 8	**9**	
10	Carryover of disallowed deduction from 1999. See page 3 of the instructions	**10**	
11	Business income limitation. Enter the smaller of business income (not less than zero) or line 5 (see instructions)	**11**	
12	Section 179 expense deduction. Add lines 9 and 10, but do not enter more than line 11 . .	**12**	
13	Carryover of disallowed deduction to 2001. Add lines 9 and 10, less line 12 ▶	**13**	

Note: *Do not use Part II or Part III below for listed property (automobiles, certain other vehicles, cellular telephones, certain computers, or property used for entertainment, recreation, or amusement). Instead, use Part V for listed property.*

Part II   MACRS Depreciation for Assets Placed in Service Only During Your 2000 Tax Year (Do not include listed property.)

Section A—General Asset Account Election

14   If you are making the election under section 168(i)(4) to group any assets placed in service during the tax year into one or more general asset accounts, check this box. See page 3 of the instructions . . . . ▶ ☐

Section B—General Depreciation System (GDS) (See page 3 of the instructions.)

(a) Classification of property	(b) Month and year placed in service	(c) Basis for depreciation (business/investment use only—see instructions)	(d) Recovery period	(e) Convention	(f) Method	(g) Depreciation deduction
15a 3-year property						
b 5-year property						
c 7-year property						
d 10-year property						
e 15-year property						
f 20-year property						
g 25-year property			25 yrs.		S/L	
h Residential rental property			27.5 yrs.	MM	S/L	
			27.5 yrs.	MM	S/L	
i Nonresidential real property			39 yrs.	MM	S/L	
				MM	S/L	

Section C—Alternative Depreciation System (ADS) (See page 5 of the instructions.)

16a Class life					S/L	
b 12-year			12 yrs.		S/L	
c 40-year			40 yrs.	MM	S/L	

Part III   Other Depreciation (Do not include listed property.) (See page 5 of the instructions.)

17	GDS and ADS deductions for assets placed in service in tax years beginning before 2000 .	**17**	
18	Property subject to section 168(f)(1) election	**18**	
19	ACRS and other depreciation	**19**	

Part IV   Summary (See page 6 of the instructions.)

20	Listed property. Enter amount from line 26.	**20**	
21	**Total.** Add deductions from line 12, lines 15 and 16 in column (g), and lines 17 through 20. Enter here and on the appropriate lines of your return. Partnerships and S corporations—see instructions	**21**	
22	For assets shown above and placed in service during the current year, enter the portion of the basis attributable to section 263A costs . . .	**22**	

For Paperwork Reduction Act Notice, see page 9 of the instructions.   Cat. No. 12906N   Form **4562** (2000)

Form 4562 (2000)   Page **2**

Part V | **Listed Property** (Include automobiles, certain other vehicles, cellular telephones, certain computers, and property used for entertainment, recreation, or amusement.)

Note: For any vehicle for which you are using the standard mileage rate or deducting lease expense, complete **only** 23a, 23b, columns (a) through (c) of Section A, all of Section B, and Section C if applicable.

Section A—Depreciation and Other Information (Caution: See page 7 of the instructions for limits for passenger automobiles.)

23a Do you have evidence to support the business/investment use claimed? ☐ **Yes** ☐ **No**   **23b** If "Yes," is the evidence written? ☐ **Yes** ☐ **No**

(a) Type of property (list vehicles first)	(b) Date placed in service	(c) Business/ investment use percentage	(d) Cost or other basis	(e) Basis for depreciation (business/investment use only)	(f) Recovery period	(g) Method/ Convention	(h) Depreciation deduction	(i) Elected section 179 cost
24 Property used more than 50% in a qualified business use (See page 6 of the instructions.):								
		%						
		%						
		%						
25 Property used 50% or less in a qualified business use (See page 6 of the instructions.):								
		%					S/L –	
		%					S/L –	
		%					S/L –	

26 Add amounts in column (h). Enter the total here and on line 20, page 1 . . . . . . **26**
27 Add amounts in column (i). Enter the total here and on line 7, page 1 . . . . **27**

Section B—Information on Use of Vehicles
Complete this section for vehicles used by a sole proprietor, partner, or other "more than 5% owner," or related person.
If you provided vehicles to your employees, first answer the questions in Section C to see if you meet an exception to completing this section for those vehicles.

	(a) Vehicle 1	(b) Vehicle 2	(c) Vehicle 3	(d) Vehicle 4	(e) Vehicle 5	(f) Vehicle 6
28 Total business/investment miles driven during the year (**do not** include commuting miles— see page 1 of the instructions)						
29 Total commuting miles driven during the year						
30 Total other personal (noncommuting) miles driven						
31 Total miles driven during the year. Add lines 28 through 30.						

	Yes	No	Yes	No	Yes	No	Yes	No	Yes	No	Yes	No
32 Was the vehicle available for personal use during off-duty hours?												
33 Was the vehicle used primarily by a more than 5% owner or related person?												
34 Is another vehicle available for personal use?												

Section C—Questions for Employers Who Provide Vehicles for Use by Their Employees
Answer these questions to determine if you meet an exception to completing Section B for vehicles used by employees who **are not** more than 5% owners or related persons. See page 8 of the instructions.

	Yes	No
35 Do you maintain a written policy statement that prohibits all personal use of vehicles, including commuting, by your employees?		
36 Do you maintain a written policy statement that prohibits personal use of vehicles, except commuting, by your employees? See page 8 of the instructions for vehicles used by corporate officers, directors, or 1% or more owners		
37 Do you treat all use of vehicles by employees as personal use?		
38 Do you provide more than five vehicles to your employees, obtain information from your employees about the use of the vehicles, and retain the information received?		
39 Do you meet the requirements concerning qualified automobile demonstration use? See page 8 of the instructions . .		

Note: If your answer to 35, 36, 37, 38, or 39 is "Yes," do not complete Section B for the covered vehicles.

Part VI | **Amortization**

(a) Description of costs	(b) Date amortization begins	(c) Amortizable amount	(d) Code section	(e) Amortization period or percentage	(f) Amortization for this year
40 Amortization of costs that begins during your 2000 tax year (See page 8 of the instructions.):					

41 Amortization of costs that began before 2000 . . . . **41**
42 **Total.** Add amounts in column (f). See page 9 of the instructions for where to report . . . **42**

Form **4562** (2000)

Form **8829**	**Expenses for Business Use of Your Home**	OMB No. 1545-1266
Department of the Treasury Internal Revenue Service (99)	► File only with **Schedule C (Form 1040). Use a separate Form 8829 for each** home you used for business during the year. ► **See separate instructions.**	**2000** Attachment Sequence No. **66**

Name(s) of proprietor(s)

Your social security number

Part I   Part of Your Home Used for Business

1	Area used regularly and exclusively for business, regularly for day care, or for storage of inventory or product samples. See instructions	**1**	
2	Total area of home	**2**	
3	Divide line 1 by line 2. Enter the result as a percentage	**3**	%

• For day-care facilities not used exclusively for business, also complete lines 4–6.
• All others, skip lines 4–6 and enter the amount from line 3 on line 7.

4	Multiply days used for day care during year by hours used per day .	**4**		hr.	
5	Total hours available for use during the year (366 days × 24 hours). See instructions	**5**	8,784 hr.		
6	Divide line 4 by line 5. Enter the result as a decimal . . .	**6**			
7	Business percentage. For day-care facilities not used exclusively for business, multiply line 6 by line 3 (enter the result as a percentage). All others, enter the amount from line 3 . . . . ►	**7**			%

Part II   Figure Your Allowable Deduction

8	Enter the amount from Schedule C, line 29, **plus** any net gain or (loss) derived from the business use of your home and shown on Schedule D or Form 4797. If more than one place of business, see instructions		**8**	
	See instructions for columns (a) and (b) before completing lines 9–20.	**(a)** Direct expenses	**(b)** Indirect expenses	
9	Casualty losses. See instructions	**9**		
10	Deductible mortgage interest. See instructions .	**10**		
11	Real estate taxes. See instructions	**11**		
12	Add lines 9, 10, and 11.	**12**		
13	Multiply line 12, column (b) by line 7		**13**	
14	Add line 12, column (a) and line 13		**14**	
15	Subtract line 14 from line 8. If zero or less, enter -0-		**15**	
16	Excess mortgage interest. See instructions . .	**16**		
17	Insurance	**17**		
18	Repairs and maintenance	**18**		
19	Utilities	**19**		
20	Other expenses. See instructions	**20**		
21	Add lines 16 through 20	**21**		
22	Multiply line 21, column (b) by line 7	**22**		
23	Carryover of operating expenses from 1999 Form 8829, line 41 . .	**23**		
24	Add line 21 in column (a), line 22, and line 23		**24**	
25	Allowable operating expenses. Enter the **smaller** of line 15 or line 24		**25**	
26	Limit on excess casualty losses and depreciation. Subtract line 25 from line 15		**26**	
27	Excess casualty losses. See instructions	**27**		
28	Depreciation of your home from Part III below	**28**		
29	Carryover of excess casualty losses and depreciation from 1999 Form 8829, line 42	**29**		
30	Add lines 27 through 29		**30**	
31	Allowable excess casualty losses and depreciation. Enter the **smaller** of line 26 or line 30 . .		**31**	
32	Add lines 14, 25, and 31		**32**	
33	Casualty loss portion, if any, from lines 14 and 31. Carry amount to **Form 4684,** Section B . .		**33**	
34	Allowable expenses for business use of your home. Subtract line 33 from line 32. Enter here and on Schedule C, line 30. If your home was used for more than one business, see instructions ►		**34**	

Part III   Depreciation of Your Home

35	Enter the **smaller** of your home's adjusted basis or its fair market value. See instructions . .	**35**	
36	Value of land included on line 35	**36**	
37	Basis of building. Subtract line 36 from line 35	**37**	
38	Business basis of building. Multiply line 37 by line 7	**38**	
39	Depreciation percentage. See instructions	**39**	%
40	Depreciation allowable. Multiply line 38 by line 39. Enter here and on line 28 above. See instructions	**40**	

Part IV   Carryover of Unallowed Expenses to 2001

41	Operating expenses. Subtract line 25 from line 24. If less than zero, enter -0-	**41**	
42	Excess casualty losses and depreciation. Subtract line 31 from line 30. If less than zero, enter -0- .	**42**	

For Paperwork Reduction Act Notice, see page 4 of separate instructions.   Cat. No. 13232M   Form **8829** (2000)

Form 6251

Department of the Treasury
Internal Revenue Service

Alternative Minimum Tax—Individuals

▶ See separate instructions.

▶ Attach to Form 1040 or Form 1040NR.

OMB No. 1545-0227

2000

Attachment
Sequence No. 32

Name(s) shown on Form 1040 | Your social security number

Part I Adjustments and Preferences

1	If you itemized deductions on Schedule A (Form 1040), go to line 2. Otherwise, enter your standard deduction from Form 1040, line 36, here and go to line 6	1
2	Medical and dental. Enter the smaller of Schedule A (Form 1040), line 4 or 2½% of Form 1040, line 34	2
3	Taxes. Enter the amount from Schedule A (Form 1040), line 9	3
4	Certain interest on a home mortgage **not** used to buy, build, or improve your home	4
5	Miscellaneous itemized deductions. Enter the amount from Schedule A (Form 1040), line 26	5
6	Refund of taxes. Enter any tax refund from Form 1040, line 10 or line 21	6 ( )
7	Investment interest. Enter difference between regular tax and AMT deduction	7
8	Post-1986 depreciation. Enter difference between regular tax and AMT depreciation	8
9	Adjusted gain or loss. Enter difference between AMT and regular tax gain or loss	9
10	Incentive stock options. Enter excess of AMT income over regular tax income	10
11	Passive activities. Enter difference between AMT and regular tax income or loss	11
12	Beneficiaries of estates and trusts. Enter the amount from Schedule K-1 (Form 1041), line 9	12
13	Tax-exempt interest from private activity bonds issued after 8/7/86	13
14	Other. Enter the amount, if any, for each item below and enter the total on line 14.	

a Circulation expenditures
b Depletion
c Depreciation (pre-1987)
d Installment sales
e Intangible drilling costs
f Large partnerships
g Long-term contracts

h Loss limitations
i Mining costs
j Patron's adjustment
k Pollution control facilities
l Research and experimental
m Section 1202 exclusion
n Tax shelter farm activities
o Related adjustments

		14
15	Total Adjustments and Preferences. Combine lines 1 through 14 ▶	15

Part II Alternative Minimum Taxable Income

16	Enter the amount from **Form 1040, line 37.** If less than zero, enter as a (loss) ▶	16
17	Net operating loss deduction, if any, from Form 1040, line 21. Enter as a positive amount	17
18	If Form 1040, line 34, is over $128,950 (over $64,475 if married filing separately), and you itemized deductions, enter the amount, if any, from line 9 of the worksheet for Schedule A (Form 1040), line 28	18 ( )
19	Combine lines 15 through 18 ▶	19
20	Alternative tax net operating loss deduction. See page 6 of the instructions	20
21	**Alternative Minimum Taxable Income.** Subtract line 20 from line 19. (If married filing separately and line 21 is more than $165,000, see page 7 of the instructions.) ▶	21

Part III Exemption Amount and Alternative Minimum Tax

22 **Exemption Amount.** (If this form is for a child under age 14, see page 7 of the instructions.)

IF your filing status is . . .	AND line 21 is not over . . .	THEN enter on line 22 . . .	
Single or head of household	$112,500	$33,750	
Married filing jointly or qualifying widow(er)	150,000	45,000	22
Married filing separately	75,000	22,500	

If line 21 is **over** the amount shown above for your filing status, see page 7 of the instructions.

23	Subtract line 22 from line 21. If zero or less, enter -0- here and on lines 26 and 28 and stop here ▶	23
24	If you reported capital gain distributions directly on Form 1040, line 13, **or** you completed Schedule D (Form 1040) and have an amount on line 25 or line 27 (or would have had an amount on either line if you had completed Part IV) (as refigured for the AMT, if necessary), go to Part IV of Form 6251 to figure line 24. **All others:** If line 23 is $175,000 or less ($87,500 or less if married filing separately), multiply line 23 by 26% (.26). Otherwise, multiply line 23 by 28% (.28) and subtract $3,500 ($1,750 if married filing separately) from the result ▶	24
25	Alternative minimum tax foreign tax credit. See page 7 of the instructions	25
26	Tentative minimum tax. Subtract line 25 from line 24 ▶	26
27	Enter your tax from Form 1040, line 40 (minus any tax from Form 4972 and any foreign tax credit from Form 1040, line 43)	27
28	**Alternative Minimum Tax.** Subtract line 27 from line 26. If zero or less, enter -0-. Enter here and on Form 1040, line 41 ▶	28

For Paperwork Reduction Act Notice, see page 8 of the instructions.   Cat. No. 13600G   Form **6251** (2000)

Form 6251 (2000)   Page 2

Part IV Line 24 Computation Using Maximum Capital Gains Rates

Caution: *If you did not complete Part IV of Schedule D (Form 1040), see page 8 of the instructions before you complete this part.*

29 Enter the amount from Form 6251, line 23 . . . .   **29**

30 Enter the amount from Schedule D (Form 1040), line 27 (as refigured for the AMT, if necessary). See page 8 of the instructions. **30**

31 Enter the amount from Schedule D (Form 1040), line 25 (as refigured for the AMT, if necessary). See page 8 of the instructions. **31**

32 Add lines 30 and 31 . . . .   **32**

33 Enter the amount from Schedule D (Form 1040), line 22 (as refigured for the AMT, if necessary). See page 8 of the instructions **33**

34 Enter the **smaller** of line 32 or line 33 . . . .   **34**

35 Subtract line 34 from line 29. If zero or less. enter -0- . . . . ▶   **35**

36 If line 35 is $175,000 or less ($87,500 or less if married filing separately), multiply line 35 by 26% (.26). Otherwise, multiply line 35 by 28% (.28) and subtract $3,500 ($1,750 if married filing separately) from the result **36**

37 Enter the amount from Schedule D (Form 1040), line 36 (as figured for the regular tax). See page 8 of the instructions **37**

38 Enter the **smallest** of line 29, line 30, or line 37 . . . . ▶   **38**

39 Multiply line 38 by 10% (.10) **39**

40 Enter the **smaller** of line 29 or line 30 . . . .   **40**

41 Enter the amount from line 38 . . . .   **41**

42 Subtract line 41 from line 40 . . . . ▶   **42**

43 Multiply line 42 by 20% (.20) **43**

Note: *If line 31 is zero or blank, skip lines 44 through 47 and go to line 48.*

44 Enter the amount from line 29 . . . .   **44**

45 Add lines 35, 38, and 42. . . . .   **45**

46 Subtract line 45 from line 44 . . . .   **46**

47 Multiply line 46 by 25% (.25) **47**

48 Add lines 36, 39, 43, and 47 . . . .   **48**

49 If line 29 is $175,000 or less ($87,500 or less if married filing separately), multiply line 29 by 26% (.26). Otherwise, multiply line 29 by 28% (.28) and subtract $3,500 ($1,750 if married filing separately) from the result **49**

50 Enter the **smaller** of line 48 or line 49 here and on line 24 . . . .   **50**

Form **6251** (2000)

✪

Form **8832**
(December 1996)
Department of the Treasury
Internal Revenue Service

Entity Classification Election

OMB No. 1545-1516

Please Type or Print	Name of entity	Employer identification number (EIN)
	Number, street, and room or suite no. If a P.O. box, see instructions.	
	City or town, state, and ZIP code. If a foreign address, enter city, province or state, postal code and country.	

1   Type of election (see instructions):

a ☐ Initial classification by a newly-formed entity (or change in current classification of an existing entity to take effect on January 1, 1997)

b ☐ Change in current classification (to take effect later than January 1, 1997)

2   Form of entity (see instructions):

a ☐ A domestic eligible entity electing to be classified as an association taxable as a corporation.

b ☐ A domestic eligible entity electing to be classified as a partnership.

c ☐ A domestic eligible entity with a single owner electing to be disregarded as a separate entity.

d ☐ A foreign eligible entity electing to be classified as an association taxable as a corporation.

e ☐ A foreign eligible entity electing to be classified as a partnership.

f ☐ A foreign eligible entity with a single owner electing to be disregarded as a separate entity.

3   Election is to be effective beginning (month, day, year) (see instructions)   . . . . ▶ ___ / ___ / ___

4 Name and title of person whom the IRS may call for more information	**5** That person's telephone number

Consent Statement and Signature(s) (see instructions)

Under penalties of perjury, I (we) declare that I (we) consent to the election of the above-named entity to be classified as indicated above, and that I (we) have examined this consent statement, and to the best of my (our) knowledge and belief, it is true, correct, and complete. If I am an officer, manager, or member signing for all members of the entity, I further declare that I am authorized to execute this consent statement on their behalf.

Signature(s)	Date	Title

For **Paperwork Reduction Act Notice, see page 2.**   Cat No 22598R   Form **8832** (12-96)

General Instructions

Section references are to the Internal Revenue Code unless otherwise noted.

Paperwork Reduction Act Notice

We ask for the information on this form to carry out the Internal Revenue laws of the United States You are required to give us the information. We need it to ensure that you are complying with these laws and to allow us to figure and collect the right amount of tax.

You are not required to provide the information requested on a form that is subject to the Paperwork Reduction Act unless the form displays a valid OMB control number. Books or records relating to a form or its instructions must be retained as long as their contents may become material in the administration of any Internal Revenue law. Generally, tax returns and return information are confidential, as required by section 6103.

The time needed to complete and file this form will vary depending on individual circumstances. The estimated average time is:

Recordkeeping . . .1 hr., 20 min.
**Learning about the
law or the form** . . .1 hr., 41 min.
**Preparing and sending
the form to the IRS** . . . . .17 min.

If you have comments concerning the accuracy of these time estimates or suggestions for making this form simpler, we would be happy to hear from you. You can write to the Tax Forms Committee, Western Area Distribution Center, Rancho Cordova, CA 95743-0001. **DO NOT** send the form to this address. Instead, see **Where To File** on page 3.

Purpose of Form

For Federal tax purposes, certain business entities automatically are classified as corporations. See items **1** and **3** under the definition of corporation on this page. Other business entities may choose how they are classified for Federal tax purposes. Except for a business entity automatically classified as a corporation, a business entity with at least two

members can choose to be classified as either an association taxable as a corporation or a partnership, and a business entity with a single member can choose to be classified as either an association taxable as a corporation or disregarded as an entity separate from its owner.

Generally, an eligible entity that does not file this form will be classified under the default rules described below. An eligible entity that chooses not to be classified under the default rules or that wishes to change its current classification must file Form 8832 to elect a classification. The IRS will use the information entered on this form to establish the entity's filing and reporting requirements for Federal tax purposes.

Default Rules

Existing entity default rule.—
Certain domestic and foreign entities that are already in existence before January 1, 1997, generally do not need to make an election to continue that classification. However, for an eligible entity with a single owner that claimed to be a partnership under the law in effect before January 1, 1997, that entity will now be disregarded as an entity separate from its owner. If an existing entity decides to change its classification, it may do so subject to the rules in Regulations section 301.7701-3(c)(1)(iv). A foreign eligible entity is treated as being in existence prior to the effective date of this section only if the entity's classification is relevant at any time during the 60 months prior to January 1, 1997.

Domestic default rule.—Unless an election is made on Form 8832, a domestic eligible entity is:

1. A partnership if it has two or more members.

2. Disregarded as an entity separate from its owner if it has a single owner.

Foreign default rule.—Unless an election is made on Form 8832, a foreign eligible entity is:

1. A partnership if it has two or more members and at least one member does not have limited liability.

2. An association if all members have limited liability.

3. Disregarded as an entity separate from its owner if it has a single owner that does not have limited liability.

Definitions

Business entity.—A business entity is any entity recognized for Federal tax purposes that is not properly classified as a trust under Regulations section 301.7701-4 or otherwise subject to special treatment under the Code. See Regulations section 301.7701-2(a).

Corporation.—For Federal tax purposes, a corporation is any of the following:

1. A business entity organized under a Federal or state statute, or under a statute of a federally recognized Indian tribe, if the statute describes or refers to the entity as incorporated or as a corporation, body corporate, or body politic.

2. An association (as determined under Regulations section 301.7701-3).

3. A business entity organized under a state statute, if the statute describes or refers to the entity as a joint-stock company or joint-stock association.

4. An insurance company.

5. A state-chartered business entity conducting banking activities, if any of its deposits are insured under the Federal Deposit Insurance Act, as amended, 12 U.S.C. 1811 et seq., or a similar Federal statute.

6. A business entity wholly owned by a state or any political subdivision thereof.

7. A business entity that is taxable as a corporation under a provision of the Code other than section 7701(a)(3).

8. A foreign business entity listed in Regulations section 301.7701-2(b)(8). However, a foreign business entity listed in those regulations generally will not be treated as a corporation if all of the following apply:

a. The entity was in existence on May 8, 1996.

b. The entity's classification was relevant (as defined below) on May 8, 1996.

c. No person (including the entity) for whom the entity's classification was relevant on May 8, 1996, treats the entity as a corporation for purposes of filing that person's Federal income tax returns, information returns, and withholding documents for the tax year including May 8, 1996.

d. Any change in the entity's claimed classification within the 60 months prior to May 8, 1996, was a result of a change in the organizational documents of the entity, and the entity and all members of the entity recognized the Federal tax consequences of any change in the entity's classification within the 60 months prior to May 8, 1996.

e. The entity had a reasonable basis (within the meaning of section 6662) for treating the entity as other than a corporation on May 8, 1996.

f. Neither the entity nor any member was notified in writing on or before May 8, 1996, that the classification of the entity was under examination (in which case the entity's classification will be determined in the examination).

Binding contract rule.—If a foreign business entity described in Regulations section 301.7701-2(b)(8)(i) is formed after May 8, 1996, under a written binding contract (including an accepted bid to develop a project) in effect on May 8, 1996, and all times thereafter, in which the parties agreed to engage (directly or indirectly) in an active and substantial business operation in the jurisdiction in which the entity is formed, **8** on page 2 is applied by substituting the date of the entity's formation for May 8, 1996.

Eligible entity.—An eligible entity is a business entity that is not included in items **1** or **3** through **8** under the definition of corporation on page 2.

Limited liability.—A member of a foreign eligible entity has limited liability if the member has no personal liability for any debts of or claims against the entity by reason of being a member. This determination is based solely on the statute or law under which the entity is organized (and, if relevant, the entity's organizational documents). A member has personal liability if the creditors of the entity may seek satisfaction of all or any part of the debts or claims against the entity from the member as such. A member has personal liability even if the member makes an agreement under which another person (whether or not a member of the entity) assumes that liability or agrees to indemnify that member for that liability.

Partnership.—A partnership is a business entity that has **at least** two members and is not a corporation as defined on page 2.

Relevant.—A foreign eligible entity's classification is relevant when its classification affects the liability of any person for Federal tax or information purposes. The date the classification of a foreign eligible entity is relevant is the date an event occurs that creates an obligation to file a Federal tax return, information return, or statement for which the classification of the entity must be determined.

Effect of Election

The resulting tax consequences of a change in classification remain the same no matter how a change in entity classification is achieved. For example, if an organization classified as an association elects to be classified as a partnership, the organization and its owners must recognize gain, if any, under the rules applicable to liquidations of corporations.

Who Must File

File this form for an **eligible entity** that is one of the following:

● A domestic entity electing to be classified as an association taxable as a corporation.

● A domestic entity electing to change its current classification (even if it is currently classified under the default rule).

● A foreign entity that has more than one owner, all owners have limited liability, and it elects to be classified as a partnership.

● A foreign entity that has at least one owner without limited liability, and it elects to be classified as an association taxable as a corporation.

● A foreign entity with a single owner having limited liability, and it elects to have the entity disregarded as an entity separate from its owner.

● A foreign entity electing to change its current classification (even if it is currently classified under the default rule).

Do not file this form for an eligible entity that is:

● Tax-exempt under section 501(a), or

● A real estate investment trust (REIT), as defined in section 856.

When To File

See the instructions for line 3.

Where To File

File Form 8832 with the Internal Revenue Service Center, Philadelphia, PA 19255. Also attach a copy of Form 8832 to the entity's Federal income tax return for the tax year of the election. If the entity is not required to file a return for that year, a copy of its Form 8832 must be attached to the Federal income tax or information returns of all direct or indirect owners of the entity for the tax year of the owner that includes the date on which the election took effect. Although failure to attach a copy will not invalidate an otherwise valid election, each member of the entity is required to file returns that are consistent with the entity's election. In addition, penalties may be assessed against persons who are required to, but who do not, attach Form 8832 to their returns. Other penalties may apply for filing Federal income tax or information returns inconsistent with the entity's election.

Specific Instructions

Employer Identification Number (EIN)

Show the correct EIN on Form 8832. If the entity does not have an EIN, it generally must apply for one on **Form SS-4,** Application for Employer Identification Number. If the filing of Form 8832 is the only reason the entity is applying for an EIN, check the "Other" box on line 9 of Form SS-4 and write "Form 8832" to the right of that box. If the entity has not received an EIN by the time Form 8832 is due, write "Applied for" in the space for the EIN. **Do not** apply for a new EIN for an existing entity that is changing its classification. If you are electing to disregard an entity as separate from its owner, enter the owner's EIN.

Address

Include the suite, room, or other unit number after the street address. If the Post Office does not deliver mail to the street address and the entity has a P.O. box, show the box number instead of the street address.

Line 1

Check box 1a if the entity is choosing a classification for the first time **and** the entity does not want to be classified under the applicable default classification. **Do not** file this form if the entity wants to be classified under the default rules.

Check box 1b if the entity is changing its current classification to take effect later than January 1, 1997, whether or not the entity's current classification is the default classification. However, once an eligible entity makes an election to change its classification (other than an election made by an existing entity to change its classification as of January 1, 1997), the entity cannot change its classification by election again during the 60 months after the effective date of the election. However, the IRS may permit (by private letter ruling) the entity to change its classification by election within the 60-month period if more than 50% of the ownership interests in the entity as of the effective date of the election are owned by persons that did not own any interests in the entity on the effective date of the entity's prior election.

Line 2

Check the appropriate box if you are changing a current classification (no matter how achieved), or are electing out of a default classification. **Do not** file this form if you fall within a default classification that is the desired classification for the new entity.

Line 3

Generally, the election will take effect on the date you enter on line 3 of this form or on the date filed if no date is entered on line 3. However, an election specifying an entity's classification for Federal tax purposes can take effect no more than 75 days prior to the date the election is filed, nor can it take effect later than 12 months after the date on which the election is filed. If line 3 shows a date more than 75 days prior to the date on which the election is filed, the election will take effect 75 days before the date it is filed. If line 3 shows an effective date more than 12 months from the filing date, the election will take effect 12 months after the date the election was filed.

Regardless of the date filed, an election will in no event take effect before January 1, 1997.

Consent Statement and Signatures

Form 8832 must be signed by:

1. Each member of the electing entity who is an owner at the time the election is filed; or

2. Any officer, manager, or member of the electing entity who is authorized (under local law or the organizational documents) to make the election and who represents to having such authorization under penalties of perjury.

If an election is to be effective for any period prior to the time it is filed, each person who was an owner between the date the election is to be effective and the date election is filed, and who is not an owner at the time the election is filed, must also sign.

If you need a continuation sheet or use a separate consent statement, attach it to Form 8832. The separate consent statement must contain the same information as shown on Form 8832.

Form **6765**	**Credit for Increasing Research Activities**	OMB No. 1545-0619
Department of the Treasury Internal Revenue Service	▶ See separate instructions. ▶ Attach to your return.	**2000** Attachment Sequence No. **81**
Name(s) shown on return		Identifying number

Part I   Current Year Credit (Members of controlled groups or businesses under common control, see instructions.)

Section A—Regular Credit. Skip this section and go to Section B if you are electing or previously elected the alternative incremental credit.

1	Basic research payments paid or incurred to qualified organizations (see instructions). . . .	1	
2	Qualified organization base period amount	2	
3	Subtract line 2 from line 1. If zero or less, enter -0-	3	
4	Wages for qualified services (do not include wages used in figuring the work opportunity credit)	4	
5	Cost of supplies	5	
6	Rental or lease costs of computers (see instructions).	6	
7	Enter the applicable percentage of contract research expenses (see instructions)	7	
8	Total qualified research expenses. Add lines 4 through 7	8	
9	Enter fixed-base percentage, but not more than 16% (see instructions)	9	%
10	Enter average annual gross receipts (see instructions)	10	
11	Multiply line 10 by the percentage on line 9	11	
12	Subtract line 11 from line 8. If zero or less, enter -0-	12	
13	Multiply line 8 by 50% (.50)	13	
14	Enter the **smaller** of line 12 or line 13	14	
15	Add lines 3 and 14	15	
16	**Regular credit.** If you are not electing the reduced credit under section 280C(c), multiply line 15 by 20% (.20), enter the result, and see the instructions for the schedule that must be attached. If you are electing the reduced credit, multiply line 15 by 13% (.13) and enter the result. Also, write "Sec. 280C" on the dotted line to the left of the entry space	16	

Section B—Alternative Incremental Credit. Skip this section if you completed Section A.

17	Basic research payments paid or incurred to qualified organizations (see the line 1 instructions)	17	
18	Qualified organization base period amount	18	
19	Subtract line 18 from line 17. If zero or less, enter -0-	19	
20	Multiply line 19 by 20% (.20)	20	
21	Wages for qualified services (do not include wages used in figuring the work opportunity credit)	21	
22	Cost of supplies	22	
23	Rental or lease costs of computers (see the line 6 instructions)	23	
24	Enter the applicable percentage of contract research expenses (see the line 7 instructions) . .	24	
25	Total qualified research expenses. Add lines 21 through 24	25	
26	Enter average annual gross receipts (see the line 10 instructions)	26	
27	Multiply line 26 by 1% (.01)	27	
28	Subtract line 27 from line 25. If zero or less, enter -0-	28	
29	Multiply line 26 by 1.5% (.015)	29	
30	Subtract line 29 from line 25. If zero or less, enter -0-	30	
31	Subtract line 30 from line 28	31	
32	Multiply line 26 by 2% (.02)	32	
33	Subtract line 32 from line 25. If zero or less, enter -0-	33	
34	Subtract line 33 from line 30	34	
35	Multiply line 31 by 2.65% (.0265)	35	
36	Multiply line 34 by 3.2% (.032)	36	
37	Multiply line 33 by 3.75% (.0375)	37	
38	Add lines 20, 35, 36, and 37	38	
39	**Alternative incremental credit.** If you are not electing the reduced credit under section 280C(c), enter the amount from line 38, and see the line 16 instructions for the schedule that must be attached. If you are electing the reduced credit, multiply line 38 by 65% (.65) and enter the result. Also, write "Sec. 280C" on the dotted line to the left of the entry space	39	

Section C—Total Current Year Credit for Increasing Research Activities

40	Pass-through research credit(s) from a partnership, S corporation, estate, or trust	40	
41	**Total current year credit.** Add line 16 **or** line 39 to line 40, and **go to Part II** on the back . .	41	

For Paperwork Reduction Act Notice, see separate instructions.   Cat. No. 13700H   Form **6765** (2000)

Form 6765 (2000)   Page **2**

Part II   **Suspended and Allowable Current Year Credits**

42	Enter the amount from line 41	**42**
43	Credit attributable to the first suspension period. Multiply line 42 by the applicable suspension percentage (see instructions). **43**	
44	Credit attributable to the second suspension period. Multiply line 42 by the applicable suspension percentage (see instructions). . . . **44**	
45	Add lines 43 and 44	**45**
46	Subtract line 45 from line 42	**46**

Part III   **Tax Liability Limit** (See **Who Must File Form 3800** to find out if you complete Part III or file Form 3800.)

47 Regular tax before credits:
* Individuals. Enter the amount from Form 1040, line 40 . . . .
* Corporations. Enter the amount from Form 1120, Schedule J, line 3; Form 1120-A, Part I, line 1; or the amount from the applicable line of your return **47**
* Estates and trusts. Enter the sum of the amounts from Form 1041, Schedule G, lines 1a and 1b, or the applicable line of your return . . . .

48 Alternative minimum tax:
* Individuals. Enter the amount from Form 6251, line 28 . . . .
* Corporations. Enter the amount from Form 4626, line 15 . . . . **48**
* Estates and trusts. Enter the amount from Form 1041, Schedule I, line 39 . .

49 Add lines 47 and 48 . . . . **49**

50a	Foreign tax credit **50a**	
b	Credit for child and dependent care expenses (Form 2441, line 9) . **50b**	
c	Credit for the elderly or the disabled (Schedule R (Form 1040), line 20) **50c**	
d	Education credits (Form 8863, line 18) **50d**	
e	Child tax credit (Form 1040, line 47) **50e**	
f	Mortgage interest credit (Form 8396, line 11) **50f**	
g	Adoption credit (Form 8839, line 14) **50g**	
h	District of Columbia first-time homebuyer credit (Form 8859, line 11) **50h**	
i	Possessions tax credit (Form 5735, line 17 or 27) **50i**	
j	Credit for fuel from a nonconventional source **50j**	
k	Qualified electric vehicle credit (Form 8834, line 19) **50k**	
l	Add lines 50a through 50k **50l**	
51	Net income tax. Subtract line 50l from line 49 . . . . **51**	

52 Tentative minimum tax (see instructions):
* Individuals. Enter the amount from Form 6251, line 26 . . . . .
* Corporations. Enter the amount from Form 4626, line 13 . . . . **52**
* Estates and trusts. Enter the amount from Form 1041, Schedule I, line 37 . . . .

53	Net regular tax. Subtract line 50l from line 47. If zero or less, enter -0- **53**	
54	Enter 25% (.25) of the excess, if any, of line 53 over $25,000 (see instructions) **54**	
55	Enter the greater of line 52 or line 54 . . . . **55**	
56	Subtract line 55 from line 51. If zero or less, enter -0- **56**	
57	**Total credit allowed for the current year. Individuals, estates, and trusts:** Enter the **smallest** of line 42, line 56, or the amount from the formula in the instructions for line 57. **Corporations:** Enter the **smaller** of line 42 or line 56. . . . . **57**	
58	**Suspended credit allowed for the current year.** Subtract line 46 from line 57. If zero or less, enter -0- (see instructions for when and how to claim) **58**	
59	**Credit for increasing research activities allowed on current year return.** Subtract line 58 from line 57. Enter here and on Form 1040, line 49; Form 1120, Schedule J, line 6d; Form 1120-A, Part I, line 4a; Form 1041, Schedule G, line 2c; or the applicable line of other returns. . . . **59**	

⊕

Form **6765** (2000)

Department of the Treasury
Internal Revenue Service

Instructions for Form 6765

Credit for Increasing Research Activities

Section references are to the Internal Revenue Code.

General Instructions

Purpose of Form

Use Form 6765 to figure and claim the credit for increasing research activities (research credit).

Who Must File

An individual, estate, trust, organization, or corporation claiming a credit for increasing research activities; or any S corporation, partnership, estate, or trust that allocates the credit to its shareholders, partners, or beneficiaries must complete this form and attach it to its income tax return.

Qualified Research

The research credit is generally allowed for qualified research. **Qualified research** means research for which expenditures may be treated as section 174 expenses. This research must be undertaken for discovering information that is technological in nature, and its application must be intended for use in developing a new or improved business component of the taxpayer. In addition, substantially all of the activities of the research must be elements of a process of experimentation relating to a new or improved function, performance, reliability, or quality.

The research credit is generally **not** allowed for the following types of activities:

- Research conducted after the beginning of commercial production.
- Research adapting an existing product or process to a particular customer's need.
- Duplication of an existing product or process.
- Surveys or studies.
- Research relating to certain internal-use computer software.
- Research conducted outside the United States, Puerto Rico, or a U.S. possession.
- Research in the social sciences, arts, or humanities.
- Research funded by another person (or governmental entity).

If you incur qualified clinical testing expenses relating to drugs for certain rare diseases, you may elect to claim the orphan drug credit on these expenses instead of taking the research credit. See **Form 8820**, Orphan Drug Credit.

See section 41 for other definitions and special rules.

Special Rules

See section 41(f) for special rules related to:

- Allocation of the credit by partnerships, estates, and trusts;
- Adjustments if a major portion of a business is acquired or disposed of; and
- Short tax years.

For special rules concerning the allocation and apportionment of research and experimental expenditures between U.S. and foreign source income, see sections 861 through 864.

If you cannot use the research credit because of the tax liability limit, carry it back 1 year then forward up to 20 years. See **Form 3800**, General Business Credit, for details, and see the instructions for Part II for when and how any suspended credit may be claimed.

Specific Instructions

Part I—Current Year Credit

You may claim the regular credit (Section A) or elect the alternative incremental credit (Section B). Under the alternative incremental credit, a smaller three-tiered fixed-base percentage and reduced three-tiered credit rate apply. You may want to figure your credit both ways to see which gives you the larger credit. However, once elected, the alternative incremental credit applies to the current tax year and all later tax years, unless you receive IRS consent to revoke the election.

Members of Controlled Groups or Businesses Under Common Control

For purposes of figuring the credit, all members of a controlled group of corporations (as defined in section 41(f)(5)), and all members of a group of businesses under common control, are treated as a single taxpayer. The credit allowed each member is based on its proportionate shares of the group's qualified research expenses and basic research payments. Use Section A or B of Part I to figure the credit for the entire group, but enter only this member's share of the credit on line 16 or line 39, whichever applies. Attach a statement showing how this member's share of the credit was figured, and write "See attached" next to the entry space for line 16 or line 39.

Section A—Regular Credit

Skip this section and go to Section B if you are electing or previously elected the alternative incremental credit (and have not requested and received permission to revoke the election).

Line 1

Corporations (other than S corporations, personal holding companies, and service organizations) may be eligible for a "basic research" credit if payments in cash to a qualified university or scientific research organization (under a written contract) exceed a base period amount (based on their general university giving and certain other maintenance-of-effort levels for the 3 preceding years). Enter your payments on this line. See section 41(e) for details.

Line 2

Enter the qualified organization base period amount as defined in section 41(e). The amount on line 2 (not to exceed the amount on line 1), although not eligible for the basic research credit, can be treated as contract research expenses on line 7 subject to the 65% (or 75%) limitation.

Line 6

Enter the amount you paid or incurred for the rental or lease of computers used in qualified research. The computer must be located off your premises and you must not be the operator or primary user of the computer. Reduce this amount by the amount that you (or any member of a controlled group of corporations or businesses under common control) received or accrued for the right to use substantially identical property.

Line 7

Include 65% of any amount you paid or incurred for qualified research performed on your behalf. Prepaid contract research expenses are considered paid in the year the research is actually done. Also, include 65% of that portion of the line 1 basic research payments that does not exceed the line 2 base amount.

However, use 75% in place of 65% for payments made to a qualified research consortium. A qualified research consortium is a tax-exempt organization described in section 501(c)(3) or 501(c)(6) that is organized and operated primarily to conduct scientific research and is not a private foundation.

Line 9

The fixed-base percentage depends on whether you are an existing company or a start-up company.

A start-up company is a taxpayer that had **both** gross receipts and qualified research expenses either:

• For the first time in a tax year beginning after 1983, or
• For fewer than 3 tax years beginning after 1983 and before 1989.

The fixed-base percentage for a start-up company is figured as follows.

• For the first 5 tax years beginning after 1993 for which you have qualified research expenses, the percentage is 3%.
• For the 6th tax year beginning after 1993 for which you have qualified research expenses, divide the aggregate qualified research expenses for the 4th and 5th such tax years by the aggregate gross receipts for those tax years, and multiply the result by 0.1667.

Page 2

Note: See section 41(c)(3)(B)(ii) to figure the fixed-base percentage for any tax year after the 6th tax year beginning after 1993 for which you have qualified research expenses.

The fixed-base percentage for an existing company (any company that is not a start-up company) is figured by dividing the aggregate qualified research expenses for the tax years beginning after 1983 and before 1989 by the aggregate gross receipts for those tax years.

The fixed-base percentage for all companies (existing and start-up) must be rounded to the nearest 1/100th of 1% (i.e., four decimal places) and cannot exceed 16%. In addition, when figuring your fixed-base percentage, you must reflect expenses for qualified research conducted in Puerto Rico or a U.S. possession for the prior tax years included in the computation.

If gross receipts or qualified expenses are de minimis in a tax year or short tax years are involved, see sections 41(c)(3) and 41(f)(4).

Note: Reduce gross receipts by returns and allowances. For a foreign corporation, include only gross receipts that are effectively connected with a trade or business in the United States (or in Puerto Rico or a U.S. possession, if applicable).

Line 10

Enter the average annual gross receipts (reduced by returns and allowances) for the 4 tax years preceding the tax year for which the credit is being determined. You may be required to annualize gross receipts for any short tax year. For a foreign corporation, include only gross receipts that are effectively connected with a trade or business in the United States (or in Puerto Rico or a U.S. possession, if applicable).

Line 16

If you do not elect the reduced credit, you must reduce your otherwise allowable deduction for qualified research expenses or basic research expenses by the amount of the credit on this line. If the credit exceeds the amount allowed as a deduction for the tax year, reduce the amount chargeable to the capital account for the year for such expenses by the amount of the excess.

Attach a schedule to your tax return that lists the deduction amounts (or capitalized expenses) that were reduced. Identify the lines of your return (schedule or forms for capitalized items) on which the reductions were made.

Section B—Alternative Incremental Credit

Complete this section **only** if you are electing or previously elected the alternative incremental credit instead of the regular credit (and have not requested and received permission to revoke the election).

Line 18

Enter the qualified organization base period amount as defined in section 41(e). The amount on line 18 (not to exceed the amount on line 17), although not eligible for the basic research credit, can be treated as contract research expenses on line 24 subject to the 65% (or 75%) limitation.

246   APPENDIX D

Section C—Current Year Credit

Line 40
Enter the amount of credit that was allocated to you as a shareholder, partner, or beneficiary.

Line 41
Pass-through entities should report the amount on line 41 as follows.
Estates and trusts. Allocate the research credit on line 41 between the estate or trust and the beneficiaries in the same proportion as income was allocated. In the margin for line 41, the estate or trust should enter its share of the credit. Label it "1041 Portion" and use this amount in Parts II and III (or on Form 3800, if required) to figure the credit to take on Form 1041. On Schedule K-1, show the credit allocated to each beneficiary.
S corporations and partnerships. Attach Form 6765 to Form 1120S or 1065, and on Schedule K-1 show the credit allocated to each shareholder or partner. Electing large partnerships should include this credit in "general credits."

Part II—Suspended and Allowable Current Year Credits
Any research credit attributable to the **first suspension period** (July 1, 1999, through September 30, 2000) may not be claimed or otherwise taken into account before October 1, 2000. Any research credit attributable to the **second suspension period** (October 1, 2000, through September 30, 2001) may not be claimed or otherwise taken into account before October 1, 2001. See the instructions for lines 43 and 44 to figure the credit attributable to each suspension period.

The suspended credit allowed for the current year may **not** be claimed on your original income tax return. Instead, see the instructions for line 58 for when and how to claim it.

Any credit not allowed for the current year that is attributable to either suspension period may not be claimed as a carryback or carryforward until the day after the end of the suspension period. The credit not allowed for the current year is the excess of line 42 over line 57 (or the amount of the research credit included on Form 3800, line 18b, if applicable). You must apply the credit **not** allowed for the current year in the following order.

- Any credit not attributable to either suspension period.
- Any credit attributable to the first suspension period.
- Any credit attributable to the second suspension period.

Line 43
Multiply the amount on line 42 by the applicable suspension percentage. The applicable suspension percentage is the number of months in your tax year included in the first suspension period divided by the total number of months in your tax year. However, if you have a research credit in a flow-through entity that has a tax year different from your tax year, you must instead multiply that portion of the credit by the number of months in the entity's tax year

included in the first suspension period divided by the total number of months in the entity's tax year.

Line 44
Multiply the amount on line 42 by the applicable suspension percentage. The applicable suspension percentage is the number of months in your tax year included in the second suspension period (see above) divided by the total number of months in your tax year. However, if you have a research credit on line 40 from a flow-through entity that has a tax year different from your tax year, you must instead multiply that portion of the credit by the number of months in the entity's tax year included in the second suspension period divided by the total number of months in the entity's tax year.

Who Must File Form 3800
Complete Form 3800 instead of Part III of Form 6765, to figure the tax liability limit for the credit if for this year you have:

- More than one of the credits included in the general business credit (see list below),
- A carryback or carryforward of any of the credits,
- A research credit from a passive activity, or
- General credits from an electing large partnership (Schedule K-1 (Form 1065-B)).

The general business credit consists of the following credits.
- Investment (Form 3468).
- Work opportunity (Form 5884).
- Welfare-to-work (Form 8861).
- Alcohol used as fuel (Form 6478).
- Research (Form 6765).
- Low-income housing (Form 8586).
- Enhanced oil recovery (Form 8830).
- Disabled access (Form 8826).
- Renewable electricity production (Form 8835).
- Indian employment (Form 8845).
- Employer social security and Medicare taxes paid on certain employee tips (Form 8846).
- Orphan drug (Form 8820).
- Contributions to selected community development corporations (Form 8847).
- Trans-Alaska pipeline liability fund.

The empowerment zone employment credit (Form 8844), while a component of the general business credit, is figured separately on Form 8844 and is never carried to Form 3800.

Part III—Tax Liability Limit

Line 52
Although you may not owe alternative minimum tax (AMT), you generally must still compute the tentative minimum tax (TMT) to figure your credit. For a small corporation exempt from the AMT under section 55(e), enter zero. Otherwise, enter the TMT that was figured on the appropriate AMT form or schedule.

Line 54.

See section 38(c)(3) for special rules that apply to married couples filing separate returns, controlled corporate groups, regulated investment companies, real estate investment trusts, and estates and trusts.

Line 57

For an individual, estate, or trust, the credit(s) on line 16, 39, or 40 is limited to the amount of tax attributable to your taxable income from the sole proprietorship or your interest in the partnership, S corporation, estate, or trust (pass-through entity) generating the credit. Figure the research credit limitation separately for each business enterprise by using the following formula:

(Line 51 – Line 54) x Taxable income attributable to the sole proprietorship or your interest in the pass-through entity / Taxable income for the year (Form 1040, line 39, or Form 1041, line 22)

The credit is limited to 100% of line 51 minus line 54. If in the current tax year you had no taxable income attributable to a particular business interest, you cannot claim any research credit this year for that business.

Line 58

The amount on line 58 (or on Form 3800, line 18c, if applicable) is allowed for the current year, but is temporarily suspended and may not be claimed on your original income tax return. Instead, this amount may be claimed only on **Form 1045,** Application for Tentative Refund, or **Form 1139,** Corporation Application for Tentative Refund (Rev. September 2000), **Form 1040X,** Amended U.S. Individual Income tax Return, **Form 1102X,** Amended U.S. Corporation Income Tax Return, or other amended return form. The portion attributable to the **first** suspension period (the **smaller** of **(a)** line 58 (or Form 3800, line 18c) or **(b)** Form 6765, line 43) may not be claimed before October 1, 2000. Any remaining portion of the amount on line 58 is attributable to the **second** suspension period and may not be claimed before October 1, 2001.

You must make a separate request for a refund of the suspended credit attributable to each suspension period. Do not request the refund before you file your tax return.

To request the refund, complete the applicable form as follows.

- **Form 1045.** Skip lines 3 and 9 through 29 and enter the amount to be refunded on line 30.
- **Form 1139.** Skip lines 3, 9, and 11 through 28 and enter the amount to be refunded on line 29.
- **Form 1040X.** Skip lines 1 through 22 and enter the amount to be refunded on line 23.
- **Form 1120X.** Skip lines 1 through 9 and enter the amount to be refunded on line 10.

Write **Application for Expedited Refund—Suspended Research Credit** at the top of the applicable form. Attach a copy of the Form 6765 you filed with your tax return. Also attach a copy of the tax return form (Form 1040, 1120, etc.), and Form 3800, if you filed it with your tax return. **Do not** amend or otherwise change any of the amounts on any of these forms, even if you are filing them with an amended tax return form. If you want to apply any of the refund as an estimated tax payment, enter the amount you want applied on Form 1040X, line 24, or attach a statement to Form 1045, 1139, or 1120X.

Paperwork Reduction Act Notice. We ask for the information on this form to carry out the Internal Revenue laws of the United States. You are required to give us the information. We need it to ensure that you are complying with these laws and to allow us to figure and collect the right amount of tax.

You are not required to provide the information requested on a form that is subject to the Paperwork Reduction Act unless the form displays a valid OMB control number. Books or records relating to a form or its instructions must be retained as long as their contents may become material in the administration of any Internal Revenue law. Generally, tax returns and return information are confidential, as required by section 6103.

The time needed to complete and file this form will vary depending on individual circumstances. The estimated average time is:

Recordkeeping.. 18 hr., 39 min.
Learning about the law or the form .... 1 hr., 47 min.
Preparing and sending the form to the IRS................. 2 hr., 10 min.

If you have comments concerning the accuracy of these time estimates or suggestions for making this form simpler, we would be happy to hear from you. See the instructions for the tax return with which this form is filed.

Form **SS-8** (Rev. January 2001) Department of the Treasury Internal Revenue Service	**Determination of Worker Status for Purposes of Federal Employment Taxes and Income Tax Withholding**	OMB No. 1545-0004

Name of firm (or person) for whom the worker performed services	Worker's name	
Firm's address (include street address, apt. or suite no., city, state, and ZIP code)	Worker's address (include street address, apt. or suite no., city, state, and ZIP code)	
Trade name	Telephone number (include area code) ( )	Worker's social security number
Telephone number (include area code) ( ) Firm's employer identification number	Worker's employer identification number (if any)	

Important Information Needed To Process Your Request

If this form is being completed by the worker, the IRS must have your permission to disclose your name to the firm. Do you object to disclosing your name and the information on this form to the firm? . . . . ☐ **Yes** ☐ **No**
If you answered "Yes" or did not check a box, stop here. The IRS cannot act on your request and a determination will not be issued.

You must answer ALL items OR mark them "Unknown" or "Does not apply." If you need more space, attach another sheet.

A This form is being completed by: ☐ Firm ☐ Worker; for services performed _____ to _____ .
                                                                                                    (beginning date)   (ending date)

B Explain your reason(s) for filing this form (e.g., you received a bill from the IRS, you believe you received a Form 1099 or Form W-2 erroneously, you are unable to get worker's compensation benefits, you were audited or are being audited by the IRS). -----------------------------
----

C Total number of workers who performed or are performing the same or similar services _____

D How did the worker obtain the job? ☐ Application   ☐ Bid   ☐ Employment Agency   ☐ Other (specify) _____

E Attach copies of all supporting documentation (contracts, invoices, memos, Forms W-2, Forms 1099, IRS closing agreements, IRS rulings, etc.). In addition, please inform us of any current or past litigation concerning the worker's status. If no income reporting forms (Form 1099-MISC or W-2) were furnished to the worker, enter the amount of income earned for the year(s) at issue $ _____ .

F Describe the firm's business. --

G Describe the work done by the worker and provide the worker's job title. --------------------------------------
----

H Explain why you believe the worker is an employee or an independent contractor. -------------------------------
----

I Did the worker perform services for the firm before getting this position? . . . . ☐ **Yes** ☐ **No** ☐ **N/A**
If "Yes," what were the dates of the prior service? ---
If "Yes," explain the differences, if any, between the current and prior service. -----------------------------------
----

J If the work is done under a written agreement between the firm and the worker, attach a copy (preferably signed by both parties). Describe the terms and conditions of the work arrangement. ---

---

For Privacy Act and Paperwork Reduction Act Notice, see page 5.   Cat. No. 16106T   Form **SS-8** (Rev. 1-2001)

Part I   Behavioral Control

1 What specific training and/or instruction is the worker given by the firm? ....

2 How does the worker receive work assignments? ....

3 Who determines the methods by which the assignments are performed? ....

4 Who is the worker required to contact if problems or complaints arise and who is responsible for their resolution? ....

5 What types of reports are required from the worker? Attach examples. ....

6 Describe the worker's daily routine (i.e., schedule, hours, etc.). ....

7 At what location(s) does the worker perform services (e.g., firm's premises, own shop or office, home, customer's location, etc.)? ....

8 Describe any meetings the worker is required to attend and any penalties for not attending (e.g., sales meetings, monthly meetings, staff meetings, etc.). ....

9 Is the worker required to provide the services personally? . . . . ☐ Yes   ☐ No

10 If substitutes or helpers are needed, who hires them? ....

11 If the worker hires the substitutes or helpers, is approval required? . . . . ☐ Yes   ☐ No
If "Yes," by whom? ....

12 Who pays the substitutes or helpers? ....

13 Is the worker reimbursed if the worker pays the substitutes or helpers? . . . . ☐ Yes   ☐ No
If "Yes," by whom? ....

Part II   Financial Control

1 List the supplies, equipment, materials, and property provided by each party:
The firm ....
The worker ....
Other party ....

2 Does the worker lease equipment? . . . . ☐ Yes   ☐ No
If "Yes," what are the terms of the lease? (Attach a copy or explanatory statement.) ....

3 What expenses are incurred by the worker in the performance of services for the firm? ....

4 Specify which, if any, expenses are reimbursed by:
The firm ....
Other party ....

5 Type of pay the worker receives: ☐ Salary   ☐ Commission   ☐ Hourly Wage   ☐ Piece Work
☐ Lump Sum   ☐ Other (specify) ....
If type of pay is commission, and the firm guarantees a minimum amount of pay, specify amount $ _____ .

6 If the worker is paid by a firm other than the one listed on this form for these services, enter name, address, and employer identification number of the payer. ....

7 Is the worker allowed a drawing account for advances? . . . . ☐ Yes   ☐ No
If "Yes," how often? ....
Specify any restrictions. ....

8 Whom does the customer pay? . . . . ☐ Firm   ☐ Worker
If worker, does the worker pay the total amount to the firm?   ☐ Yes   ☐ No   If "No," explain. ....

9 Does the firm carry worker's compensation insurance on the worker? . . . . ☐ Yes   ☐ No

10 What economic loss or financial risk, if any, can the worker incur beyond the normal loss of salary (e.g., loss or damage of equipment, material, etc.)? ....

Form **SS-8** (Rev. 1-2001)

250 APPENDIX D

Part III   Relationship of the Worker and Firm

1   List the benefits available to the worker (e.g., paid vacations, sick pay, pensions, bonuses). ....

2   Can the relationship be terminated by either party without incurring liability or penalty?   . . . . ☐ **Yes**   ☐ **No**
If "No," explain your answer. ....

3   Does the worker perform similar services for others?   . . . . ☐ **Yes**   ☐ **No**
If "Yes," is the worker required to get approval from the firm? . . . . ☐ **Yes**   ☐ **No**

4   Describe any agreements prohibiting competition between the worker and the firm while the worker is performing services or during any later period. Attach any available documentation. ....

5   Is the worker a member of a union?   . . . . ☐ **Yes**   ☐ **No**

6   What type of advertising, if any, does the worker do (e.g., a business listing in a directory, business cards, etc.)? Provide copies, if applicable.

7   If the worker assembles or processes a product at home, who provides the materials and instructions or pattern? ....

8   What does the worker do with the finished product (e.g., return it to the firm, provide it to another party, or sell it)? ....

9   How does the firm represent the worker to its customers (e.g., employee, partner, representative, or contractor)? ....

10   If the worker no longer performs services for the firm, how did the relationship end? ....

Part IV   For Service Providers or Salespersons—Complete this part if the worker provided a service directly to customers or is a salesperson.

1   What are the worker's responsibilities in soliciting new customers? ....

2   Who provides the worker with leads to prospective customers? ....
3   Describe any reporting requirements pertaining to the leads. ....

4   What terms and conditions of sale, if any, are required by the firm? ....
5   Are orders submitted to and subject to approval by the firm? . . . . ☐ **Yes**   ☐ **No**
6   Who determines the worker's territory? ....
7   Did the worker pay for the privilege of serving customers on the route or in the territory? . . . . ☐ **Yes**   ☐ **No**
If "Yes," whom did the worker pay? ....
If "Yes," how much did the worker pay?   . . . . $_____
8   Where does the worker sell the product (e.g., in a home, retail establishment, etc.)? ....

9   List the product and/or services distributed by the worker (e.g., meat, vegetables, fruit, bakery products, beverages, or laundry or dry cleaning services). If more than one type of product and/or service is distributed, specify the principal one. ....

10   Does the worker sell life insurance full time?   . . . . ☐ **Yes**   ☐ **No**
11   Does the worker sell other types of insurance for the firm? . . . . ☐ **Yes**   ☐ **No**
If "Yes," enter the percentage of the worker's total working time spent in selling other types of insurance.   . . . _____%
12   If the worker solicits orders from wholesalers, retailers, contractors, or operators of hotels, restaurants, or other similar establishments, enter the percentage of the worker's time spent in the solicitation.   . . . . _____%
13   Is the merchandise purchased by the customers for resale or use in their business operations? . . . . ☐ **Yes**   ☐ **No**
Describe the merchandise and state whether it is equipment installed on the customers' premises. ....

Part V   Signature (see page 4)

Under penalties of perjury, I declare that I have examined this request, including accompanying documents, and to the best of my knowledge and belief, the facts presented are true, correct, and complete.

Signature ▶ _____   Title ▶ _____   Date ▶ _____
(Type or print name below)

General Instructions

Section references are to the Internal Revenue Code unless otherwise noted.

Purpose

Firms and workers file Form SS-8 to request a determination of the status of a worker for purposes of Federal employment taxes and income tax withholding.

A Form SS-8 determination may be requested only in order to resolve Federal tax matters. The taxpayer requesting a determination must file an income tax return for the years under consideration before a determination can be issued. If Form SS-8 is submitted for a tax year for which the statute of limitations on the tax return has expired, a determination letter will not be issued. The statute of limitations expires 3 years from the due date of the tax return or the date filed, whichever is later.

The IRS does not issue a determination letter for proposed transactions or on hypothetical situations. We may, however, issue an information letter when it is considered appropriate.

Definition

Firm. For the purposes of this form, the term "firm" means any individual, business enterprise, organization, state, or other entity for which a worker has performed services. The firm may or may not have paid the worker directly for these services. **If the firm was not responsible for payment for services, please be sure to complete question 6 in Part II of Form SS-8.**

The SS-8 Determination Process

The IRS will acknowledge the receipt of your Form SS-8. Because there are usually two (or more) parties who could be affected by a determination of employment status, the IRS attempts to get information from all parties involved by sending those parties blank Forms SS-8 for completion. The case will be assigned to a technician who will review the facts, apply the law, and render a decision. The technician may ask for additional information before rendering a decision. The IRS will generally issue a formal determination to the firm or payer (if that is a different entity), and will send a copy to the worker. A determination letter applies only to a worker (or a class of workers) requesting it, and the decision is binding on the IRS. In certain cases, a formal determination will not be issued; instead, an information letter may be issued. Although an information letter is advisory only and is not binding on the IRS, it may be used to assist the worker to fulfill his or her Federal tax obligations. This process takes approximately 120 days.

Neither the SS-8 determination process nor the review of any records in connection with the determination constitutes an examination (audit) of any Federal tax return. If the periods under consideration have previously been examined, the SS-8 determination process will not constitute a reexamination under IRS reopening procedures. Because this is not an examination of any Federal tax return, the appeal rights available in connection with an examination do not apply to an SS-8 determination. However, if you disagree with a determination and you have additional information concerning the work relationship that you believe was not previously considered, you may request that the determining office reconsider the determination.

Completing Form SS-8

Please answer all questions as completely as possible. Attach additional sheets if you need more space. Provide information for all years the worker provided services for the firm. Determinations are based on the entire relationship between the firm and the worker.

Additional copies of this form may be obtained by calling 1-800-TAX-FORM (1-800-829-3676) or from the IRS Web Site at **www.irs.gov.**

Fee

There is no fee for requesting an SS-8 determination letter.

Signature

The Form SS-8 must be signed and dated by the taxpayer. A stamped signature will not be accepted.

The person who signs for a corporation must be an officer of the corporation who has personal knowledge of the facts. If the corporation is a member of an affiliated group filing a consolidated return, it must be signed by an officer of the common parent of the group.

The person signing for a trust, partnership, or limited liability company must be, respectively, a trustee, general partner, or member-manager who has personal knowledge of the facts.

Where To File

Send the completed Form SS-8 to the address listed below for the firm's location. However, for cases involving Federal agencies, send the form to the Internal Revenue Service, Attn: CC:CORP:T:C, Ben Franklin Station, P.O. Box 7604, Washington, DC 20044.

Firm's location:	Send to:
Alaska, Arizona, Arkansas, California, Colorado, Hawaii, Idaho, Illinois, Iowa, Kansas, Minnesota, Missouri, Montana, Nebraska, Nevada, New Mexico, North Dakota, Oklahoma, Oregon, South Dakota, Texas, Utah, Washington, Wisconsin, Wyoming, American Samoa, Guam, Puerto Rico, U.S. Virgin Islands	Internal Revenue Service SS-8 Determinations P.O. Box 1231 Stop 4106 AUCSC Austin, TX 78767
Alabama, Connecticut, Delaware, District of Columbia, Florida, Georgia, Indiana, Kentucky, Louisiana, Maine, Maryland, Massachusetts, Michigan, Mississippi, New Hampshire, New Jersey, New York, North Carolina, Ohio, Pennsylvania, Rhode Island, South Carolina, Tennessee, Vermont, Virginia, West Virginia, all other locations not listed	Internal Revenue Service SS-8 Determinations 40 Lakemont Road Newport, VT 05855-1555

Instructions for Workers

If you are requesting a determination for more than one firm, complete a separate Form SS-8 for each firm.

> ⚠ *Form SS-8 is not a claim for refund of social security and Medicare taxes or Federal income tax withholding.*

If you are found to be an employee, you are responsible for filing an amended return for any corrections related to this decision. A determination that a worker is an employee does not necessarily reduce any current or prior tax liability. For more information, call 1-800-829-1040.

Time for filing a claim for refund. Generally, you must file your claim for a credit or refund within 3 years from the date your original return was filed or within 2 years from the date the tax was paid, whichever is later.

Form SS-8 does not prevent the expiration of the time in which a claim for a refund must be filed. If you are concerned about a refund, and the statute of limitations for filing a claim for refund for the year(s) at issue has not yet expired, you should file **Form 1040X,** Amended U.S. Individual Income Tax Return, to protect your statute of limitations. File a separate Form 1040X for each year.

On the Form 1040X you file, do not complete lines 1 through 24 on the form. Write "Protective Claim" at the top of the form, sign and date it. In addition, you should enter the following statement in Part II, Explanation of Changes to Income, Deductions, and Credits: "Filed Form SS-8 with the Internal Revenue Service Office in (Austin, TX; Newport, VT; or Washington, DC; as appropriate). By filing this protective claim, I reserve the right to file a claim for any refund that may be due after a determination of my employment tax status has been completed."

Filing Form SS-8 does not alter the requirement to timely file an income tax return. Do not delay filing your tax return in anticipation of an answer to your SS-8 request. You must file an income tax return for related tax years before a determination can be issued. In addition, if applicable, do not delay in responding to a request for payment while waiting for a determination of your worker status.

Instructions for Firms

If a **worker** has requested a determination of his or her status while working for you, you will receive a request from the IRS to complete a Form SS-8. In cases of this type, the IRS usually gives each party an opportunity to present a statement of the facts because any decision will affect the employment tax status of the parties. Failure to respond to this request will not prevent the IRS from issuing an information letter to the worker based on the information he or she has made available so that the worker may fulfill his or her Federal tax obligations. However, the information that you provide is extremely valuable in determining the status of the worker.

If **you** are requesting a determination for a particular class of worker, complete the form for **one** individual who is representative of the class of workers whose status is in question. If you want a written determination for more than one class of workers, complete a separate Form SS-8 for one worker from each class whose status is typical of that class. A written determination for any worker will apply to other workers of the same class if the facts are not materially different for these workers. Please provide a list of names and addresses of all workers potentially affected by this determination.

If you have a reasonable basis for not treating a worker as an employee, you may be relieved from having to pay employment taxes for that worker under section 530 of the 1978 Revenue Act. However, this relief provision cannot be considered in conjunction with a Form SS-8 determination because the determination does not constitute an examination of any tax return. For more information regarding section 530 of the 1978 Revenue Act and to determine if you qualify for relief under this section, you may visit the IRS Web Site at **www.irs.gov.**

Privacy Act and Paperwork Reduction Act Notice. We ask for the information on this form to carry out the Internal Revenue laws of the United States. This information will be used to determine the employment status of the worker(s) described on the form. Subtitle C, Employment Taxes, of the Internal Revenue Code imposes employment taxes on wages. Sections 3121(d), 3306(a), and 3401(c) and (d) and the related regulations define employee and employer for purposes of employment taxes imposed under Subtitle C. Section 6001 authorizes the IRS to request information needed to determine if a worker's or firm is subject to these taxes. Section 6109 requires you to provide your taxpayer identification number. Neither workers nor firms are required to request a status determination, but if you choose to do so, you must provide the information requested on this form. Failure to provide the requested information may prevent us from making a status determination. If any worker or the firm has requested a status determination, and you are being asked to provide information for use in that determination, you are not required to provide the requested information. However, failure to provide such information will prevent the IRS from considering it in making the status determination. Providing false or fraudulent information may subject you to penalties. Routine uses of this information include providing it to the Department of Justice for use in civil and criminal litigation, to the Social Security Administration for the administration of social security programs, and to cities, states, and the District of Columbia for the administration of their tax laws. We may also provide this information to the affected worker(s) or the firm as part of the status determination process.

You are not required to provide the information requested on a form that is subject to the Paperwork Reduction Act unless the form displays a valid OMB control number. Books or records relating to a form or its instructions must be retained as long as their contents may become material in the administration of any Internal Revenue law. Generally, tax returns and return information are confidential, as required by section 6103.

The time needed to complete and file this form will vary depending on individual circumstances. The estimated average time is: **Recordkeeping,** 22 hrs.; **Learning about the law or the form,** 47 min.; and **Preparing and sending the form to the IRS,** 1 hr., 11 min. If you have comments concerning the accuracy of these time estimates or suggestions for making this form simpler, we would be happy to hear from you. You can write to the Tax Forms Committee, Western Area Distribution Center, Rancho Cordova, CA 95743-0001. **Do not** send the tax form to this address. Instead, see **Where To File** on page 4.

APPENDIX E

Glossary

The following are terms that often come up in a discussion of income taxes. I have tried to keep the definitions simple, so not all the variations and exceptions are noted.

Accelerated Cost Recovery System (ACRS)   A method of computing depreciation for tax returns, generally for assets placed in service from 1981 to 1986.

Accelerated depreciation   Any method of depreciation that results in a higher depreciation deduction in the earlier years of the life of the asset than in later years.

Accrual-method accounting   The method of accounting that records (recognizes) income when it is earned and expenses when they are incurred, regardless of the time when payment is made. (Somewhat modified for IRS purposes. See Chapter 4.)

Accumulated earnings   The net total of income and losses since the first day of business, reduced by owners' draws (or dividends) from the business.

Adjusted gross income (AGI)   On an individual income tax return, the total income minus certain adjustments, before the subtraction of itemized deductions and personal exemptions. (AGI is the bottom line on page 1 of Form 1040.)

Alternative minimum tax (AMT)   A second income tax system designed to snare those who pay little or no tax. (Only the government can get away with sending you two bills and telling you to pay whichever one is higher.)

Annuity   An agreement by one entity to pay an individual a certain sum of money periodically for life. Usually offered by insurance companies, but individuals can so agree with another individual. (There are lots of variations, as "variable" annuities.)

Assets   Economic resources that a business owns. Assets can be tangible (desks, bulldozers, buildings) or intangible (goodwill, franchises).

Basis   Usually the cost of an asset minus the accumulated total of depreciation claimed on the asset to date. Other factors can affect it (as when it is property contributed by a partner to a partnership).

Beneficiary   See *Trust.*

Book value   The value of assets as recorded on the accounting books of a business. Usually, that will be at cost, minus any depreciation that has been or could have been deducted. Generally means about the same as the IRS term of *basis.*

Brother-sister corporation   Two corporations, each owned by the same parent corporation.

Cash-method accounting   The "opposite" of the accrual method. Income and expenses are recognized when cash (or other form of payment) changes hands.

Corporation (C or S)   A separate entity, owned by one or more stockholders, usually formed to conduct business. A C corporation pays its own income taxes before it distributes earnings to stockholders. An S corporation pays no tax (with exceptions), but the stockholders pay income tax on the earnings of the corporation.

Deduction   Almost an IRS synonym for *expense,* but some expenses are not deductions. (If you spend $50 taking a customer to lunch, that is a $50 expense. But the IRS will let you take only a $25 deduction.)

Depletion   An item that the IRS allows a taxpaying entity to deduct from income if the entity is using up, in a business, natural resources he, she, or it owns. Depletion is similar to depreciation, but the calculation is complex and varies with the type of natural resource.

Depreciation   Any method of allocating the cost of an asset over the period that the asset will be used. (Applicable only to assets with a useful life of more than one year.)

Distribution   A payment of part or all of the earnings of a business operation to its owners.

Dividend   A distribution made from a C corporation to its stockholders.

Equity   The value of the ownership of a business. Computed by subtracting total liabilities from total assets. The computation can be based on *book value* or *market value* of assets. *Net worth* is a synonym for equity.

Estate   The financial empire of an individual that is left after death.

Exemption, personal   An amount ($2,800 in 2000) that the IRS allows as a deduction for every taxpayer (with exceptions) and each dependent of the taxpayer.

Expenditure   In nontax life, usually refers to the act of writing a check or handing over cash. The IRS seems to use this term when it does not want to use the terms *expense* or *deduction*. The term is often used when the discussion applies to both cash-basis and accrual-basis taxpayers.

Expense   In the tax and accounting world, a cost of generating income in a business. The time an expense happens will depend on whether the entity is on a cash or accrual method of accounting.

Fiduciary   An institution or individual who holds money or other assets for the benefit of someone else. The term usually arises in trusts and estates and refers to the trustee of a trust or executor of an estate.

FIFO   A system of identifying which inventory items are taken off the shelf and sold first. FIFO stands for *first-in, first-out*.

Gain   The amount by which the proceeds of selling an asset exceed the basis of the asset. Gain is similar to *profit,* but profit usually refers to the daily operations of a business, whereas *gain* is usually used in the context of sales of equipment, real estate, and similar transactions.

Gift   A transfer of property without at least a reasonable payment or consideration in return.

Income   What has been earned by sale of goods or services *or* cash received for sales made or to be made. (See *Cash-method accounting* and *Accrual-method accounting.*)

Installment sale   A sale made in exchange for periodic future payments. In some cases, the taxable gain from sale of equipment, real estate, ownership of a business, and certain other gains can be reported on the installment basis. That is, tax need not be paid on the gain until the cash rolls in later.

Intangible asset   An asset that has no physical properties but does have value. Copyrights and patents are most frequently used as examples, but such things as future costs that have been paid for but not yet applied to an accounting period are also intangible assets.

Inventory   Usually the merchandise on the shelf, ready to be sold to customers. Inventory can also refer to a stock of other items, such as an inventory of spare parts for a machine or an inventory of office supplies.

Kiddie tax   A tax resulting from the decision by Congress that all children under 14 should pay tax on their investment income at their parents' rate. (Except for the first $1,200 of investment income.)

Liabilities   Debts of a business.

LIFO   A system of identifying which inventory items are taken off the shelf and sold first. LIFO stands for *last-in, first-out.*

Limited liability company (LLC)   A business entity that can be formed in many, but not all states. Essentially, it is taxed as a partnership but the owners of the business have the protection of limited liability (as if the business were a corporation).

Loss   The opposite of profit. Loss occurs when expenses are more than sales. Also used as the opposite of *gain* (when an individual sells an asset for less than its basis).

Market value   The value of assets determined to be what they would bring at a sale.

Modified Accelerated Cost Recovery System (MACRS)   A method of computing depreciation for tax returns, generally for assets placed in service in 1987 and later.

Net operating loss Basically, the same as a simple loss, but generally used to define that loss that can be added to last years' loss and used to offset the hoped-for income next year. (Usually a loss can be carried back two years.)

Net worth See *Equity.*

Parent corporation A corporation that owns enough stock in another corporation (a subsidiary corporation) to control it. For income tax purposes, to be classified as a parent corporation generally requires 80 percent ownership of the subsidiary corporation.

Partner An owner in a partnership of two or more entities.

Partnerships A business composed of two or more owners that is not incorporated. The term probably does not include LLCs, although they are taxed as partnerships.

Passive activity loss Losses that arise from an enterprise in which an investor takes no active management part. Passive activity losses can be used to offset only passive income.

Private Letter Ruling A ruling by the IRS national office as to how to treat a specific tax situation of a specific taxpayer. It does not bind the IRS to follow the same course in another similar situation, but it does provide some idea as to how the IRS is thinking. See *Revenue Ruling.*

Recapture The taking back of a tax benefit that the IRS had allowed you. For instance, if you take a Section-179 deduction (up to $20,000) for the purchase of new equipment and then sell the equipment the following year, the IRS will *recapture* the benefit of that deduction. (You will pay tax as if you never took the Section-179 deduction, although you will pay the tax in the year you sell the equipment.)

Regulation, IRS Issued by the IRS national office in two categories. The first is *interpretative* rulings: These rulings interpret a specific section of the Internal Revenue Code so that we taxpayers can understand the law. (As you can see from some of the regulations reprinted in the appendix to this book, many of the interpretative regulations need further interpreting.) They present the thinking of the people at the IRS as to what Congress meant by a section of the tax law. In court, it is possible to argue that the IRS interpretation is wrong. The second category is *legislative*. They are issued when Congress enacts a new tax law written in general terms and delegates the details to the Commissioner of Internal Revenue. These regulations have the force of law, so the only defense against them is that the IRS overstepped its authority or that the regulations are unconstitutional.

Revenue Ruling   A ruling by the IRS national office as to how a certain situation should be taxed or not taxed. A Revenue Ruling usually arises from a request by either an IRS auditor or a taxpayer. The IRS publishes the ruling as a guide to how it would treat similar circumstances. See *Private Letter Ruling.*

Revenue   A term not often used by the IRS, except in its own name. Accountants often use it to refer to the gross, or total, income from sales of goods and services.

Safe harbor   A set of circumstances that if you can fit into, will protect you from IRS attack. For instance, showing a profit in your business in three out of five consecutive years usually will keep the IRS from considering your business to be no more than a hobby. (See Chapter 5.)

Self-employment tax   The social security tax that is levied on self-employed individuals.

Standard deduction   An amount that can be deducted from an individual's income in lieu of itemized deductions.

Subsidiary corporation   A corporation owned by another corporation. See *Parent corporation.*

Taxable income   The income that is subject to tax. Taxable income is the bottom line, after all adjustments, deductions, and exemptions have been subtracted from income. For a C corporation, taxable income is the result obtained by subtracting expenses from gross income.

Trust   An entity that is organized for the purpose of taking care of assets (usually investments) for other people (the beneficiaries). A trust is taxed separately if it keeps the income in the trust. If it distributes the income to the beneficiaries, the beneficiaries are taxed on the income. (Lots of technical exceptions here, but this is the essence of the concept.)

INDEX

R 5/28